Cromwell's
Wars at Sea

Cromwell's Wars at Sea

John Barratt

Pen & Sword
MILITARY

First published in Great Britain in 2006 by
Pen & Sword Military
an imprint of
Pen & Sword Books Ltd
47 Church Street
Barnsley
South Yorkshire
S70 2AS

ISBN 1 84415 459 9

A CIP catalogue record for this book is available
from the British Library

Typeset in Sabon by Phoenix Typesetting, Auldgirth

Printed and bound in Engand by Biddles Ltd, King's Lynn

Pen & Sword Books Ltd incorporates the Imprints of Pen & Sword
Aviation, Pen & Sword Maritime, Pen & Sword Military, Wharncliffe
Local History, Pen and Sword Select, Pen and Sword Military Classics
and Leo Cooper.

For a complete list of Pen & Sword titles please contact
PEN & SWORD BOOKS LIMITED
47 Church Street, Barnsley, South Yorkshire, S70 2AS, England
E-mail: enquiries@pen-and-sword.co.uk
Website: www.pen-and-sword.co.uk

Contents

List of Plates

(between pages 128 and 129)

Maps

Preface

Compared with their predecessors in the Age of Drake, Nelson and his 'Band of Brothers', and their successors in more recent times, the story of Oliver Cromwell's sailors in the decade from 1650 is much less well-known. Whilst Frobisher, John Hawkins, Collingwood, Jellicoe and Cunningham are familiar names to students of English naval history, Cromwell's commanders, Ayscue, Lawson, Mountagu and even the greatest of them, Robert Blake, are largely forgotten.

But they are no less worthy of remembrance than their betterknown compatriots. Victorious against English Royalists and a variety of foreign foes, the Dutch and Spaniards foremost among them, Cromwell's captains played as great a role as the much better-known New Model Army in securing the survival of the English Commonwealth and Protectorate against its host of enemies.

Previous writers, chief among them Bernard Capp, J.R. Powell and R.C. Anderson, have, through their researches, thrown much light on the administration, organisation and nature of 'Cromwell's Navy'. I gladly acknowledge my debt to them in the preparation of this book, which is intended to focus mainly on the 'State's Navy' and its officers and men in action, in victory and defeat. A special debt is owed to Bernard Capp, whose monumental work on Cromwell's Navy has been a constant source and point of reference in my discussion of the social aspects of the Navy.

As usual, I owe my thanks to the excellent and professional team at Pen and Sword, to Derek Stone for his excellent maps, and to the staff of a number of libraries, chief among them the Sydney Jones Library, University of Liverpool, the British Library, London, and the Bodleian Library, Oxford.

John Barratt
Henllan, May 2006

Chronology

1649

21 January	Rupert sails from Holland with Royalist fleet to Kinsale
30 January	Charles I executed, English Republic established
February	Rank of General at Sea established by Act of Parliament
March	Admiralty Committee set up
May	Blake begins blockade of Royalist fleet in Kinsale
23 October	Rupert leaves Kinsale for Lisbon

1650

10 March–September	Blake blockades Rupert in Lisbon
26 July	Indecisive action between Blake and Portuguese-Royalist fleet
7 September	Second indecisive action between the above
14 September	Blake seizes part of Plate Fleet
27 September	Blake withdraws to Cadiz
12 October	Rupert heads for Mediterranean
20 October–16 November	Most of Royalist fleet captured or destroyed by Blake
12 December	Spain recognizes Commonwealth

1651

1 April	Blake and Ayscue ordered to take Scilly Isles
18 April	Tresco taken
3 June	Grenville surrenders Scillies
20 September	Council of State orders capture of Channel Islands
15 October	Ayscue arrives at Barbados
22 October	Commonwealth forces land on Jersey
12 December	Elizabeth Castle, Jersey, surrenders
19 December	Guernsey surrenders

1652

11 January	Barbados surrenders to Ayscue
19 May	Clash off Dover between Blake and Tromp triggers First Dutch War
7 June	War declared between Commonwealth and Dutch
24 July	Clash off Shetland Islands between Blake and Tromp prevented by bad weather
16 August	Ruyter bests Ayscue in action in English Channel
27 August	Badiley narrowly defeated by van Galen off Monte Cristo
4 September	Blake captures French convoy off Calais
28 September	Battle of Kentish Knock. Blake defeats de With
28 November	Tromp defeats Blake off Dungeness

1653

18–20 February	Battle off Portland Bill. Blake defeats Tromp
4 March	Badiley defeated by van Galen off Leghorn
20 March	'Fighting Instructions' issued
April	Rump Parliament overthrown. Cromwell becomes Lord Protector
2 June	Battle of Gibbard Shoal. Monck defeats Tromp
31 July	Battle of Scheveningen. Tromp defeated and killed by Monck. Last major battle of First Dutch War

1654

September	Peace settlement between Protectorate and Dutch
October	Blake's squadron despatched to Mediterranean as Cromwell prepares for war with Spain

1655

4 April	Blake attacks Turkish ships at Porto Farina
14–18 April	Commonwealth forces attack Santo Domingo, but repulsed
11–17 May	Commonwealth forces take Jamaica
June–September	Blake off Cadiz awaiting confirmation of war with Spain

1656

22 January	Mountagu appointed General-at-Sea
20 April	Mountagu and Blake begin blockade of Cadiz
9 September	Stayner captures Plate Fleet

1657

March	Cromwell makes full alliance with France against Spain
23 April	Battle of Santa Cruz; Blake defeats Spanish squadron
4 September	English forces take Mardyke

1658

4 June	English and French defeat Spanish at Battle of the Dunes
3 September	Death of Oliver Cromwell

1659

October	Rump Parliament removed by Army
14 December	Vice-Admiral Lawson and squadron declare support for Rump and blockade London
26 December	Rump Parliament restored

1660

8 May	Charles II restored
12 May	Mountagu and fleet sent to bring Charles from Holland
23 May	State's Navy becomes Royal Navy
25 May	Charles II lands at Dover

Glossary

Abeam	the direction at right angles to a ship's centre line
Beach	to run a ship aground or ashore
Beat up	to work to windward by successive tacks, to proceed obliquely to windward with the wind first to one side and then the other
Boatswain	warrant officer responsible for a ship's sails, rigging and tackle
Bring to	to heave-to or stop, usually by backing one or more sails
Broadside	1) the number of guns mounted or bearing on one side 2) the simultaneous firing of all these guns
Close-hauled	steering as nearly towards the wind as possible
Convoy	a body of merchant ships under escort
Course	the direction of a ship's movement
Coxswain	a petty officer in charge of a boat's crew
Culverin	a long gun firing a shot of about 18lb
Demi-culverin	a long gun firing a shot of about 9lb
Fireship	a small warship fitted with combustibles in order to destroy enemy ships by setting herself on fire and running alongside them
Flag captain	captain of a flagship
Frigate	a small warship of fine lines and high speed
Galleon	a type of armed merchant ship used by the Spanish for long-distance trade
Hoy	a type of sailing barge, square-rigged on a single mast

Impress, press	to recruit men by force
Ketch	a small vessel square or fore and aft-rigged with a main mast, and a smaller mizzen aft
Larboard	relating to the port or left-hand side of the ship
Laid-up	a ship out of service or in reserve
League	a measure of distance (three miles)
Lee	the direction towards which the wind is blowing
Lee-shore	a coastline towards which the wind is blowing
Leeward	relating to the direction towards which the wind is blowing
Line abreast	a formation in which ships of a squadron sail on the same course abeam of each other
Line ahead	a formation in which one or more ships follow a leader, conforming to his movements
Line of battle	a fighting formation in which ships of a fleet form a straight line in pre-determined order
Luff, Luff up	to turn into the wind
Mizzen	the aftermost mast of a ship or ketch
Mole	a breakwater; a barrier protecting a harbour from the force of the sea
Onshore	towards or on the shore
Privateer	a privately-owned warship licensed by letter of marque by a government to capture enemy ships for profit
Prize	a captured enemy ship
Prize-money	proceeds of selling a prize
Rate	one of six classes into which larger warships were divided
Sail: make sail	to hoist or spread sail; shorten sail to reduce or take in sail
Seawards	in the direction of the open sea

Shallop	a small cruising warship
Shoal	a sandbank, reef or area of shallow water
Sloop	a small cruising warship, usually with one deck
Starboard	relating to the right-hand side of a ship
Tack	the course held by a ship beating to windward; (verb) 'to shift tack' go about to turn into the wind and so on to the opposite tack; 2) to beat to windward by successive tacks
Tarpaulin	an officer brought up in merchant ships; a person of low birth
Wear	to alter course from one tack to another by turning before the wind
Weather gauge	the windward position in relation to another ship or fleet
Windward	relating to direction from which the wind is blowing
Yawl	type of ship's boat

Chapter 1
A Republic at Bay: 1649

'Our forces are such at sea as our enemies looked
not for'

On the cold foggy afternoon of 30 January 1649, England's
Parliament and Army executed their king, and embarked on a
perilous future. The first and most critical question was whether
the infant Republic could even survive. At home both friends and
enemies were keenly aware that the monarchy had been abolished
only on the authority of the 'Rump' Parliament, a mere fragment
of one House of a Parliament elected eight years earlier, supported
and in part impelled by the Army.[1]

Although the new Republic, known as the Commonwealth,
moved rapidly to abolish the monarchy and set up in its place a
new executive body, the Council of State, and claimed to represent
all the people of England, even its most enthusiastic supporters
were uneasy. The majority of the population, whilst not necessarily
in sympathy with the policies of the late king, had little enthusiasm
for the violent and radical change of regime, still less for the
prospect of *de facto* military rule. It was apparent that the Republic
depended on the Army for its survival; indeed the new Council of
State was formed from senior army officers and only civilians
known to be in sympathy with them. Both crypto-Royalists and the
great majority of moderate Presbyterians felt themselves excluded
from a government formed largely of Independents and other
religious radicals.[2]

The new rulers of England cared little for popular opinion, and on the mainland the Royalists were for the moment silenced, but on a wider view the situation was much less favourable. The Scottish government had opposed Charles I and his religious policies, but he had been king of Scotland as well as of England, and his summary trial and execution by the English Parliament without consultation with his Scottish subjects had aroused considerable resentment north of the Border. This was expressed by the prompt declaration in Edinburgh of the Prince of Wales as Charles II. Though Scotland remained nominally England's ally, there was every possibility, if Charles accepted Presbyterianism and other conditions, that he could before long find himself on the Scottish throne, at war with England.

Ireland presented a more immediate threat. Apart from Dublin and a few other garrisons, the bulk of the country was under the control of an Irish-Royalist alliance, at least nominally subjects of the Crown. Irish privateers, based in the southern ports of Wexford, Waterford and Kinsale, had for years been a scourge of English merchant shipping, and the possibility of Charles II making his way to Ireland to head an invasion of England could not be ruled out.

A purely Royalist threat also remained. The king's men still held the Scilly Isles, Channel Islands and Isle of Man, as well as most of the English possessions in the New World. Privateers continued to operate from the Royalist bases, which also acted as refuges for the disaffected. A more serious potential threat was presented by that part of the Navy which had mutinied during the Second Civil War of the summer of 1648, and which, after the failure of the Royalist uprisings, had taken refuge in the neutral Dutch port of Helvoetsluys, from where, unless constantly confined by blockade, it might sally forth to wreak havoc on English trade routes.

Equally uncertain was the attitude of England's Continental neighbours. The Commonwealth was born without a friend in the world, with most governments, whatever their views on Charles I, fearful of the wider consequences of the English act of regicide. Exhausted by the recently concluded Thirty Years' War, no European power was anxious to embroil itself in conflict with Commonwealth, but they also saw it in their interests for England to remain weak and divided. For this reason, as well as the sympathies of its current Stadtholder William III for the Stuarts, the Dutch United Provinces were willing to give refuge to Charles II and his exiled Court. In an effort to gain sympathy, in May 1649 the Commonwealth sent as its envoy to the Hague Isaac Dorielaus, but in July Dorielaus was murdered by Royalist exiles, against whom the Dutch States General took no action. Indeed they had recognised Charles, Prince of Wales, as king of England, and continued to allow him to use Dutch territory from which to plot possible invasions of England mounted from Scotland and Ireland.[3]

The attitude of other European countries was similar. The Swedes were allowing the Royalist Marquis of Montrose to fit out an expedition to Scotland, whilst privateers purportedly acting in the name of Charles II were operating from Spanish Flanders and French Dunkirk.

Ultimately, as the new rulers of England recognised, only proven military strength would bring them grudging recognition. The threats presented by Scotland and Ireland could be countered largely by the New Model Army, but the Royalist threat from overseas and the danger of European intervention would have to be dealt with by the Navy.

A practical demonstration of naval success against the Royalists might be expected to modify European hostility, or at least render it more circumspect, but the Council of State had well-founded doubts regarding the willingness and ability of its Navy to undertake this task.

The core of the English navy remained the 'ship-money fleet' of Charles I – so called because the bulk of the funds for building it had been provided from the proceeds of the notorious 'Ship Money' tax, the unpopularity of which had played a role in bringing about the First Civil War. The 1st rate men-of-war of this fleet, like the mighty 1,500-ton *Sovereign of the Seas*, mounting 100 guns, had been built as much with the aim of intimidating potential Continental enemies and to display the monarchy's prestige as for practical use. Although some of *Sovereign*'s consorts were smaller and handier, they shared the common feature of being built largely as floating gun platforms, designed to meet a similar European fleet in full-scale battle.[4]

In practice their main role in the years immediately preceding the

Civil War had been against the elusive Barbary corsairs, whose raids extended as far as the English coast. They had proved to be almost entirely unsuitable for this role, which unfortunately was very similar to that demanded of them throughout the Civil War, when attacks on merchant shipping by privateers at least nominally in the service of the king was a major problem.

The most important contribution by the Navy, which almost in its entirety had sided with Parliament, was in supplying and supporting coastal garrisons and ports such as Hull, Plymouth and Lyme. Though not invariably successful in this (the Navy proved unable to prevent Royalist forces from taking, for example, Exeter and Dartmouth in 1643), its intervention was the most important single factor which enabled other garrisons to defy the Cavaliers. The other major contribution of the Navy lay in its sustained efforts to cut off the flow to the king of munitions from the Continent and troops from Ireland.[5]

However, the political developments of the closing stages of the First Civil War and its immediate aftermath caused growing discontent among many officers and some seamen. Unlike the New Model Army, the majority of naval officers were moderate Presbyterians in religion and relatively conservative in political outlook, who viewed with disquiet the rise of the religious Independents and political radicalism within the Army.[6]

The Navy's respected Lord Admiral, the Earl of Warwick, had laid down his command in 1645 under the terms of the Self-Denying Ordnance, which in theory barred members of both Houses of Parliament from holding military commands. Warwick was succeeded by his vice-admiral, William Batten, another political moderate, who, during the growing crisis between the Army and Parliament, allowed many of the soldiers' moderate political opponents to escape abroad.[7]

The increasingly powerful Independents responded by engineering the appointment of new admiralty commissioners, who included known radicals such as Henry Marten and Thomas Rainsborough. Batten, feeling unable to work with the new appointees, resigned, much to the anger of many moderate officers and seamen. He was replaced as vice-admiral by Rainsborough, who as colonel of a regiment of foot was clearly an Army nominee, though he had in fact commanded a warship until 1643. The reasons for Rainsborough's appointment were actually more complicated than they appeared, for the Independents distrusted him as a sympathiser with the extreme radical Leveller movement, and felt that he would be less dangerous out of the way at sea in the essentially conservative Navy.

It was certainly the aim of the more radical members of the House of Commons and Navy Commissioners to weed out and replace those captains whose political reliability was seen as suspect. Unfortunately for them, before this process could be carried very far, the series of uprisings known as the Second Civil War broke out in the summer of 1648. The immediate result was the outbreak of mutiny among a significant part of the Navy, although the two largest 1st rates, *Sovereign of the Seas* and *Prince*, were both laid up in Chatham docks and unready for sea.

Rainsborough was sent ashore by the mutineers, and Parliament responded by re-appointing the Earl of Warwick in an unsuccessful attempt to quell the rising discontent. All that Warwick actually achieved was to split the Navy into two opposing groups, with, by July, half of the thirty-nine ships of the intended Summer Guard either in rebel hands or totally or potentially unreliable.[8]

This defection of a large part of the Navy came as a tremendous shock to both radical politicians and the Army. Particularly alarming were the political demands made by the mutineers, including the disbanding of the Army.

For much of the summer the mutinous section of the fleet hovered off Kent or in the mouth of the Thames, with William Batten restored as their commander. On several occasions a pitched battle between the mutineers and the 'loyalist' portion of the fleet led by the Earl of Warwick appeared imminent, but in the late summer, with the failure of the various insurrections on land, and the defeat of the Scottish invasion, the mutinous part of the fleet, now aligned with the Royalists, took refuge in the Dutch port of Helvoetsluys.

The reliability of the remainder of the fleet was of vital concern to the English authorities. At the end of 1648, still under the command of the Earl of Warwick, who was himself politically suspect, most of it was anchored in the Downs. Warwick was under instructions to make no move without Parliament's express permission. As well as being politically unreliable, Warwick was elderly and in poor health, but his popularity with the seamen made his removal a delicate operation. Parliament's first move was to expand the role of the existing Navy Committee from purely financial responsibilities to include the full range of naval matters. Its political reliability was assured by the appointment to its membership of an increased radical element, including Army officers such as Oliver Cromwell and Henry Ireton. In February 1649, Warwick was retired, followed by a far-reaching command reorganisation in which the post of Lord Admiral was not filled. Thomas Rainsborough had been killed by the Royalists in 1648, and the opportunity presented itself for the now dominant Army to bring the Navy within its own control.[9]

The Army aimed to achieve this by appointing reliable soldiers as senior commanders. The post of General at Sea was established, and three officers, Robert Blake, Richard Deane and Edward Popham, appointed jointly to it. The rather shadowy Popham had the most directly relevant experience, having commanded warships in the decade prior to the Civil War, though he had served on land, mainly in the West Country, during the actual conflict.[10] Given that most naval commanders of the period were expected to depend heavily upon experienced seamen for advice, lack of relevant previous service was not necessarily seen as a disadvantage. Deane certainly had none to offer, but, described by his old commander, the Earl of Essex, as an 'honest, judicious, and stout man', was a reliable officer who served both in the Parliamentarian army of the Earl of Essex and in the New Model Army.[11] Robert Blake is more difficult to characterise. The son of a Somerset merchant, Blake may have had some limited experience at sea in merchant shipping prior to the war, although it seems unlikely. He won his command because of political reliability and the reputation which he had gained, particularly with his West Country colleagues, for his sturdy defence of Lyme and Taunton during the First Civil War, during the first of which sieges he had received ample testament to the value of naval power.[12]

The new Generals at Sea were not vested with the far-reaching powers of a Lord Admiral. It was stipulated that they were 'to hold and execute by yourselves, or any two of you, the place of Admiral and General of the said Fleet'[13] the implication being that major decisions should be if possible made by two, each serving as a safeguard for the other's reliability. In normal circumstances, none was intended to act alone; two signatures were required for their orders to be legal. The Council of State was determined to keep ultimate power in its own hands, though it delegated most non-controversial matters to the Admiralty Committee, which was also responsible for the selection of naval officers. Its leading member was the highly experienced and influential Independent leader Sir Henry Vane, who had been Treasurer of the Navy since 1642. Another was Cromwell's brother-in-law, Valentine Walton. Though at times proving cumbersome, on the whole the Admiralty Committee would function effectively, even at times of great pressure such as the Dutch War.

The most immediate problem in early 1649 was the reliability of the Navy's personnel. On 16 January Parliament appointed sixteen 'Regulators' to investigate all branches of the Navy and to purge 'manifest distempers of the Navy, and the great decay of Customs, occasioned by evil, malignant, unfaithful and supernumerary officers, employed by both sea and land, to the great prejudice of the Commonwealth'.[14] Batten, who had returned to England after quitting command of the defecting ships, was naturally removed, though not prosecuted. Also seen as a monarchist sympathiser and dismissed was Richard Cranley, Master of Trinity House, the governing body of merchant shipping and its captains. A new Trinity House Committee was set up, its members including two Regulators and Richard Deane. Too valuable to remove was Peter Pett, head of the family that had been designing and building ships for the Navy since the reign of King Edward VI.

In the same way, it was impractical to attempt to dispense with all politically suspect dockyard craftsmen and ordinary seamen. Apparently suitably penitent dockyard workers were therefore 'pardoned' and retained. The Generals at Sea were left to excuse those ordinary seamen whom they felt reliable, a task aided by promises of a pay rise and a more equitable distribution of prize money.

The task of purging the officer corps was more difficult. However, by the summer of 1649, twenty-seven of the captains of the 1647 Summer Guard had been retired or dismissed, along with a quarter of the survivors of the 1648 crisis. Finding replacements proved difficult, although a number of men would rise rapidly.

Some were experienced seamen; Robert Moulton, commanding the Downs squadron in the summer of 1649, had served in the Navy since 1643. Edward Hall, another radical with experience at sea, would also achieve rapid promotion. In 1649 Sir George Ayscue, who had commanded ships for Parliament during the First Civil War, was given the vital Irish Sea Squadron. Among other newly-appointed commanders who would progress rapidly were Nehemiah Bourne, a settler from Massachusetts, who had returned to England on the outbreak of Civil War and had served in Rainsborough's Regiment, and John Lawson, a noted radical from Scarborough who before the war had served for many years in the East Coast collier trade, before at various times during the war fighting as a captain of foot and in command of a warship.[15]

As part of a bid to give the Navy a new identity, it was renamed 'the State's Navy', those of its ships with politically suspect or overtly monarchist names were gradually rechristened, and a new ensign was issued, bearing the cross and harp of the Commonwealth in place of the old 'disunion flag'.

Nevertheless, with the officer corps in the midst of root and branch replacement, and many of the seamen discontented, the Navy remained in a questionable condition to meet the onerous responsibilities placed on it. Scotland and Ireland presented major threats of invasion and there was a pressing need to establish Commonwealth authority in the colonies of the New World. Nearer home, though the European powers were unwilling to go to war with the Commonwealth, they were still providing support to assorted privateers operating against English shipping. In January 1649 the transfer of the Royalist squadron at Helvoetsluys, now under the energetic command of Prince Rupert, to the strategically well-placed port of Kinsale on the south-west coast of Ireland, boded ill both for Commonwealth plans for the reconquest of Ireland and for merchant trade throughout the Western Approaches.

In order to tackle these threats, a fleet larger than the regular navy employed by Elizabeth I against Spain would be needed. In the summer of 1649, the Navy consisted of thirty-nine ships, four more than on the outbreak of war in 1642, a far from adequate force. Although the Council of State proclaimed its satisfaction to its commanders, there was a sting in the tail:

'our own forces are such at sea as our enemies looked not for, and ourselves could scarce have hoped, consisting of so many good ships and faithful commanders as have not formerly been sent out in any one year. But that it was difficult to have so many set out and furnished you very well know, and how the Commonwealth will be able to continue the same in successive years is not easy to evidence.'[16]

The Council of State was warning its commanders that they had to win a decisive victory over the Royalists before resources to maintain their ships ran out.

In reality, however, this would prove unduly alarmist. From March 1649 onwards, the Commonwealth began a steady programme of naval expansion. During the next three years, twenty new warships would be built, and twenty-five others either purchased or added from captured prizes, almost doubling the size of the fleet. Steps also began to rename some particularly politically incorrectly christened existing ships. *Charles* would become *Liberty*, *Henrietta Maria*, *Paragon*, the *Royal Prince*, *Resolution*. Only the mighty *Sovereign of the Seas* would retain a truncated form of her original name when rechristened *Sovereign*, a reference to England's claim to the 'sovereignty' of the waters surrounding her coasts.

However, in the spring of 1649 the strengthening of the Navy lay in the future; for the present the new Generals at Sea would have to make do with what they had. Although two of the 'great ships', *George* and *Unicorn*, were taken out of mothballs to provide a not very effective show of strength off the Flanders coast, Parliament's policy of keeping the Navy widely dispersed to reduce the impact of any further mutinies meant that it was more difficult to meet the various threats.

One result during the spring was an upsurge in quasi-Royalist privateering in English waters. An ex-Parliamentarian captain, Thomas Plunkett, operating in the North Sea, captured thirty ships from a convoy of colliers off Newcastle, while in August eight more merchant ships were taken off Flamborough Head. Later in the summer the Council of State was alarmed by reports that sixteen privateers were fitting out in Dunkirk and Ostend, intending to attack English shipping in the Thames Estuary.

Although the Council of State made strenuous efforts to mobilise every available ship, with the exceptions of the great *Resolution* and *Sovereign*, and extended the Summer Guard's commission to eight months instead of the usual six, the task awaiting the Generals at Sea was formidable.

Chapter 2
Cromwell's Navy

'Instruments in the hands of God'
(Captain Edmund Thompson)

Administration
In 1642 there had been two principal organisations responsible for the Navy – the Admiralty and the Navy Board. The Admiralty was headed by the Lord Admiral of England, usually a leading member of the nobility, often with limited maritime experience, who was responsible to the king and his ministers for overall command matters. The Lord Admiral or his deputies also led the main fleet. Under the Lord Admiral was a body of permanent officials or civil servants known as the Navy Board, who were responsible for building and maintaining ships, dockyards and naval stores. The Treasurer of the Navy, nominally a member of the Navy Board, though in practice largely independent of it, controlled its finances. Two or more members of the Board, known as Victuallers, were responsible for the supply of food and drink, provided on a fixed price per man per month. Munitions were supplied both to land and naval forces by the Ordnance Board.

Following the outbreak of Civil War Parliament initially appointed its own Lord Admiral, but control of administrative matters ashore was passed to the Admiralty Committee, while the Navy Board was retitled the Navy Commissioners, and a Parliamentary Navy Committee was responsible for the issue of money to the Treasurer. The Commissioners were mainly shipowners, who took on the responsibility of supplying the armed merchant ship auxiliaries and privateers which were an essential supplement to the Navy in time of war, often to their own financial benefit.

After the Independent faction took control of Parliament in late 1648, a 'Committee of Members', otherwise known as Regulators, was appointed with the task of removing opponents of the regime from the Navy. The fleet, the Navy Commissioners and the Ordnance Office were all purged, as was as was Trinity House, the organisation which controlled all pilotage on the Thames, and which was also closely involved in all aspects of merchant shipping.

In March 1649 the newly established Council of State appointed a new Admiralty Committee, headed by the Treasurer of the Navy, the influential Independent political leader Sir Henry Vane. Vane was probably the ablest of the Parliamentarian political leaders during the Civil War. Architect of the 'Solemn League and Covenant' with Scotland, which played a major part in the defeat of the king, Vane was an outstanding political operator. He was a man of considerable charm and affability, despite which many, with some reason, felt him to be untrustworthy. Vane had a 'wonderful sagacity' in learning the aims and feelings of others, while concealing his own. Vane had been Treasurer since 1642, and in practice he and sometimes one of the Council of State were largely responsible for policy decisions. The Parliamentary Naval Committee, headed by Cromwell and his son-in-law, Henry Ireton, overlapped the other bodies responsible for the Navy, with membership from both.

Not surprisingly, this convoluted system proved unsatisfactory, and there were a number of problems resulting from the heavy demands of the Dutch War. General at Sea Edward Popham commented of the Admiralty Committee Secretary, Robert Coytmore: 'It is not unusual for Mr Coytmore to mistake winter for summer';[1] this opinion may have been slightly coloured by the fact that Coytmore also spied on the Generals at Sea on behalf of the Council of State.

Vane's own handling of the Navy also came under increasing criticism, and he resigned in 1652 in protest at the Dutch War. His departure did nothing to improve efficiency, and defeat at Dungeness led to a major reorganisation. Parliament removed the authority of the Navy Committee, and in future voted money to the Navy Commission, which was formed from six civilian members and the three Generals at Sea. It was once again headed by Sir Henry Vane, who took a leading role in the reforms which followed, largely bypassing the Admiralty Committee in the process.

Vane left office again on Cromwell's assumption of power in 1653 and the new leading figure was Cromwell's brother-in-law, the 'grim giant', John Desborowe. In practice, however, most administrative work for the Navy was increasingly carried out by the Navy Commissioners, who for the remainder of the Interregnum were effectively salaried permanent officials. These five men, with offices in Minary Lane near Tower Hill in London, did most of the day-to-day work of running the Navy, and were responsible during the Dutch War for fitting out and administering the largest fleet so far mustered by England. At the height of the war they employed over 2,000 men in the naval dockyards, and between 1649 and 1654 built eighteen ships in the dockyards and had thirty-six more built by contract.[2]

Most of the Naval Commissioners had close links with ship-building, and it was only to be expected that they took full financial advantage by diverting contracts to themselves and their relatives and associates. But overall, until the demands of the Dutch War reached a peak, they proved effective in carrying out their responsibilities.

Finance

Money, or more accurately the lack thereof, would be a major factor in the eventual failure of the English Republic. During the Civil War Parliament had raised three principal taxes: Customs, Excise, and the Assessment. The revenues of the Customs Tax had traditionally gone to the Navy, but during and after the war the demands of the New Model Army alone were too great for all the tax revenue raised by Parliament.

Despite significant rises in taxation, there was never enough money, and, partly because unrest among the troops was always a potential threat to the regime, and also because, following Cromwell's takeover, many of the leading figures in government were Army officers, the Army always received the bulk of what money was available. In 1649 at least £10,000 earmarked for the

Navy was diverted to the needs of the Army and the Irish expedition. For a time in 1651–2, the situation improved because of a slight reduction in the demands of the Army and revenue gained from the sale of Church lands. In 1652 the Government planned to spend £535,000 on the Navy, and £1,328,579 on the Army, just about gaining solvency. But this proved short-lived, and by the time the Dutch War broke out in 1652 Navy finance was already critical. By November 1653, the Navy had debts totalling £10,760, anticipated expenses for the coming six months of £1,200,000, and an anticipated income for the same period of only £415,000. The Rump Parliament only assigned £600,000 to the Navy for the same period. Indeed the Rump never accepted the financial needs of the Navy. In 1654 its Revenue sub-committee insisted that the maximum amount required annually by the Navy was £269,750, while the costs of the Dutch War were actually running at almost ten times that much. Throughout the war the Navy was living from hand to mouth. Its needs during the war totalled some £3 million.

Further major financial difficulties were encountered in the Spanish War. Cromwell was so convinced that the war would pay for itself that taxes were actually reduced in 1655. The Navy was left only with the proceeds of the Customs, and any special allocations which were not tapped into for the needs of the Army. By the end of 1655 the Navy's debts and current financial requirements totalled £1,400,000. In November of 1657 the Navy had debts of £1 million, with another million required for the coming year.[3] The mounting financial crisis of the Navy made it impossible for the Commissioners to borrow money or to obtain credit from contractors except at up to 50 percent above the going rates.

The Navy arguably only continued to function at all by not paying its officers and men, who ran up large arrears.

The political chaos which marked most of 1659 completed the ruin of the Navy's finances, and on the Restoration in May of the following year over £2 million was required to pay off existing debts and to finance that year's Summer Guard.

The ships
Warships were roughly grouped, by size and number of guns carried, into five classes or 'rates'. The 'great ships' like the fleet

flagship, the 1st rate *Sovereign,* might carry up to 100 guns and several hundred men, and were what would soon be termed 'line of battle ships', designed to fight in fleet actions on equal terms with the largest vessels of foreign powers, and to have the potential to overwhelm smaller opponents. The 2nd rates, also classed as 'great ships', might carry eighty guns, and were intended for a similar function.

Increasingly seen as the most useful and versatile 'maid of all work' was the 3rd rate, carrying fifty-six to seventy guns. Providing the backbone of the Commonwealth and Protectorate Navy, those constructed during the Interregnum were based on the *Speaker,* built at Woolwich in 1650 by Christopher Pett of the famous shipbuilding family dynasty. These vessels were more adaptable than the 1st and 2nd rates, which were normally not employed outside the summer months, partly because they were unable to open their lower-deck gunports in rough seas. The 3rd rates, however, were powerful enough to stand in the line of battle, and also weatherly enough to be deployed in winter operations. They frequently served as squadron flagships, or as convoy escorts.

The smaller 4th and 5th rates were the largest vessels seen as being fit to stand in the line of battle, and also acted in detached squadrons and as convoy escorts.

The term 'frigate' was somewhat indiscriminately applied. Many 4th and 5th rates certainly fell within this type. Typical of them was the long-serving *Constant Warwick.* She was designed and built by Peter Pett in late 1644 or early in the following year. At this time the main threat facing merchant shipping was the well-manned fast sailing privateers (also known as frigates) employed by a variety of enemies, including the Irish Confederates, the English Royalists and the miscellany of nationalities operating out of the port of Dunkirk.

Constant Warwick was also intended to act as a privateer, and her design was probably based on captured Dunkirk privateers. She was owned by a syndicate which included the then Lord Admiral, the Earl of Warwick. She was about eighty-five feet long, with a breadth of twenty-six feet and a displacement of 374 tons. Her complement and armament varied at different times in her career, but normally included at least ninety-six men and thirty-two guns. Serving first as a privateer, but later as a Navy ship, *Constant*

Warwick was briefly held by the Royalists after the Second Civil War of 1648, but her crew defected in November, and the ship was taken back into the State's Navy.[4]

Constant Warwick proved to be forerunner to many of the same type. By 1655 Cromwell's Navy included fifty-four ships of various sizes loosely described as 'frigates'. The largest were the two-decker 3rd rates such as the *Speaker*, whose number of guns was steadily increased from an intended forty-four to sixty.

Frigate hulls were long and unhandy, not suitable for the manoeuvres involved in Elizabethan gunnery tactics of hit and run. This led to an increasing use of broadside gunnery tactics, with boarding the enemy seen as a secondary aim. By the mid-1650s the 'great frigate' was effectively the earliest form of the 'ship of the line' and of the 156 ships comprising the Navy in 1660, seventy-five were ranked as 4th rate or above, and fit to lie in the line of battle.

The Navy and politics

The English Navy was never entirely at ease with domestic politics from 1648 onwards. In 1649 Royalist tales of dissent among the seamen following the execution of the king were largely the products of wishful thinking. But there were strongly felt grievances, as Blake and Deane discovered when they took command that spring. Some episodes of mutiny, perhaps more accurately resembling 'strikes', did occur, but these were over service conditions rather than politics, and the rebels were largely mollified by concessions such as improved distribution of prize money.

Seamen were required to swear an oath of loyalty to the new regime, which the vast majority did readily enough. Nevertheless, its political masters never felt entirely sure of the loyalty of the Navy, and in 1651, during the invasion of England by Charles II and the Scots which culminated in the Battle of Worcester, Blake was warned by the Council of State to keep a close eye on his men. In fact these fears proved almost entirely groundless. During the whole period of the Interregnum from 1649 onwards only one small ship defected to the Royalists. Many naval officers shared the religious and political views of the zealots in the Army, and, while the ideological and spiritual fervour of most of their men was rather more diluted, this was compensated for by generally held anti-'Popish' views and the opportunity which conflict with the Republic's foes might offer for prize money and booty.

The Leveller movement, which caused a potentially major crisis in the Army in 1649, had little attraction for the majority of naval officers. The Council of State, its fears coloured by the mutinies of 1648, was much more apprehensive regarding Royalist sympathies in the fleet. The outbreak of the Dutch War in 1652 was seen as a major test of the Navy's loyalty. The Royalists hoped that defeat at sea would undermine the English regime, and that the Dutch would follow the desires of the Orange party and declare open support for the Stuarts, particularly as a leading Dutch commander, van Tromp, was a Stuart sympathizer of long standing. In the event, however, the Dutch Republic proved unwilling to associate itself with Charles II, refusing the very limited help which the Royalists offered it.

Of more pressing concern to the English government were the often untested loyalties of the greatly expanded officer corps, which the Dutch War made necessary. After the English defeat at Dungeness,[5] Blake claimed that a number of officers had deliberately held back, and there were demands for a purge. In fact, as we shall see, although there was clear evidence that some captains had not engaged the enemy with enthusiasm, their reasons were not generally political. This was not to say that there were not some disaffected officers with the fleet, probably more evident among warrant officers than in more senior positions. Available replacements, especially for specialists such as gunners, were often no more trustworthy. Nevertheless, much of the apparent disaffection was of a fairly low level, such as the case of a ship's cook who was noted as being 'a very profane and wicked man, and a perfect enemy to the commonwealth.'[6]

The problem of lack of commitment, as displayed at Dungeness and elsewhere, was most marked among the crews of the hired merchant vessels which comprised much of the enlarged fleet. While in some cases latent Royalist sympathy may have played a part, a more pressing consideration was usually a reluctance by a ship's captain or owner (often one and the same), to see the means of their livelihood damaged in battle.

It was in light of these concerns that a new disciplinary code was introduced at the end of 1652, including nine articles dealing with political offences. The necessity of forcibly 'pressing' large numbers of seamen to man the expanding fleet meant that Royalist sympathizers were inevitably caught up in the net. In 1653, for example, it was found that over a third of a group of men pressed in Jersey had previously served with Prince Rupert or other Royalist captains.[7] The potential for unrest had apparently also been increased by drafting Scottish prisoners of war into the fleet, and it was stipulated that no more than six of these were to be allowed to serve together in any one ship.

In fact, despite the fears of the Council of State, and the hopes of Royalist exiles such as Edward Hyde, there was little desertion during the Dutch War; instinctive patriotism, and the lure of booty and prize money, counteracted any political doubts.

A more severe test of the Navy's loyalty came in April 1653, when the Rump Parliament was removed from office by Oliver Cromwell's military coup.[8] In the purge that followed, all of the existing Naval Commissioners, headed by the long-serving Sir Henry Vane, were removed. Much now depended on the attitude of the Generals at Sea. Whatever their personal doubts, which in the case of Robert Blake were probably considerable, the Generals felt that in time of war the needs of their country's safety must take precedence, and on 22 April Blake, George Monck and Richard Deane issued a declaration stating that they would be loyal to their trust 'for the defence of [the nation] against the enemies thereof at sea.'[9]

It was hardly a ringing endorsement of the new regime, but in the end most naval officers, though with little enthusiasm, followed their commanders' examples. Richard Deane was, however, a confidante and friend of Cromwell, and George Monck, who had replaced Edward Popham on the latter's death, was newly appointed, with no real following in the fleet. Robert Blake, potentially the most influential of the Generals at Sea, was ashore on sick leave at the time of the coup, and as a staunch supporter of Parliament must have been deeply dismayed by the turn of events. But he eventually concluded that: 'tis not for us to mind state affairs, but to keep foreigners from fooling us.'[10]

In part this may have been recognition that so long as the Army wholeheartedly supported a government, there was very little that either the Navy or anyone else could do to oppose it. By late autumn, after the failure of the brief radical experiment known as the 'Barebones Parliament', a Cromwellian-dominated Council of State was in control and new Navy Commissioners, political moderates who were to prove to be highly competent administrators, were appointed. On balance, though with some minor misgivings, the majority of naval officers, first and foremost military professionals, seem to have welcomed the stability represented by the Protectorate.

Political unrest was certainly minimised because the constitutional changes took place in the midst of war against a foreign foe. Most seamen welcomed the Dutch War, which was seen as the culmination of a long-standing series of disputes over the English claim to 'sovereignty of the seas', rights of search and other issues. As Rear-Admiral Bourne noted: 'We had a strong God on our side who would judge between the nations', while other officers expressed their satisfaction at the bringing down of 'the pride and arrogance of that insufferable nation.' Even Vice-Admiral John Lawson, the leading radical among the Navy's senior commanders, whose unease with political developments had been about to cause him to retire prior to the outbreak of war, changed his mind, feeling that 'I could not satisfy my conscience to leave at this time, being very well satisfied that this service is in order to the design of God in the exultation of Jesus Christ, and therefore with much cheerfulness shall spend myself in this cause where the glory of God and the good of his people is much concerned.'[11]

Similar views were expressed by many lower down the scale of command. Captain Edmund Thompson of Yarmouth, a merchant skipper who sold his own ship in order to serve in the Navy in the war against the Dutch, exulted:

> 'It was the day of the Lord and we rejoice in it, and tell it to our children and let them tell it to generations to come, so that the goodness of the lord may never be forgotten by us nor them. [the English] though sinful men yet instruments in the hands of God, to carrying on his own work.'[12]

Not everyone shared this mood of religious certainty, however; the veteran commander Sir George Ayscue retired in September

1653, probably more because of his unease with the war than for the reasons of ill-health which he cited. Others had doubts about the justification for fighting fellow Protestants, and overall there was probably relief when peace was proclaimed.

The new regime made various efforts to identify the Navy with the changed political order in England. Most noticeable was their selection of names for ships of the State's Navy.

Since at least Tudor times it had been common for ships to be given names associated in some way with the ruling dynasty. Thus the *Mary Rose* was named after the sister of Henry VIII. At the same time names with a religious significance continued to be used, and increasingly ones, for example *Revenge*, extolling various warlike qualities. As might be expected, the Navy of Charles I laid great emphasis on dynastic names.

A change began during the Civil War, when the bulk of the Navy was under the control of Parliament, with a trend towards names of political significance. In 1646 the new frigate *President* referred to the chairman of the Committee of Both Kingdoms, which directed the anti-Royalist war effort. But the really fundamental change came in 1649–50, following the foundation of the English Republic. Within a month of the execution of Charles I, the Council of State ordered that 'the ships in service of the state shall only bear the Red Cross in a white flag and the State's arms on the ship's stern.' In June 1649 it was decreed that that the royal arms should be removed from all ships and public buildings and replaced by the arms of the Commonwealth. Finally, on 1 January 1650, Parliament ordered that all ships whose names had associations with the former regime should be renamed. In accordance with this instruction, *Charles* became *Liberty*, *Royal Prince* was now called *Resolution*, and *St Andrew* and *St George* became simply *Andrew* and *George*.

Reflecting the regime's attempt to identify the Navy with the new order were the names given to newly constructed ships. In 1650 the *Speaker*, *President* and *Fairfax* (named after Parliament's Lord General in the latter stages of the Civil War) were added. Next year a new frigate was named after Cromwell's victory at Worcester. It is not entirely clear who was responsible for the selection of names for new vessels. Probably the task was given to the Admiralty Committee, their choices subject to approval by the Council of

State. The early 1650s saw a massive increase in naval construction, and during this time nearly all vessels were named after battles or sieges. Indeed, the names chosen have been aptly described as being 'a battle roll of the Parliament and Commonwealth Army'. It may have been partly because of the presence of so many Army officers on the Admiralty Committee that land victories were awarded such prominence. The string of ships added to the fleet included the *Bristol, Gainsborough, Preston, Langport, Newbury, Marston Moor, Nantwich, Colchester* and *Naseby*.[13]

Significantly the only ship to be named after a naval victory was the *Portland*. It was Cromwell himself and the Army whose exploits were glorified in the names of the ships of what was regarded as to some extent a subordinate service to the all-powerful Army.

After 1656 the by then much more limited naval construction programme underwent another change in naming policy. The new names chosen mostly had no real political overtones, only perhaps the *Bradford, Lichfield* and *Coventry* having some Civil War associations. This change in policy echoed Cromwell's attempts at the time to reduce the overtly military nature of his regime. Of the remaining ships of the Interregnum, the *Richard*, launched in 1658, was named after Cromwell's son and brief successor, but otherwise only the *Monck* built in 1659 carried the name of one of the leaders of the by now faltering regime.[14]

The end of the Dutch War made it easier for some of those officers who remained discontented with the Protectorate to quit active service. Others remained, though in some cases inciting dissent. Among the latter was Vice-Admiral Lawson, who was involved, with Leveller leader John Wildman, in attempts to fan unrest in the Navy.

Discontent among the seamen was seen as a threat to Cromwell's cherished 'Western Design' – his plans to attack the Spanish colonies in the West Indies and America – and William Penn and John Desborowe were sent to the fleet with a large amount of money to quiet the unrest.

The Leveller plots were eventually quelled, although, possibly because of his popularity among the seamen, the authorities claimed to have found no evidence of Lawson's involvement, and he was restored to command.

The ill-fated West Indies expedition of 1656 saw other cases of discontent among the seamen, though in this instance they seem to have resulted more from disagreements between soldiers and sailors than from any political motive. Nevertheless, throughout 1654–5 the Royalists had renewed hopes of support from the Navy, although their only real impact on the fleet came when Royalist activists managed to gain entrance to the dockyard at Woolwich, and hack the figurehead of Cromwell off the 1st rate *Naseby*![15]

The chief concern of the Government continued to centre around the activities of John Lawson and a small group of sympathizers among naval officers. Lawson remained in secret communication with the exiled Leveller leaders Saxby and Wildman.

Matters came to a head in 1656, when Lawson resigned on being appointed as vice-admiral in Blake's expedition against Spain, which he, probably correctly, viewed as being designed to get him out of harm's way. Several of his captains were dismissed or arrested, and the Government remained uneasy until Blake was safely at sea.

Even so, the outbreak of war with Spain caused further divisions among naval officers, many seeing it as primarily 'Cromwell's war', instigated because of his personal views rather than in the national interest, and some were disturbed by the failure of the 'Western Design' and the long and initially fruitless blockade of the Spanish coast by Blake. Others, however, either shared Cromwell's dislike of the Spaniards as England's 'traditional foe' or were attracted by hopes of booty.

Throughout the closing years of the Protectorate the Royalists continued to claim widespread support in the Navy, though there is little evidence to confirm this.

When Cromwell died on 3 September 1658, the fleet remained quiet, largely because of the influence of 'Cromwell's Earl', General at Sea Edward Mountagu, who issued a declaration of support for Cromwell's designated successor, his son Richard. But it would not be long before the Navy became caught up in the increasing political ferment which swept through the country, and would eventually lead to the Restoration of Charles II.[16]

The officers

During this period, a ship's captain was often the only commissioned officer on its establishment. Lieutenants were generally only to be found on the larger 1st–4th rate warships, and none ever had more than one.

Unlike later practice, officers were not permanently commissioned, but were appointed to command either in the seasonal 'guards' or for a particular campaign, with no guarantee of continued employment afterwards. During the period of rule by the Rump Parliament, officers were generally appointed by the Council of State, which made its selection from lists of nominations prepared twice a year (for the Summer and Winter Guards) by the Generals at Sea. Though this system worked well enough during the early years of the republic, it proved less satisfactory under the demands of the Dutch War, when the Generals were frequently absent on campaign.

After the war the selection system was reorganised, with the Admiralty Committee assuming responsibility for the choice of officers, largely given a free hand by the Council of State.

A chosen officer ideally met several criteria. The overriding factor was political reliability, with religious zeal of an approved type also being favourable. Senior naval commanders of approved views were asked for recommendations, while nominated officers would often provide the Admiralty Committee with testimonials to their 'godliness'. In 1653, for example, Captain Wootlead was supported by the entire congregation of his church at Sandwich, who testified that he was 'God-fearing, faithful, and skilful for a command at sea.'

However, more traditional criteria were not forgotten when selecting commanders. Foremost was a proven record of courage in action. This was sometimes testified to in original ways. Daniel Baker offered to send to the Committee as proof 'sundry great bones' taken out of his leg as the result of a wound suffered in action. Whether or not this offer was accepted is unrecorded, but Baker got his commission.[17]

One hopeful or desperate candidate even pressed his claims in verse. Francis Cranwell said of his experience in fighting the Scots:

> With thundering cannon made them fly,
>   From town and castle to mountains high.'

Carried away by his poetic enthusiasm, Cranwell envisaged that if he was given a command:

Then Spanish admiral, stand you clear,
For Cranwell means a chain of gold to wear.'

Possibly more as tribute to the Committee's sense of humour than its poetical judgement, Cranwell was granted a command.[18]

Courage in action was deemed more important in lieutenants than in captains, for it was the lieutenant's role in larger ships to lead the men in battle, with little responsibility for the day-to-day running of the ship. Captains, whose responsibilities included checking the accounts of their warrant officers, were required to have some clerical and administrative skills, qualities evidently lacking in the poetic Francis Cranwell, who complained on one occasion that the Admiralty Committee valued 'penmanship' above valour.

The Commonwealth and Protectorate Navy has traditionally been seen as offering particularly good opportunities for 'tarpaulin' sailors – professional seamen of often humble origins as opposed to the scions of the aristocracy who more usually formed the bulk of the officer corps. In fact it seems that, as with the New Model Army, everything else being equal, officers from a gentry background were still preferred. It was felt that men of this sort had more natural authority, and would also be more skilled in the diplomatic role which often fell to ships' captains.

In practice, particularly during wartime, there were not sufficient candidates with a gentry background available, which meant that birth perforce had to carry rather less weight than previously, and evidence of seamanship rather more. Considerable use was made of men with local knowledge, such as in the case of the North Sea fishing fleets, the commanders of whose escorts during the Dutch War were often Yarmouth men.[19]

It was the Rump Parliament rather than Cromwell's Government which was responsible for establishing the foundations of the officer corps of 'Cromwell's Navy'. Of its captains, some 230 were first appointed between 1649 and 1653, compared with eighty-nine who first held command under the Protectorate. About fifty-four are known to have first commanded ships during the First Civil War, with only two being naval captains prior to the war. There was also no real evidence that the upheavals of the English Revolution led to men being given commands at a younger age than in previous years. The average age of captains on gaining their first command was thirty-six, and the Generals at Sea averaged forty-one on their appointment. The only notable exception was Edward Mountagu, who was ten years younger when appointed, but that was due largely to political circumstances and his favour with Cromwell.[20]

One reason for the maturity in years of newly appointed captains was the tendency to recruit them from the ranks of experienced merchant captains. Furthermore, those candidates who were regarded as having proven political and religious reliability, as well as experience, also tended to be older. In some cases notably older men were appointed, such as Captain Harris, aged over sixty and Richard Haddock, a vice-admiral in 1652 at the age of seventy. Those captains promoted because of long previous experience as warrant officers were also naturally older.

The demands of the Dutch War led to younger men obtaining promotion more quickly, and some of the more experienced masters of merchant ships were given more important naval commands. Among them were many veterans of the American trade, including some with colonial origins, particularly from New England, with its strongly Puritan tradition. The Mediterranean and Levant trade also provided many recruits, most notable among them being Richard Badiley.

In most cases, those enticed by pecuniary motives were attracted by the prospects of booty, rather than pay, which was frequently in arrears. Such considerations were especially applicable to those merchant captains who did not own a ship themselves, and to whom the outbreak of the Dutch war threatened financial ruin.

The second major category of officer consisted of those promoted from within the Navy, from the warrant officers: masters, boatswains, gunners and carpenters. Some of these had served in the Navy since the early part of the reign of Charles I. Captain Anthony Young, for example, had first seen action at the age of ten in the Duke of Buckingham's expedition to the Ile de Ré in 1627. He became a gunner's mate, then a gunner, before gaining his first command in 1645. Captain Richard Country had been boatswain's boy – probably to his father – in 1635 in the *Vanguard*.

The third important group of captains had, in most cases, no prior maritime experience at all. These were Army officers transferred to the Navy. There were some precedents for this, stretching back to mediaeval times, of land commanders also leading at sea. Army officers were seen as possessing the required fighting qualities, as well as being politically reliable. The trend was most marked among the appropriately named Generals at Sea, five out of six of whom had previously served in the Army. Only William Penn, ironically one of the least successful, had an entirely naval background.

This military dominance even led briefly to rumours that Cromwell himself was preparing to take command at sea, and many transferees continued to be known by their Army rank. The majority of officers from an Army background, however, served as lieutenants, where their experience at leading troops in battle had obvious relevance. Some eventually rose higher. Thomas Adams, for example, had served on land as a lieutenant in the sieges of Lyme and Taunton, where he had no doubt come to the notice of Robert Blake. He served at sea firstly as a lieutenant in Blake's flagship, next commanded a Dutch prize, and then became captain of a frigate.[21]

Few Army officers can have been drawn to transfer by the attractions of pay. The captain of a 4th rate theoretically received 7s 8d a day, compared with a captain of foot's 8s and the 10s of a cavalry captain. Even the captain of a 1st rate was only paid 15s a day whilst an army major received 21s.

However, such comparisons can be deceptive. The Navy, for example, provided free board and lodging, as well as the chance of prize money. For the wider spectrum of recruits, provided they had reached the necessary standard of literacy, the Navy offered the chance of promotion. Of twenty men who rose in the 17th century from cabin boy to admiral, fourteen had obtained their first command in the Commonwealth Navy, though all of the Generals at Sea were either well-born or of gentry background.[22]

However, the notion of a career structure in the later sense was fairly rudimentary. But it was certainly aided by the almost constant warfare of the period, which made it necessary to put large fleets to sea almost every year. One result was the beginnings of a sense of naval professionalism, and some kind of order of seniority based on length of service. During the Dutch War, for example, officers who had already proved themselves were moved into better ships ahead of others whose skills had yet to be demonstrated. But this trend should not be overstated; Commonwealth officers still had no guarantee after the end of each commission that they would be re-employed, or in what capacity. Once the Dutch War had ended, opportunities naturally declined, and many commissioned officers were forced back into being warrant officers or 'reformadoes'.

These factors meant that an officer's career progress could be uncertain and erratic. Speedy promotion depended on luck, such as being given command of a prize, a timely death creating a post to be filled, or the power of patronage. The latter was widely exercised by the Generals at Sea, and to a lesser extent by individual captains. Both might promote particular friends or previous colleagues. Ideology and religious views could also play a part, if a commander wished to favour those with similar opinions to his own. Family connections might also be significant; among Robert Blake's captains were four of his relatives or former officers during the Civil War. William Penn appointed a number of his relatives.

Members of Parliament and Navy Commissioners often opened up promotion avenues for favourites, but overall, most patrons seem to have acted responsibly in their choices, though there was, naturally, sometimes discontent among those who missed out.[23]

Command at sea

At the highest level responsibility was theoretically shared between the Generals at Sea, who commanded either individually, or often in pairs. This might seem an arrangement full of potential problems, but it generally appears to have worked smoothly, mainly because of the good personal relationships between most of the Generals. This was particularly the case with the earliest Generals, Blake, Popham and Deane, and matters continued to run smoothly when George Monck was appointed following Popham's death. The only serious potential difficulties came in 1657, when the young Edward Mountagu was appointed joint commander of the Spanish expedition along with the veteran Robert Blake. Blake seems at first to have resented the politically appointed newcomer, but, largely because of Mountagu's good sense and tact, these initial difficulties were overcome and the two men eventually worked harmoniously together.

As on land, Councils of War were held before anticipated major engagements. Again following the common practice ashore, the Generals were usually able to dominate the debate when they so wished, and ensure that their opinion was accepted. On occasions when the fleet or squadron commander had no clear opinion, decision was usually reached by a process of consensus, rather than a formal vote. However, in smaller squadrons where no General was present debate often resulted in dispute or even disobedience.

There was a rapid turnover in officers, which can largely be accounted for by a high casualty rate. During the course of the Interregnum thirty-six captains were killed in action – possibly more than in the entire previous existence of the Navy. Of the Generals at Sea, Richard Deane was killed in action during the Dutch War. About thirty-eight other captains are known to have died due to illness or accident.[24]

Disability as a result of enemy action usually resulted in the award of a gratuity, though this did not always occur. Former Lieutenant John Weale, for example, who had been blinded in both eyes, was forced to attempt to earn a living as a fencing master![25]

Other officers, especially former merchant ship masters, left the service voluntarily to pursue commercial or business interests. About fifty captains and considerably more lieutenants lost their posts as the result of alleged misconduct of various kinds. This was only rarely the result of formal court martial; more commonly the Admiralty Commission simply refused to re-employ the individual concerned. The most frequent offences were absence without leave, drunkenness, embezzlement or failure to maintain adequate discipline.[26]

The degree of severity in removing officers varied according to circumstances. In time of war it was sometimes necessary to retain men who might otherwise have been dismissed, but during peacetime there was usually an ample pool of potential replacements.

Warrant officers

These comprised the various specialists – masters, boatswains, gunners, carpenters – whose skills were essential for the running of a ship. The master, whose field of expertise was navigation, was expected to be capable of taking over from the ship's captain in the event of the latter being incapacitated. As he was responsible for navigating the ship, the master would be liable for blame if a ship were lost, and could possibly face court martial. In general neither the Council of State nor the Admiralty Committee was involved in the appointment of warrant officers, which were usually the result of recommendation by Generals at Sea or senior captains. The only exception was the 'prestige' flagship, *Sovereign*, where the Council of State took a keen interest even in warrant officer appointments.

In times of severe shortages, it was sometimes necessary to employ as warrant officers former captains or lieutenants who had proved unsatisfactory in more senior command.

Other warrant officers, including boatswains, gunners and carpenters, were termed 'standing officers', in that they served on a continuous basis, often for many years at a time. They frequently regarded themselves as permanent fixtures as a result; Captain Ned Ward described his gunner as 'a little king in his own conceit'.[27] As there was no fixed retirement age, some warrant officers were notably old; one gunner was seventy-three, and the boatswain of one ship laid up in reserve was supposedly 100!

As with commissioned officers, ideological reliability was a major consideration in the selection of warrant officers. The lower-ranking warrant officers of a ship were usually appointed from suitable men within its crew. These included 'midshipmen', who at this period were experienced seamen who could take over the roles of gunners or boatswains if needed. The position of cook, also classed as a warrant officer, was often given to seamen too old or crippled for other duties.

The post of ship's purser, responsible for keeping the ship's accounts and obtaining its provisions, obviously required a fair degree of literacy and numeracy. As in later times, the job offered plenty of opportunities for profit for the unscrupulous, and hence was eagerly sought-after. Many pursers were soldiers grown too old for active service in the field.

Surgeons were a desirable, if not always available, addition to a ship's company, and were allowed between £3 and £10 to stock their medicine chest. The Company of Barber-Surgeons was required to supply surgeons, obtained if necessary by pressing. The calibre of those obtained was often very low, though there was an attempt to improve standards at the end of 1652, when a surgeon's pay was increased to £2 10s a month. Even so, the level of medical care on board ship often remained abysmal, and the lack of good surgeons made it necessary to relax the rules regarding political reliability so that known Royalist sympathisers could be employed. The best surgeons tended to gravitate to the larger ships, where conditions for them were better.

Life at sea

A large warship might have a crew of 300 or more men, and at the height of the Dutch War over 20,000 men were serving in the Navy. Conditions of life at sea seem to have lain somewhere in between those of the days of Charles I, when seamen were 'used like dogs', and the claim sometimes put forward that the Commonwealth Navy was a place of harmony and goodwill. In practice there seems to have been no overall common pattern of life aboard ship. A good ship's company might be closely bonded by the dangers and hardships which it faced, and a capable captain not only encouraged such links but also found the overall atmosphere aboard ship was improved by the volunteers who readily came forward to fill out the ranks of his crew.

On the other hand there were officers who misused their authority, resulting in discontented crews. But these seem to have been very much a minority, and on the whole the State's Navy had better relations between officers and men than would be the case for two centuries to come. The situation was helped by most of the officers being experienced seamen rather than gentry appointments, and most of them seem to have had an almost paternal care for their men, being for example horrified by the heavy losses of the Dutch War. After the heavy casualties suffered in the action off Portland it was serving officers who urged the Government to make provision for the wounded, and for the widows and orphans of those killed in the fighting. They also attempted to obtain better food for their men, while in 1653 George Monck personally undertook to pay for the care of some wounded men who were otherwise relying on the charity of civilians on whom they were billeted.

Captains often spoke out forcibly on behalf of their men, if they felt that their interests were being neglected. In late 1652, Captain John Sherwen, a frigate captain in the Irish Sea squadron, when ordered to keep his ship in commission throughout the winter, pointed out the wretched condition of his men, and added that the

Navy Commissioners were a 'company of barking whelps that mind their own prey more than the welfare of their dam, that values not the frigate so long as their self-interest is provided.'[28]

Captains were partly motivated in their concern by the need to avoid the risk of mutiny, and a good captain moving to a new ship often took a number of his men with him, some of them petitioning to continue serving under their old commander.

In general differences of rank did not form a major barrier between commissioned and warrant officers, who were frequently on friendly personal terms, and some captains had relatives among their warrant officers. In 1652 the hired merchant ship *Prosperous* had John Baker as its captain, with his son as master and his son-in-law as master's mate.[29] A popular officer might strengthen bonds by recruiting sailors from his own locality. However, there was often tension between those of a crew who were volunteers and those who had been pressed into service.

In theory the disciplinary code to which seamen were liable was ferocious. The provisions in the code introduced on 25 December 1652 had twenty-five offences which carried the death penalty. The prevailing view was still that seamen required harsh discipline. One official commented in May 1653: 'They are the rudest generation of men I ever saw.'[30] However, the code was used more as a deterrent. Only one sailor is known to have been hanged in the eleven years between 1649 and 1660, and courts martial repeatedly ignored the death penalty stipulated for crimes such as desertion. The punishment of whipping from ship to ship in a squadron was occasionally imposed, but the most common offence, of drunkenness while on duty, was only punished if the circumstances were particularly bad. A quartermaster found drunk on duty, for example, was whipped and reduced to the ranks.

Captains often ordered summary punishment without recourse to the procedure of court-martial. An offender might be put in irons, struck on the head with the boatswain's whistle or gagged and bound with a notice around his neck giving details of his crime. For a more serious offence a man might be ducked, whipped or discharged, but a serious flogging could only be administered after a full court-martial.

Crews readily complained to higher authority if they felt that they were being treated unfairly. In the majority of cases they were supported by the Admiralty Committee. In 1658 the Commissioners warned the captain of the *Newcastle* after complaints from his men about their commander's 'imperious carriage':

> 'It is necessary you should bear a command and we would not weaken your hands in it, though our advice be, that you should do it with that prudence and good temper of spirit as may not needlessly exasperate the ship's company, and make the service burdensome to them.'[31]

Even so, the Commissioners would only normally take direct action against a commander if they received overwhelming evidence to support a complaint against him. In practice, as the Commissioners undoubtedly intended, a captain had to earn the respect of his crew, and often allowed them considerable latitude when enforcing regulations. The most common problems seem to have been quarrels or feuds between commissioned and warrant officers, especially if a captain was not forceful enough to impose his authority. Cases of outright mutiny were rare; more frequent were outbreaks of disorderly conduct brought on by drink. Protests against higher authority usually involved grievances over pay, and were not directed against the ship's captain. Such unrest usually took the form of 'strikes' directed against the Admiralty Commission.

There were, however, a handful of occasions when ships' crews refused to fight the enemy when faced by what they saw as overwhelming odds. In 1652, when Rear-Admiral Richard Badiley encountered a Dutch squadron in the Straits of Gibraltar, his men refused to renew the action if the enemy engaged them on the second day, telling their commander that 'We'll fight no more, that state hath better ships, but we have no more lives.' In the event a flat calm prevented a renewal of the action. A few years later, Captain Hone of the *Parrot*, when attacked by four French privateers, was forced to surrender by his crew without firing a shot.

On the whole, life on board most ships ran fairly smoothly. However, the prospect of being deprived of what they saw as their fair share of the prize money for a captured ship might sometimes unite both officers and crew against authority. Prize regulations stipulated that the crew of a capturing vessel were entitled to all the goods aboard the prize found on or above its gun deck, but in practice captains were often to the forefront in ignoring or evading this. Some captains also took advantage of their position by taking bribes from convoy captains or falsified muster rolls in order to claim the pay of dead or runaway sailors. But although many warrant officers, especially pursers, sold ship's stores, corruption overall was probably less than at many other periods.

Life at sea was probably less harsh than some land-dwelling critics suggested. Although discipline in ships of the State's Navy was no stricter than that aboard many merchant ships, pay was lower, but overall conditions better, especially as there were usually more men available to handle the ship. The diet of a seaman was far better than he would normally have obtained ashore. He could anticipate hot meals of pork, beef or fish every day, even if these were not always of the authorised standard. If food ran short, as happened not infrequently, a sailor was given 'short allowance money' which, if in port, enabled him to buy food ashore. Another money-raising practice of the sailors was to buy clothes on credit from the ship's purser, and then sell them ashore to raise money for more pleasurable things.

In general, the sailor of Cromwell's Navy lived largely for the present, with the philosophy of ' A merry life and a short.'[32] It was common for a sailor in port to squander a whole year's pay in a week or less. As was the case throughout recorded history, much of it was spent on strong drink, officially forbidden on board ship, but often used to supplement the daily issue of a gallon of beer per man. The use of tobacco was also universal, with smoking forbidden below decks, although this rule did not prevent two ships from being lost as a result of accidental fires caused by smoking.

Other common pastimes at sea included fishing and carving and rigging model ships. One captain allowed his men to bring a dancing bear aboard for a cruise, and other popular pastimes were games of various sorts and singing, though one more godly witness described the ditties as 'vain, idle songs with ungodly words and actions.'[33]

Overall the atmosphere below decks seems to have been one of rough good humour, punctuated by the inevitable fights and quarrels.

Officers relaxed with talk around the dinner table, with music providing a common pastime, though Blake for one evidently disliked it. Staple reading matter was provided by the large numbers of contemporary newsbooks, while some ship's chaplains maintained small lending libraries of mainly devotional works. Officers could also go ashore at home and abroad, see the sights of foreign parts and buy gifts for their families. For the seamen, shore leave was a valued privilege granted only to the volunteers among a ship's company. Such excursions usually terminated in the nearest ale-house, with resultant misbehaviour which upset naval administrators concerned by the 'mad, savage spirit' of the sailors.

Though many months might pass without news from home, officers were able to write to their families, an option generally not available to the frequently illiterate seamen. In some cases wives at home had to earn a living as best they could, and it was not unknown for captains to resign from the service under pressure from their spouses. The Admiralty Commission disapproved of the practice of allowing officers' wives on board ship in home waters, though this seems to have been common. The wives of seamen were generally allowed to visit when the ship was in port.

The attitude of many ordinary seamen towards marriage was fairly casual. In 1656 Captain Thomas Wright discovered that two of his men had five wives between them, and partly as a result of hardship, infidelity was common among sailors' wives, with many turning to prostitution. Perhaps surprisingly, many officers also took a casual approach to matters matrimonial. In the mid-1650s, due to a tangle of misadventures, Captain Nicholas Foster found himself with two wives already as he was preparing to marry a third.[34] Casual sexual encounters, second perhaps only to strong drink, were the prime objective of many of all ranks when ashore, and also sometimes led to problems at sea. On the *Grantham* the captain and boatswain quarrelled over the latter's wife, though many captains attempted, with what success is unclear, to ensure that 'wives' who came on board actually were such.

Homosexuality seems to have been universally condemned, and, perhaps because crowded conditions on board ship made it difficult to conceal, rarely practised.

Manning the fleet

Providing seamen for their ships was one of the greatest challenges to face the Admiralty Committee. If the Dutch War had continued into 1654 it was estimated that 30,000 seamen would have been needed. The difficulty of the task may be gauged when it is noted that early in the reign of Charles I it was estimated that England only possessed some 18–20,000 seamen. Though this number had certainly increased by the 1650s, many were serving overseas – in 1652 between five and six thousand of them with the Dutch! Under-manning remained a problem throughout the Dutch War; it proved very difficult to replace the losses suffered in the action off Portland. In 1653 it was impossible to find crews for Dutch prizes, and the great *Sovereign* could not be manned all summer.

Volunteers were naturally preferred to pressed men, and efforts were made to include some in every ship's company. In 1652 a new category of sailor was introduced with the title of 'able seaman' – 'fit for helm, lead, top and yards' – paid just over 10d a day, which matched the wage of a soldier or farm labourer, but also came with free food board. However, the crews of merchant ships and privateers were often paid between 30 and 40s a month during wartime.

Prize money rather than wages was usually the main attraction for volunteers, certainly in time of war. Some volunteers asked to serve with a particular captain, but hopes of booty made it easier to obtain volunteers for the smaller faster ships and frigates rather than the great ships. The Admiralty Committee found it very difficult to stipulate where volunteers should serve. It was not uncommon for seamen to volunteer rather than risk being pressed with all the disadvantages that brought with it. However, there were never enough volunteers, so pressing was always the main means of manning the fleet. All trained seamen, apart from those holding senior posts in merchant ships, were liable to be pressed, with a penalty of three months' imprisonment for evasion or resistance. Each spring, press warrants were issued to conscript men between the ages of fifteen and fifty. Thousands of men were required to man the Summer Guard, and pressing normally extended over several weeks, often with an embargo on outward-bound merchant shipping until the target was met or the pressure of merchants forced the lifting of the ban.

Magistrates of coastal areas and vice-admirals of coastal shires were responsible for administering the press system. Each high and petty constable was instructed to leave a note at every seaman's house in their parish, requiring him to report to the nearest market town on a specified day. In practice the results varied. The press seems generally to have been effective in London, but elsewhere proved more patchy. Of 1,000 men called on to report at Newton Abbot in Devon in March 1653, less than 100 appeared, of whom only twenty-eight were deemed fit to press. Many would flee on the first rumours of a press, and the parish constables were often too afraid, or were bribed, not to enforce the press. Many magistrates who were also local shipowners failed to ensure that the press was carried out, while others used it as a means to get rid of local undesirables, with or without maritime experience.

In response the government ordered local military commanders to enforce the press, and warships often had to send out their own press gangs. Even then there were frequent problems in running fugitives to ground. Some would lurk out at sea in small boats, or seek work inland in order to avoid the press. Local mobs would sometimes turn out against the press gangs, and pitched battles ensued. If he was apprehended, a pressed man could apply for exemption on compassionate grounds or simply abscond, particularly as he would already have received 'conduct money' to cover his immediate expenses in making his own way to the fleet. In 1656, out of one group of thirty pressed men, less than six actually joined the fleet at Portsmouth. The only reasonable chance of compliance was if men were escorted under guard or pressed from seamen in merchant ships at sea. Even then violent clashes often took place.

The Admiralty Commissioners generally tried to enforce the press system as humanely as possible, but found that it failed to meet the required needs. The other main method of filling out ships' crews during the Dutch War was by the use of soldiers. They were officially deployed to carry out amphibious operations and also in boarding actions at sea, but in practice they were also often required to help man their ships. In theory they were supposed to make up no more than a third of a ship's total complement, but sometimes there were more, and between 3,000 and 4,000 troops served aboard the fleet during the Dutch War.[35] Those earlier soldiers turned sailors, the Generals at Sea, were unenthusiastic about the employment of troops; in January 1654 Blake and George Monck turned down an offer of more troops, saying that they were 'of little advantage to the service they being unprovided of all conveniences, and (as we have found by experience) unable to brook this winter weather.'[36] They were willing to accept soldiers only as a last resort, their enthusiasm dampened by the ill-feeling, often degenerating into brawls which frequently followed when soldiers and sailors were in close proximity.

Grievances

Although Cromwell's Navy was relatively free from major mutiny, there were a number of ongoing grievances among its personnel. The quality of provisions provided was a fairly constant source of complaint, particularly because of the frequent outbreak of diseases associated with dietary deficiencies, which sometimes resulted in entire ships' companies being incapacitated. In fact the standard of food provision was considerably better than it had been in the Tudor Navy.

Another source of complaint was the standard of clothing issued to the seamen. There was no regulation dress, and issues of clothing were often so infrequent that the men were left clad in rags. Prize money was often distributed unfairly, or only after long delays. Similar discontent was aroused by wages, which were often paid by means of a 'ticket', which sailors often found difficulty in cashing. On several occasions widespread riots followed when the majority of sailors in the fleet were discharged at the end of a campaigning season. By the end of 1658 some crews were owed two years' wages and others four. Even when discharged, seamen were sometimes only given part of what was owed to them in order to make them more inclined to re-enlist in the hope of obtaining the remainder. Men were often reduced to selling their 'tickets' to local tradesmen for whatever return they could get. Although the Admiralty Commissioners did intervene in the worst cases of seamen's grievances, they often lacked the resources to assist them. It was not uncommon for the Generals at Sea and captains to do what they could to help their men out of their own pockets.

Not surprisingly, there was evidently considerable desertion throughout the period, though no detailed statistics survive. Many merchant ship captains and privateersmen were ready to engage deserters without enquiring too closely into their circumstances, while the ongoing desperate shortage of seamen meant that those deserters who were apprehended were rarely severely punished. They were usually just returned to their original ship, forfeiting any pay which was due to them. So bad was the situation that troops were sometimes used to guard ships in port, and roads leading out of the ports, in an attempt to quell desertion.

Actual mutiny while at sea was rare, although disorders in port were much more frequent. At the end of 1652 there was widespread disorder over pay demands, and even more in 1653, when thousands of seamen headed for London, and serious rioting followed in the capital, with, on 27 October, an armed mob advancing on Whitehall and fighting with Cromwell's Life Guard before being dispersed. On the 28th, in order to restore order, Parliament imposed the death penalty on the rioters, and two men were hanged, one for drawing his sword against Monck. There were disorders in several ports, and at Portsmouth three ring-leaders were condemned to death, though their sentences were commuted to being nailed by the right hand to the mainmast, with halters around their necks.

The Protectorate learnt from the experience, and in future strenuous efforts were made to pay men everything owed to them on their discharge, and no further serious strikes or mutinies took place. Whenever possible, the authorities tried to settle such disputes by peaceful persuasion, partly because the port officials often sympathised with the grievances of the men, and also because both common sense and self-preservation tended to make officials placatory in their approach. However, as a last resort, if persuasion failed, they would use the military to restore order.

Sick and wounded

The care of sick and wounded would prove a major challenge for Cromwell's Navy. As the fleet saw little service in hot climes, the tropical diseases which had plagued, for example, Francis Drake's expeditions, were rare. In the earlier years of the Commonwealth the main causes of sickness in the fleet were 'cold weather diseases', such as exposure and pneumonia, and what was known as 'camp' 'gaol' or 'ship' fever, usually typhus, which was carried by ticks and attacked poorly clothed, ill-washed seamen in crowded conditions. But by September 1653 the flood of battle casualties in the Dutch War had all but overwhelmed the Navy Commissioners, with the result that a new Board of Sick and Wounded was set up with the task of organising medical and nursing care ashore and provision for the wounded and care for the widows of those who died. Beds were commandeered in the London hospitals, and the old Savoy Palace and Ely House were turned into military and naval hospitals. However, despite the efforts of an energetic naval physician, Dr David Whistler, no corresponding naval hospital was set up at Portsmouth, and the wounded and sick there had to be billeted in civilian homes and lodging houses. In the London hospitals the staff had strict orders to report unauthorised absences and the use of strong drink and strong language by their patients, but for those living in the wider community no such supervision was feasible, with the result that many of the patients succumbed to the temptations of liquor. As a consequence Dr Whistler preferred whenever possible to return convalescents or the lightly wounded to their ships, where they would be out of reach of such ungodly attractions.

The East Coast ports received many wounded, and here too they were quartered in farms and inns where the main problem was lack of cash for their carers in order to cover the expenses they incurred. Those who volunteered to act as nurses, most famously Elizabeth Alkin (known as 'Parliament Joan' and in some ways the Florence Nightingale of the 17th century), were unable to recoup their own expenses. The situation was only eased when General at Sea George Monck sent some Dutch prizes directly to Yarmouth to be sold there to raise funds.

Religion
It is not surprising that religion played a central role in the life of Cromwell's Navy. Most of the senior officers were men of strong radical religious and political views. In the period prior to the Restoration, William Penn, for example, was noted for his strong religious beliefs, with his journals dotted with scriptural references. In some, these religious protestations may have been somewhat exaggerated for the sake of their owner's advancement, though of the Generals at Sea only George Monck had little apparent

religious enthusiasm – though even he adopted 'godly' rhetoric on appropriate occasions.

Many of the Admiralty Commissioners were known as radical religious activists, and they naturally appointed men of similar doctrine to senior posts. At least 100 captains (a quarter of the total) are known to have been Puritan, and in reality there were almost certainly more. The religious Generals at Sea seem to have had a significant bonding effect on the officer corps as a whole, frequently holding prayer meetings with their officers. In early 1653, Blake held such a meeting on board his flagship, and the company 'asked God to tell us where [the Dutch] were'. When, next day, the Dutch fleet was sighted and the battle of Portland began, it was seen by many as a sign of divine intervention. As in the army, a number of officers were well known for preaching to their men.

The most common religious conviction among naval officers was that they were God's instruments for carrying out his work. Blake and Deane, for example, would often report their successes with the same kind of religious exultation common among Parliamentarian and Commonwealth generals on land. Just before the encounter off Portland Blake wrote to Parliament: 'We dare not in this great business to promise anything but for or to ourselves, because it is God alone who giveth courage and conduct.'

Most officers attributed good or ill fortune to the workings of 'providence'. Many of them saw the wars with the Dutch and Spanish as heralding Christ's approaching kingdom, coupling this with an instinctive strongly anti-Catholic feeling.

Not surprisingly, the Sabbath was strictly observed and enforced aboard most naval vessels. However, the degree of religious activism can be exaggerated. Most naval officers resembled Cromwell in having undenominational, broadly Puritan, beliefs. They were not, for the most part, deep religious thinkers. Overall, Puritans were a minority in the fleet. In most ships, short daily services took place, and 'profaness', a term which could cover a wide range of misdemeanours, was forbidden. If a ship had a chaplain or minister, then it was he who conducted the service. If not, it would be one of the officers. On Sunday the service would be accompanied by a sermon.

Between 1649 and 1660 at least 175 chaplains served with the fleet. Of the twenty-nine ships sent to the Baltic in 1658, twenty-two had chaplains. A chaplain was regarded as an officer, but only received the pay of an ordinary seaman, though this was sometimes doubled by deductions from the pay of the crew. The harsh nature of life at sea proved not to the taste of many clergymen, and several chaplains were killed in action. The choice of chaplain was usually left to each ship's captain, and the degree of care taken in selection consequently varied. Most were of Independent or Presbyterian persuasion, though a few ex-clergy of the formally abolished Established Church were also appointed, as well as some lay preachers. Their impact also varied from ship to ship. In some of the smaller, less closely scrutinised vessels, there was virtually no religious observance, and in general a great deal depended upon the attitude of individual captains. The impact of religion on crews was often limited; some indeed found that both the officers and seamen in their charge were beyond redemption; one complained that 'There is so much swearing in the sea, as if both hell, the damned, and all the devils in it were let loose.'[37]

However, many seamen seem, in a rather generalised way, to have welcomed the presence on board of a minister in times of danger or when faced by death. A few commanders, such as Robert Blake, were able to instil some apparent religious enthusiasm in their men, even if they did so partly by compulsion. Overall, however, the ordinary seamen were often not particularly drawn to religion. They remained a superstitious breed, swayed by omens and a belief in evil spirits, that storms and shipwrecks were the work of witchcraft, and that astrology could tell their futures.[38]

Chapter 3
Defeating the Royalists: I:
Blake versus Rupert

'This vagabond German; a Prince of Fortune'
(Charles Vane)

The rival commanders
Robert Blake, the stocky fifty-year-old five foot six son of a
Somerset merchant, provided a striking physical contrast to Prince
Rupert, aged twenty-nine, over six foot in height and powerfully
built. In the past decade, Rupert, largely as a result of his exploits
as a Royalist cavalry commander during the First Civil War, had
earned an international military reputation,[1] while Blake, although
his dogged defence of Lyme and Taunton had earned him respect
in Parliamentarian military circles, remained a largely unknown
figure beyond them.

However, the two commanders had more in common than was
at first apparent. Both were austere in personality and quick-
tempered and more at ease in the company of military men than in
social situations. Both seem to have been at best uneasy in the
company of women.

Naval command was an entirely new experience for both Blake
and Rupert. Though they had seasoned seamen to advise them,
and, in Rupert's case at least, a pre-war interest in naval matters,
Prince Rupert and Robert Blake were entering literally unknown
waters, with a great deal resting on the decisions that they took.

Both had problems with the men and ships under their command, but the situation which Rupert inherited was probably worse. As we have seen,[2] after its failures in the Second Civil War what remained of the Royalist fleet had retired to the neutral Dutch port of Helvoetsluys, where, blockaded by a Parliamentarian

squadron under the Earl of Warwick, it was split by dissension and dispute, with defections by several ships and a steady stream of desertions among the seamen.

Prince Rupert played some part in this unrest; ambitious and energetic, he pressed for the removal of the uninspiring William Batten, and to assume command himself. The Earl of Clarendon, no friend of Rupert, would later accuse the Prince of intriguing for the post, although he admitted that 'there was in truth nobody in view to whom the charge of the fleet could be committed but Prince Rupert'.[3]

At the end of October 1649 Rupert was appointed Admiral, 'with all the powers he formerly exercised on land', and with unlimited authority 'on the coasts of the three kingdoms'.[4]

Rupert's first objective was to support the Irish-Royalist forces of the Marquis of Ormonde, currently on the offensive. His opportunity came when the Earl of Warwick, following the contemporary practice of laying up most fighting ships during the winter months, on 21 November raised the blockade and sailed for the anchorage in the Downs between Folkestone and Dover.

There was still a great deal to be done, with scanty resources, before the Royalist fleet was ready for sea. At the end of October Rupert's squadron in Helvoetsluys consisted of seven heavy ships, together with several smaller craft. Flagship, and largest, was the fifty-two gun 2nd rate, *Constant Reformation*. Rupert's faithful brother, Prince Maurice, was Vice-Admiral in the forty-six gun *Convertine*, with Sir John Mennes, a Royalist soldier who had served at sea before the Civil War, as Rear Admiral aboard *Swallow* (forty guns). The other significant vessels included three frigates.[5]

Before he could think of putting to sea, Rupert had to deal with his crews. Many of the sailors were pressed men, with little enthusiasm for either Parliament or king. In occasional meetings on shore, they had noted the better clothing and more regular pay of the Earl of Warwick's crews, and became increasingly restless. Particularly troublesome were the crew of the frigate *Antelope*. In an effort to prevent further defections to the enemy, soon after taking over command Rupert had ordered his ships to be unrigged. The men of the *Antelope* refused to obey.

Rupert's response was characteristic:

His Highness went on board himself, with some half score resolute gentlemen, and called positively for twenty of the best foremast men, and walked upon the deck to see his commands obeyed; when the seamen, instead of complying, gathered about his Highness, and one bold fellow among the rest called out: 'One and all', upon which the Prince immediately caught him in his arms and held him overboard, as if he would have thrown him into the sea. The suddenness of this action wrought such a terror upon the rest, that they returned forthwith to their duty.'[6]

Rupert sets sail

Rupert obtained some money with the help of his mother, the exiled Queen of Bohemia, who pawned some of her jewels, and from the proceeds of several privateering cruises by his smaller vessels. The frigate *Antelope*, the least seaworthy of the Royalist flotilla, was stripped of her guns, which were sold, and was left behind in port when, on 21 January, Rupert put to sea with *Constant Reformation*, *Convertine*, *Swallow*, *Charles*, *Thomas*, *James*, *Mary* (ketch) and *Elizabeth* (hoy).[7] Two frigates currently at sea, the *Roebuck* and *Blackmoor Lady*, were under orders to join Rupert at his destination, the south-western Irish port of Kinsale. Here the Royalists, in co-operation with the Irish privateers, would be poised to strike at vital English trade routes.

Rupert's squadron was accompanied on its voyage down the Channel by three large Dutch Indiamen, powerful ships which could give a good account of themselves in action. It may have been their presence which deterred Vice-Admiral Robert Moulton, commanding the small Parliamentarian 'Winter Guard' stationed in the Downs, from attempting an interception.

Most of the Royalist squadron reached Kinsale on 5 February 1649. When he himself entered port, five days later, Prince Rupert, characteristically, had adventures of his own to relate. While separated from the remainder of the squadron, *Constant Reformation* had encountered the *Assurance*,[30] flagship of William Penn, Vice-Admiral of the Irish Sea Squadron. Mistaking Rupert's flagship for an Irish privateer, Penn had closed with her, 'and being almost within shot perceived his error and made more haste to get out than he had done to come in.'[8]

Rupert, with no more than about 600 seamen in his whole squadron, was no doubt relieved that the critically under-manned *Constant Reformation* had not been forced to fight, even against a more lightly armed vessel. Safely within the strong harbour defences of Kinsale, he was soon reported to have a squadron of thirteen ships, which must have included some additional prizes taken during the voyage. If he could link up with the larger Irish privateers from Waterford, the Prince might soon command a fleet of around thirty ships, which added to the depredations of privateers operating from the Scilly and Channel Isles, and the Isle of Man, would leave the Parliamentarian fleet sorely stretched.

Privateering operations

Around 12 February, Rupert received the shattering news of the execution of his uncle, King Charles I. A letter from Edward Hyde, Secretary of State to the new king, Charles II, included a commission for Rupert as Lord High Admiral, and the Prince responded with a declaration in which he vowed vengeance on 'those Arch-Traitors, pretending the name of Parliament, and keeping a perpetual Sessions, of blood-thirstiness and murdering massacre at Westminster.'[9]

Such vows were easier to proclaim than perform. Still critically short of men, all that the Royalist commander could do for the moment was to despatch Sir John Mennes, flying his flag in *Swallow*, along with three other vessels, *Charles*, *Roebuck* and *Thomas*, to communicate with Sir John Grenville's Royalist garrison in the Scilly Isles, and to attack trade in the Western Approaches to the Channel.

By mid-April Mennes and his squadron were back at Kinsale, bringing five prizes with them, and their depredations were sufficiently alarming for the Council of State to order one of the Generals at Sea, Edward Popham, to sail immediately for the western end of the Channel with such ships as were available.

Popham soon had an encouraging success to report. On 9 April Rupert had despatched four of his frigates, *Thomas*, *James*, *Charles* and *Roebuck*, with orders to prey once again on shipping around the Scillies. This time, their luck ran out. On around 20 April the

Royalist *Charles* was captured by the Commonwealth's *Leopard* and *Constant Warwick*, which also took an Irish privateer, the *Fame* of Waterford. To add to Royalist discomfiture, the small *Thomas* was also captured, probably around 20 May.[10]

Although soon afterwards three merchantmen, two Dutch and one English, were taken off the Scillies, probably by Grenville's privateers, this was the last significant Royalist success for some time, for the Commonwealth's plans to open up a major new campaign in Ireland led to a significant increase in their naval presence off the Irish coast. By now they had about sixty ships in commission, while Robert Blake and Richard Deane were hard at work preparing others. On 18 April Blake embarked aboard his flagship, the 2nd rate *Triumph*, at Tilbury, and on the 24th reached the Downs, where he was joined by the *Andrew* (fifty-six) and *Victory* (sixty-two).[11]

Andrew bore the flag of Sir George Ayscue, Admiral of the Irish Sea Squadron, and picking up off Portsmouth his Vice-Admiral, William Penn, with the *Lion,Garland* and *Hercules*, Ayscue joined Popham at Plymouth by 10 May, with Blake and Deane arriving on the 13th.[12]

Blockading Kinsale

The united Commonwealth fleet was now ready for action; its most urgent objective was to prevent Rupert from interfering with the massive fleet which was preparing to transport Cromwell's troops over to Ireland. On 18 May the majority of the Plymouth squadron sailed for Kinsale, although Popham, whose skills and personal preferences were suited more to an administrative role than command at sea, was sent back to London to hasten supplies for the ships under Blake and Deane which were to blockade Kinsale.

Fearing that the Royalists might try to slip away 'in the darkest time of the night', Blake anchored his ships as close to the mouth of the bay as possible, and the small frigate *Rebecca* was stationed with some ships' boats near to the harbour entrance in order to give prompt warning of any Royalist movements.

The first weeks of Commonwealth operations were severely hindered by bad weather. A storm began to blow on 28 May, and by 1 June the wind 'blew hard westerly with much sea'. In danger of being driven ashore, the Commonwealth squadron had to cut its cables, abandoning its anchors, and take refuge at Milford Haven in South Wales. There were fears that Rupert might take advantage of the blockaders' absence to put to sea. Blake assured the Council of State that if this were to happen, he would 'follow him where-soever he shall go'.[13] Blake was back on station by 20 June, to find Rupert still in port. The Prince remained critically short of crewmen, although recruiting agents were scouring the Irish ports in an attempt to bring the Royalist squadron up to strength. At first the Prince hoped to attack the blockading squadron, but a later meeting of the Royalist Council of War reversed this decision, and he decided instead to refit their seven best ships and escape to sea on a suitably dark night.[14]

Blake informed the Council of State that his aim was the 'reduce-ment of that perfidious crew, who are sheltered in this harbour.'[15] But within a few days he had got wind of Rupert's intention to try to slip away, and was concerned that he might not be able to prevent this. The Commonwealth squadron was expected not only to bottle up Kinsale, but also to watch the Irish privateering ports of Waterford and Wexford, while its strength was depleted when Richard Deane had to take one ship to Plymouth to pick up supplies.

Rupert, whose attempts to recruit more men were hindered by his inability to offer them prize money, was not entirely inactive. On the night of 4 July his larger ships escorted to the mouth of the harbour a twenty-three gun shallop and a nine-gun sixteen-oared frigate, (the latter probably an ex-Dunkirk privateer) which managed to put to sea. However, next day they were sighted, chased and taken by Captain Ball's *Nonsuch*. The captured vessels proved to be the *Teresa* (probably an Irish privateer), and the *Daisy*. Aboard the latter were two of Rupert's close associates, Colonel Will Legge and Sir Hugh Wyndham, who were carrying despatches for the king.

As July opened, Blake grew more concerned about the range of responsibilities which confronted him. He had not only to blockade Kinsale, but also to attempt to isolate the Royalist garrison in the Scillies. A new concern was the campaign in Ireland by Commonwealth forces under Oliver Cromwell. A major fear was that Rupert might slip through the blockade and fall on Cromwell's transports and supply ships in the Irish Sea. The Marquis of

Ormonde, commanding Royalist forces in Ireland, had the same hope, but on 22 July Blake intercepted a despatch from the Prince to Ormonde which eased his concern. Rupert admitted that his squadron was not yet fit for sea, but reported that it would be fully provisioned by the end of September, when 'since the enemy dare not venture so far from their own coasts, and we, by reason of our safe harbours, and short voyages between the coast of Spain and France and those parts, shall be able to cross the whole Trade through both Channels; and every south and westerly wind, which shuts them up in their harbours, if they were ready, shall bring ships from the southern and easterly ports into our lap.'[16]

This came as a relief for Blake, as the wear and tear of the blockade had forced him to send two of his largest ships, *Triumph* and *Victory*, home for repairs. Not only the weather, but also the general monotony of blockade duty was affecting the ships and men of the Commonwealth squadron, and Blake probably won the respect of his crews when he declined an offer from Cromwell to appoint him Major-General of Foot in the army being employed in Ireland. It has plausibly been suggested that Blake's lack of close family ties made him prefer the comradeship of service at sea to the less close relationships of a senior command ashore.

By late September Blake had only five ships to maintain the blockade of Kinsale. Virtually all of the remaining Commonwealth vessels were either in port for refit, engaged in supporting Cromwell's operations or on convoy escort duty. In such a situation, Blake could not afford damage to his remaining force, and when the weather deteriorated he was again forced, on 16 October, to take shelter in Milford Haven.

By now Cromwell's success at Drogheda and his storming of Wexford on 11 October was bringing his army steadily closer to Rupert at Kinsale. This was plainly no longer a safe refuge for the Royalist squadron, and 'Rupert, three days after Cork declaring for the Parliament, [20 October] in great haste sailed from Kinsale with seven ships.' They were the *Constant Reformation* (fifty-two), *Convertine* (forty-six), *Swallow* (forty), *Blackamoor Lady* (eighteen), *Mary* (twenty-four), *Scot* (thirty), and *Black Knight* (fourteen).[17]

Rupert's departure from Kinsale would ultimately result in a considerable lessening of the threat to Commonwealth seaborne trade. With none of the remaining Royalist bases in the Scillies, Channel Islands or the Isle of Man suitable for Rupert's force, he could only operate from a neutral port, with all the restrictions on him that was likely to involve.

Initially, however, Rupert's intentions were unclear. When weather conditions permitted Blake to put to sea again, he was engaged for several days in securing Cork and in providing transport to land troops at newly submitted Youghal. It was thought most likely that Rupert would head for his old hunting grounds off the Scillies, and Edward Popham, with three ships, was ordered to patrol off Land's End.

Blake, in suggesting that Rupert might be heading for the Straits of Gibraltar in order to attack English merchant ships heading home with the spices of the Levant, came closest to divining the Prince's real intentions. As early as March Rupert had begun sounding out King John IV of Portugal regarding the possibility of basing himself at Lisbon, and, receiving a favourable response, now made that port his objective.

Rupert at Lisbon

Rupert had an eventful voyage. His flagship, *Constant Reformation*, became separated from the rest of the squadron by storms in the Bay of Biscay. Rupert recounted in a despatch to King Charles:

> . . . it happened that in the night by a mistake of a fight all our Fleet except Sir John Mennes lost me, and the next morning a Ship appearing which we chased all day in vain, we were put to Leeward of our first rendezvous the Isle of Bayone [Bayona Islands off NW Spain] whither we imagined our Fleet had sailed. We therefore plied as much to windward as we could; two days after we made early in the morning 7 ships to windward we gave chase to them and they to us which proved to be our Fleet. Marchal [Captain Marshall of a frigate] being come in with a prize and my Brother having taken another made up the 7 ships. Marchal's prize was a Newfoundland man out of which we took all her fish and fired the hulk thereof.[18]

This was the real beginning of the often apparently indiscriminate seizure of merchant shipping which was to be a constant feature of Rupert's operations. The aim was to obtain funds, not only to maintain the Royalist fleet, but also for the Court in exile. Rupert, in practice, made a very wide interpretation of what constituted ships belonging to the Commonwealth or those countries which he thought in sympathy with the new English Republic. It was not only the Prince's English enemies who would accuse him of piracy.

After a brief but hot engagement, Rupert took two more English prizes, the *John Adventure* and the *Hopeful Adventure*, and entered Lisbon around 20 November.

King John was personally sympathetic, although his ministers, fearing that support for the Royalists would force the new English regime into alliance with Portugal's enemy, Spain, were much less enthusiastic. For the moment, however, King John had his way. Not only were the Royalists permitted to add two of their prizes, *Roebuck* (thirty-six) and *John Adventure*, renamed *Second Charles*, with forty guns, to their fleet, which now included about eleven vessels, but King John signed an agreement with Rupert, whereby the Royalists 'should have power to make adjudication of such prizes as should be taken at sea by his Majesty's fleet; and after such adjudication to sell and dispose of the same, in any of the ports of the kingdom of Portugal.'[19]

But although Rupert had some success in selling off his prizes, tension remained, particularly over the circumstances of the capture of the *Roebuck*, whose cargo was Portuguese. For the moment the Royalists were safe in harbour, but it remained to be seen if the Portuguese government would withstand pressure from the English Republic.

By 11 November it was known in England that Rupert had been sighted off the Portuguese coast. On 5 December the Council of State decided that Blake should lead the force to be sent after Rupert, whilst Vice-Admiral William Penn took over the small squadron watching the remaining Royalist ships in Kinsale. On 10 January 1650 Blake was in London conferring with the Council of State, and, aware that his mission was as much to impress the Portuguese as fight with Rupert, he asked to be provided with trumpeters, and, in words which hint at some lack of musical appreciation on Blake's part, 'particularly a complete noise for the ship appointed for us.'[20]

Blake returned to Plymouth to complete fitting out his squadron, and on 17 January received the expected order to 'pursue, seize, scatter or destroy, all ships of the revolted fleet, and all other adhering to them.'[21] On 1 March Blake sailed from Cowes. Under his command was a powerful squadron consisting of his flagship, the 2nd rate *St George* (fifty-four), Vice-Admiral Robert Moulton in *Leopard* (fifty-six), Rear Admiral Badiley, in *Entrance* (forty-six), *Bonaventure* (forty-two), the frigates *Adventure* (forty), *John* (thirty), *Assurance* (thirty-two), *Constant Warwick* (thirty-two), *Tiger* (thirty-six), *Providence* (thirty) and *Expedition* (thirty). Also with Blake were the fireship *Signet*, and the small ketches *Tenth Whelp*, *William* and *Patrick*.

Responsibility for the delicate negotiations with the Portuguese, who had no diplomatic relations with the Commonwealth, was given to Sir Henry Vane's younger brother, Charles, who also sailed with the expedition.

Blake arrived off Lisbon on 10 March. Although the king remained a supporter of Rupert, his chief minister, the Count de Miro, was more concerned about the effect which the unwelcome presence of the Royalist squadron was having on Portuguese trade with England. In consequence he put pressure on Portuguese merchants to cease trading with Rupert. Meanwhile Prince Maurice had been preparing to put to sea in search of further prizes, but he was informed that Portugal felt that it 'would be no way convenient to make a war or show any hostility, nor yet to give any assistance or favour against those English that follow the Parliament; and that his Majesty should rather equally entertain all of the English nation, for with it he had renewed the contracts of peace and amity that was always between the two nations.'[22]

Early in the new year, on 27 January, Rupert received a more direct indication that in some quarters at least he had outstayed his welcome, when de Miro informed him that it was desired that 'your Serenity should re-embark all into your ships, and with all brevity hasten your departure.'[23]

Rupert and Maurice responded by strengthening their links with the Portuguese king and joining him on hunting parties, and courting popularity with the Portuguese common people and priests, who 'began to fill the pulpits with how shameful a thing it was for a Christian King to treat with rebels.'[24]

Blake's blockade

As a result, when Blake arrived off the Tagus, Rupert's squadron was still anchored in Oerias Road, two miles above Blake's anchorage.

Blake sent an officer ashore with a message to King John, saying that he was sure that the Portuguese authorities would have no objection to 'the extermination of the nefarious tribes of pirates' and asked that he might 'freely use your port, without placing any obstacle in the way . . . Since the brothers Rupert and Maurice are an important part of them, who have now for several years been carrying on piracy with the ships of the British Commonwealth . . . we cannot but deem it the work of some special providence that they have been detained in your harbour until the arrival of our fleet.'[25] He had in effect issued the Portuguese with an ultimatum which he had neither the strength nor authority to enforce. It was a clumsy move by an inexperienced commander which the older and wiser Blake of future years would not make.

Blake and his Council of War met the next day, 21 March, and 'craved direction from the great God'. The decision they reached was to enter Lisbon harbour by force if necessary and engage Rupert. In his flagship, *St George*, followed by *Leopard*, *Bonaventure* and *Entrance*, Blake led the way into the approaches to Lisbon harbour. As the English vessels drew near, Portuguese gunners in St Julian's Castle and Fort Bugro fired several shots at them, though none found their mark. But before an engagement could begin, the wind dropped and Blake and his ships were forced to drop anchor in a highly vulnerable situation.

A stand-off followed, with Blake remaining where he was, complaining that he could not move his squadron further out to sea as it would be 'very inconsistent to the accommodation and security' of his ships. As the diplomatic fencing continued, the Portuguese urged Blake to move his squadron out of sight of land, after which they would try to persuade Rupert to leave Lisbon.

Charles Vane, now conducting negotiations ashore, reached an agreement that Blake would not pass the Portuguese defences without permission, though in a carefully worded get-out clause reserved the right to enter Oeiras Bay in case of bad weather. Unsurprisingly, the same day, 28 March, because of 'foul weather', Blake brought his squadron in and anchored two miles below Rupert's ships, which rode under the protection of the guns of Belem Castle.

A lengthy stalemate followed. With the Portuguese anxious to avoid clashes between their unwelcome guests, Blake agreed not to allow any of his sailors ashore, other than parties sent to purchase provisions. Blake claimed, however, that a number of Rupert's men deserted to the Commonwealth ships: 'Many of his men run ashore, some whereof are come to us, his chief expectation is of assistance from France – for by information come from Toulon, four frigates of good sort and many men are coming to him.'[26]

On 1 April Vice-Admiral Moulton was sent ashore bearing four new proposals. The first, with little prospect of being accepted, was that Rupert's fleet should be surrendered. Alternatively Moulton was instructed to demand permission to attack it. Failing that, both squadrons should be required to leave harbour at the same time, or, if this was refused, Blake should be allowed a safer anchorage further into the harbour.

The only concession King John was willing to make was to allow Blake the freedom of the harbour while negotiations continued. The Portuguese knew Blake's squadron had a considerable naval advantage over the Portuguese fleet and King John hoped to play for time, but Blake was not deceived, commenting that the king's plan was 'to contribute what he can to the increase of Rupert's strength and the lessening of ours.'[27] He asked Vane to demand a plain answer from the prevaricating Portuguese monarch 'and to let them know that we should take it far better at his hands that he did openly declare for Rupert, than by such indirect policies, to undermine us – and lead us along by the nose with an opinion of his neutrality – as we may clearly perceive by that order given to his forts, the contrary was intended.'[28]

King John's response was to decree that no more English ships would be allowed to enter Lisbon harbour, leaving Rupert with at least a numerical advantage over that part of Blake's squadron actually in port.

On 5 April Blake's foreboding of French intervention came true when two French frigates, of forty and thirty-two guns, arrived and mistakenly anchored among the Commonwealth squadron. Blake seized control of the ships, only to be forced to back down by concerted protests from the French Ambassador and King John and allow them to join Rupert.

Deadlock continued, broken by brawls ashore between men of Blake and Rupert's fleets in tavern encounters, and an alleged attempt by seamen from the Commonwealth squadron to assassinate Rupert and Maurice while the latter were on a hunting party.

Rupert was not one to take such an insult without retaliating, and soon afterwards;

> . . . that they might know that he had wit as well as courage, he . . . endeavoured a requital; for having fitted a bomb-ball in a double-headed barrel, with a lock in the bowels to give fire to a quick-match, sent it aboard their Vice-Admiral [the *Leopard*] in a town-boat with one of his soldiers clad in a Portugal habit, to put into the stern-boat as a barrel of oil, to keep it for him till he hailed up the side without, 'refreshing for the men'; but being come to the ship's stern, those ports being unfortunately shut, before he could get to the transom-port, he was known, and taken.[29]

A spirited war of words was also continuing. In an effort to stiffen Portuguese resolve, Rupert made a typically colourful declaration to the king, denouncing the enemy as ' nothing else, but tumultuous, factious and seditious soldiers, . . . retaining nothing of the ancient form and Government of lawful Parliaments', and calling on the Portuguese not to tolerate 'such insolency to be committed by these People, who being Rebels to their Prince, and having in Law no right of privilege in War, are to be deemed and esteemed as Pirates and Sea Rovers'.[30]

Blake's envoy, Charles Vane, proved himself if anything an even greater master of colourful invective, when he declared his government's friendship for Portugal, and added:

> . . . neither do we take it for any disparagement to us, our parliament and nation, that we are so vile in the

esteem of this Vagabond German, a Prince of Fortune, whose highness is nothing else than haughtiness, his Principality mere piracy, the plurality of his person an affectation so singular that no real prince can choose but to smile at it, who after he was cudgelled out of England from his trade of plundering did in a short time set up at sea.[31]

These exchanges no doubt gave satisfaction to all concerned, but brought a resolution of the deadlock no nearer. At the end of May, possibly hoping to lure Rupert out to sea, Blake withdrew his squadron to the mouth of the harbour. He may also have been influenced by news that his government was losing patience with the Portuguese, and that the Council of State was considering breaking off relations with Portugal.

English attitudes had indeed hardened. On 25 May Edward Popham left Plymouth to reinforce Blake with his flag aboard the *Resolution* (sixty-eight), *Andrew* (forty-two), *Phoenix* (thirty-six), *Satisfaction* (twenty-six), four armed merchant ships and a much-needed store ship. Popham carried with him instructions that the English squadron was to attack Rupert, and any French ships accompanying him, anywhere that they were encountered. If the Portuguese refused to co-operate, their ships were also to be seized.

The fleets clash

Even before Popham's arrival, the confrontation at Lisbon had escalated. On 21 May, the outward-bound Portuguese fleet to Brazil left port, and Blake seized ten English merchant ships which had been chartered as part of it. King John retaliated by ordering the arrest of all English subjects in Lisbon known to sympathize with the Commonwealth. (Vane had prudently withdrawn to the safety of Blake's squadron beforehand.) He also ordered his elderly naval commander-in-chief, Jose de Sequerra Varejo, to prepare thirteen ships, each probably carrying from twenty-four to forty guns, to support Rupert in a break-out attempt.

Popham joined Blake on 26 May, and on 5 June another Council of War was held, at which it was decided to send King John a further ultimatum, demanding that Rupert's ships be handed over, failing which the English would do 'what we could to right ourselves by force' and demanding an answer by 10 June.

The Portuguese response came one day late, and was dismissed as being 'delusory or at least dilatory'. Over the next few days Blake seized a number of Portuguese fishing boats. But with Lisbon no longer open to him, the English commander was forced to send Rear Admiral Badiley with several ships to obtain supplies from Cadiz, and three other vessels were despatched to Bayonne to relieve a critical shortage of drink aboard the squadron, leaving Blake with only seven warships and four armed merchantmen. By now Rupert was ready for sea, and seeing an excellent opportunity to take advantage of a weakened opponent, King John instructed Varejo to be prepared to support his sortie.

Blake was warned of the Portuguese and Royalist preparations by a Swedish merchant ship and, cheered by reports that Badiley was on his way back from Cadiz, prepared for action.

On the night of 21–22 July, some twenty-two Portuguese and Royalist ships, accompanied by a large number of smaller vessels, moved down into Oreias Bay. To oppose them Blake and Popham had ten of their own squadron and nine of the former Brazil Fleet vessels.

Rupert's plan was for the Portuguese squadron to use their lights to lure Blake closer inshore while Rupert's ships slipped away under cover of darkness.

Between 9 and 10am on 26 July, 'with much noise', Rupert's fleet came out of the Bay. The wind was blowing from east-south-east, putting Blake's squadron well to leeward of the harbour. The Commonwealth commanders hoped to get between the Portuguese and Royalists and the entrance to the harbour, so forcing Rupert out to sea. Seeing the enemy approach, Blake weighed anchor and stood out to sea on the port tack, with the enemy lying to windward, and 'having got a reasonable berth [distance] from the shore', hove to, awaiting attack, but then, with the wind shifting to the south, tacked and got to windward of the enemy. The Portuguese and Royalists also tacked to conform, so that both fleets were now on a parallel course towards Cape Espichel.

It quickly became apparent that the Portuguese had little appetite for pitting their generally inferior ships against Blake. While his allies hung back, Rupert, his line headed by a large forty-gun

French ship and four fire ships, followed by the Prince himself in *Constant Reformation*, about a mile astern, came on. At first only the *Resolution*, *Phoenix* and *Mayflower* of Blake's squadron were able to come up, but once the wind veered to the south the remainder of the Commonwealth force 'filled our sails, tacked and got the wind . . .'

As the leading ships of each squadron drew closer to each other, shots were exchanged, and firing continued for much of the afternoon. Popham described how shots were exchanged 'between us and the Frenchman, but we could never get within shot of Rupert, do what we could.' The Royalists, however, claimed that the Prince's flagship lost its foretopmast in the exchange. But, according to Popham:

> Rupert and the Frenchman bearing up still as we neared them, threatening to get us too leeward by following them, that the fire ships might the better do their work upon us, but the *Phoenix* put them off . . . we bore large upon the Frenchman, being betwixt us and the *Reformation*, but as fast as we bore upon him, he bore away large towards the harbour and Rupert likewise (his mizzen always hauled up).[32]

Although firing was apparently occasionally quite heavy, it was also largely ineffective. The French ship, the most heavily engaged vessel on the Allied side, suffered only three dead and five or six men wounded.[33] The Royalists claimed that once they found that they could not weather Cape Espichel, they tacked and stood to the north, with the Commonwealth squadron following suit. However, with night coming on, and finding themselves facing the danger of being on a lee shore, Blake's ships stood out to sea, while the Allies dropped anchor at the mouth of Lisbon harbour.

Further indecisive manoeuvring followed over the next two days, without action being joined. By 30 July, the Allies had withdrawn up the Tagus out of Blake's reach. Rupert's break-out attempt had failed, though this was as much the result of the reluctance of the Portuguese to give battle as of Blake's actions.

A long period of inactivity followed. The Council of State, finding difficulty in keeping Blake's large squadron supplied, suggested that Blake send home any vessels not required, and on 3 September Popham left for England with half the squadron, Blake retaining his flagship, *George, Lion, Bonaventure, Phoenix, Expedition, Constant Warwick, John, Hercules* and *Merchant*. His intention was to remain on station for about a month, after which the approach of winter would force him to abandon the blockade. However, early on the morning of 7 September, when cruising in foggy conditions off the Rock of Lisbon, Blake briefly sighted Rupert and the Allied fleet. He lost contact until about 4pm, when, with only his flagship, *Phoenix* and *Expedition*, Blake spotted the whole Allied fleet of about thirty-six sail. The enemy lay to leeward of the Commonwealth squadron, with Rupert in *Constant Reformation* to windward of the rest of the Allied fleet, so that he and Blake were standing towards each on opposite tacks. The *George's* Master pointed out to Blake that it was very doubtful if the flagship could weather *Constant Reformation*, to which Blake allegedly responded: 'Can you stem [ram] him?' 'Yes', the Master replied, 'but then we shall hazard both ships.' 'I'll run that hazard,' Blake declared, 'rather than bear up for the enemy.'[34]

Faced by the three Commonwealth ships, it was Rupert who gave way, and as he passed by, each of Blake's ships delivered a broadside, which brought down the Royalist flagship's foretopmast, after which Rupert took refuge in the body of the Allied fleet.

The descent of more fog ended the encounter, with the Allies withdrawing again to Lisbon.

Capture of the Brazil Fleet

A week later, on 14 September, Blake sighted the homeward-bound Portuguese Brazil Fleet, laden with the rich goods of the Portuguese colony. With a fresh north-easterly breeze behind him, Blake moved in to the attack. Accounts of the action which followed differ in detail, but there is no doubt that Blake scored a major success. The thirty-two gun Portuguese flagship escaped with the loss of her mainmast, but Blake then engaged the thirty-six gun flagship of the Portuguese Rear Admiral. The sea was by now rising, so that the English flagship was unable to open her lower gun ports, and a hotly fought-engagement lasting for three hours took place before the Portuguese ship surrendered. Blake's brother, Benjamin, commanding *Assurance*, boarded and captured the

Portuguese Vice-Admiral, and around six other ships, carrying a rich cargo, including 4,000 chests of sugar, were also taken.

By now Blake was running severely short of supplies and water and, taking his battered prizes with him, headed for Cadiz, where he arrived on 27 September. He was received by the Spaniards with 'much honour', tinged with nervousness, for Anthony Ascham, the Commonwealth Envoy in Madrid, had just been murdered by English Royalists, and the Spanish Government was anxious not to do anything which might provoke Blake into reprisals. From Cadiz, Blake sent home four of his prizes, escorted by Richard Badiley and four ships of the Commonwealth squadron. With the remainder, Blake returned to his station off Lisbon, to find Rupert gone.

The loss of the Brazil fleet had made clear to King John that he could no longer afford to harbour his increasingly unwelcome guest, and, with his ships refitted and resupplied, Rupert was visited by the king in person, to tell him to be gone. On 12 October the Prince left Lisbon with *Constant Reformation, Swallow, Black Prince, Scot, Charles, Henry* and *Mary* (having sold *Convertine*). The overall situation for the Royalists was increasingly grim. With the end of organised resistance in Ireland, there was no safe base left for the Royalist squadron, which, fast descending into a condition of near-piracy, with Rupert indeed now the 'German vagabond' described by Charles Vane, could only head for the Mediterranean and the hope of assistance from the French. The author of the *Royalist Sea Narrative* commented sadly: 'Now misfortunes being no novelty to us, we plough the sea for a subsistence, and being destitute of a port, we take the confines of the Mediterranean Sea for our harbour; poverty and despair being companions, and revenge our guide.'[35]

Hunting down the Royalists

Rupert headed through the Straits of Gibraltar. By 20 October the Commonwealth squadron was five leagues off the Straits. Blake was not particularly concerned by Rupert's escape, and indeed had expected him to take advantage of the lifting of the blockade. He probably felt that Rupert at sea, rather than lurking in Lisbon, was decidedly preferable. Proof of this came when the same day Blake's frigates, spread out in line of search, captured a thirty-six gun French ship, the *Jules*, which in company with the Royalist *Second Charles*, had been making its way to join Rupert. According to one version of events, the captain of the *Jules* initially surrendered believing Blake's flagship to be more powerful than was actually the case, and on discovering the truth, withdrew his surrender. Blake returned the Frenchman to his ship, but *Jules*'s crew refused to renew the fight! The Royalist ship made off, while Blake returned to Cadiz to pick up his heavy ships. On 28 October he learned that Rupert had been at Malaga two days earlier.

In a night action Rupert had captured two English merchant-men who had mistaken Rupert's squadron for Blake's, but in the process had lost touch with the *Second Charles*, and then headed deeper into the Mediterranean. After being dissuaded by the fire of the Spanish defences from seizing an English merchant ship in the small port of Estepona, the Prince continued towards the more important harbour of Malaga. However, his plan to send in one of his ships, the *Henry*, in the guise of an English merchant ship in order to anchor in such a position as to cut off the escape of any other English ships in the harbour misfired

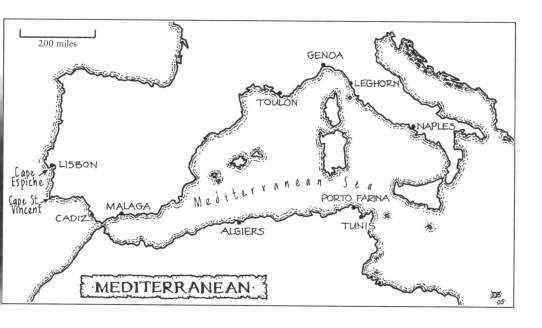

when some of *Henry*'s crew deserted in the ship's boat and raised the alarm.

Thwarted of one objective, Rupert sailed a little further eastwards up the coast to Velez Malaga, where four English ships had taken refuge. A bout of diplomatic haggling followed with the Spanish Governor of the town, as Rupert endeavoured to persuade him to surrender the English ships. Eventually, Rupert agreed not to fire on the English ships unless they fired first, but, stretching that agreement somewhat beyond the bounds of plausibility, the Royalists then prepared a fireship to attack them. Versions of what ensued differ, the Spaniards claiming that the Royalists fired two of the merchant ships and Rupert claiming that they were burnt by their own captains.

Whatever the truth of the matter, and the Spanish version seems rather more likely, Rupert had done neither his reputation nor his relations with the Spaniards any good, and followed up the incident at Velez Malaga by burning three more English ships in the port of Motril, on this occasion being fired on by the Spanish defences.

By early November Rupert's squadron was dangerously strung out in search of prizes across some one hundred miles of the Mediterranean between Cape de Gate and Cape Palos. The Royalists were vulnerable to attack, and Blake, having learned at Cadiz on 28 October of Rupert's latest activities, was closing in. On 2 November he caught up with the *Henry*, whose crew refused to fight and surrendered without a shot being fired.

At the same time five other Royalist ships were chasing a fleet of eighteen merchant ships that turned out to be Dutch. But the pursuit had brought the Royalists within sight of Blake's squadron, who at once went in pursuit. Blake's ships were in better condition and faster than some of their opponents, and overtook the frigate *Black Prince* at dusk. The Royalist ship was temporarily saved by the onset of night, but at dawn, finding itself cut off by the Commonwealth squadron, the Royalist vessel was beached and burnt by its own crew. The remaining four Royalist ships, *Second Charles*, *Mary* and two recently captured prizes, the *Malagonian* and *William and John*, managed to reach the temporary safety of Cartagena harbour.

Blake blockaded the Royalist squadron, and tried to persuade the Governor of Cartagena to allow him to enter the port to destroy 'these notorious pirates and destroyers of all trade . . . before they join themselves unto the French, which is likely to be their refuge.' The Governor hesitated, pending instructions from Madrid, but the Royalists, on 16 November, settled their own fate when they attempted to run for the open sea, were caught by a sudden squall and all driven ashore and wrecked.

Rupert and Maurice, in *Constant Reformation* and *Swallow*, were still at large, having left the area in pursuit of an English ship, but their fleet had been effectively shattered. The princes by late December had taken refuge in the French port of Toulon.[36] Blake, having failed to make contact with these remnants of the Royalist fleet, had been recalled to England, and was replaced in the Mediterranean by Vice-Admiral William Penn, with a squadron of eight ships. Penn's views on Rupert were energetically expressed: 'The Lord forgive the bloody wretch, and convert him, if he belongeth unto him; otherwise, if his Holiness please, suddenly destroy him.'[37]

On 29 March 1652 Penn left Cadiz 'intending (with God's assistance) to find Prince Rupert out, and endeavour the destroying of him and his adherents.'

Rupert, meanwhile, had wintered in Toulon, refitting his three remaining ships, and when the captains of the ships lost at Cartagena eventually joined him, apportioning blame for the disaster. The chief culprits were held to be Captain Barley of the *Henry*, accused, though evidence was lacking, of giving intelligence to Blake, and Captain Thomas Allen of the *Charles*, blamed for deserting the rest of the squadron during the action between Blake and the *Black Prince*. Barley was dismissed from service, and Allen, who escaped before sentence was passed, would later have a distinguished career in the Restoration Navy. In fact, the Royalist squadron would have been no match for Blake even if it had stayed together. Any blame that there was would seem to have been primarily Rupert's, for allowing the squadron to become so scattered in search of prey.

Rupert, using the crews of the ships lost at Cartagena when they eventually joined him, fitted out three prizes to increase the size of his squadron. Then 'conceiving all disasters past, he fixed his resolution to take revenge upon the Spaniards.'

To some extent the Prince may have been pressured into this stance by his French hosts, but it was another step in the descent of the Royalist squadron into little more than a pirate flotilla. From now onwards its overriding aim, without a secure base left in the world, was to maintain itself on the proceeds of increasingly indiscriminate prize-taking.

Rupert spread reports that his next destination was to be Sardinia, and Penn obligingly headed in that direction, leaving the Straits of Gibraltar unguarded for the Royalist squadron to make its departure from the Mediterranean in mid-June. Rupert, as it transpired, had escaped from the Navy of the Commonwealth for good, but on the wider strategic scene it scarcely mattered. Ahead of the Prince and his dwindling squadron lay almost a year of adventure and disaster in the Canaries, Cape Verde Islands, off the West coast of Africa and in the West Indies. But its details relate much more to the story of Prince Rupert than to the wider scene. The Prince and his squadron were barely more than a nuisance to the English Commonwealth, operating as they were in seas far distant from vital trade routes, and unable to face the English Navy in battle.

Eventually, after losing most of his ships and his brother Maurice, who perished in a hurricane, Rupert limped into the River Loire aboard the *Swallow*, last survivor of his original squadron, on 4 March 1653. Apart from a handful of privateers, nominally acting in the king's name, there would henceforward be no Royalist presence at sea.

The campaigns of Rupert's squadron had brought few lasting advantages for the Royalists. Although they had taken some prizes, the effects of the continual operations of the smaller privateers from bases such as the Channel Islands and the Scillies were of greater significance in terms of the number and value of prizes which they took, and their effects on English trade. Rupert had handled his squadron with varying degrees of skill, but was hindered throughout by the poor quality of many of his seamen, and his inability to face the Commonwealth fleet in action.

Blake, admittedly having advantages in terms of men and ships, certainly came out better from the contest. His determination and patience in blockade, and his generally skilful handling of the Portuguese, had prevented Rupert from either interfering with Cromwell's operations in Ireland or maintaining a continuous threat to English trade, and in the end had destroyed the Royalist fleet as a serious fighting force.

Chapter 4
Defeating the Royalists: 2:
Scillies, Channel Islands and Barbadoes

'. . . these piratical rocks . . .'
(Sir George Ayscue, May 1652)

Blake's men were jubilant over their successes against Rupert; Captain Charles Salton of the *John* wrote to the Secretary of the Admiralty Committee:

> . . . the Lord had proved us exceedingly, since we have had but little of the arm of the flesh amongst us – I mean, sir, since our great and powerful fleet of many ships were reduced to a small squadron of ten ships under the command of General Blake, for since then we have taken the Brazil fleet, and after that our squadron being now but three ships and four frigates, we have taken three French ships, and [of] all Rupert's ships, seven in number, only two now remains – thus God hath owned us in the midst of our implacable enemies, so that the terror of God is amongst them – the Spaniards are now exceeding kind unto us, and the King of Spain hath made large expressions to our general how acceptable our service hath been unto him since our coming into the Straits.[1]

The Commonwealth no longer seemed so certainly a loser, and on 2 November, the same day that Salton wrote his letter, the

Spanish king despatched his Ambassador to England to apologise for the murder of Ascham, promising punishment for his killers. Blake's fleet, he assured the Council of State, would be allowed the use of Spanish ports. On 12 December the Spanish Ambassador went a step further by affording formal recognition to the English Commonwealth. In a warning to those countries which might be prepared to risk incurring the new Republic's displeasure, the French ambassador was ordered out of England, and the Portuguese envoy refused a hearing.

On 10 February 1651 Robert Blake reached England, and a gratified Parliament awarded their General at Sea £31,000 in recognition of his 'good and faithful service.' Blake went ashore for some much-needed rest, but his respite was brief.

Although Blake's campaign had undoubtedly impressed some of the Commonwealth's European neighbours, the threat from those English outposts still in Royalist hands remained. Ireland was largely subdued, but Scotland remained defiant and Charles II was preparing to strike from there into England. The New World colonies remained nominally Royalist, but of more immediate concern were the privateer bases in the Scilly Isles, Channel Islands and Isle of Man.

Taking the Scillies

The most pressing danger seemed to come from the Scilly Isles, where the activities of their Royalist Governor, Sir John Grenville, appeared to be about to trigger a confrontation with the Dutch.

Lying some twenty-six miles to the south-west of Land's End, the Scillies consisted of four inhabited islands and over fifty small islets and rocky outcrops. The main island, St Mary's, had been fortified in the closing years of the sixteenth century with Star Castle, which also served as the Governor's residence. During the First Civil War the Scillies had been held by the Royalists, and used as a base for privateers, but had surrendered to Parliament in August 1646. For the next two years the islands remained in Parliamentarian hands, until in September 1648 the garrison became involved in the general ferment of the Second Civil War, mutinied and declared for the king. On news of the revolt reaching the mainland, Sir John Grenville, twenty-five-year-old son of the famous Sir Bevil and nephew of the infamous Sir Richard Grenville, arrived as the king's Governor.[2]

During the following years the Scillies became a rallying point for disaffected West Country Royalists and, anticipating an attempt by Parliament to recover the islands, Grenville worked to strengthen their defences, principally by constructing new batteries on St Mary's and lesser fortifications on the other inhabited islands, notably on Tresco.

As more Royalist refugees and troops arrived, supplying their necessities became a major problem, and it was partly for this reason that Grenville resumed privateering operations. In the region of twenty Royalist privateers seem to have used the Scillies, although not all were permanently based there. Unlike his counterpart in the Channel Islands, Sir George Cartaret, and despite orders from the king to desist, Grenville made Dutch merchant ships as

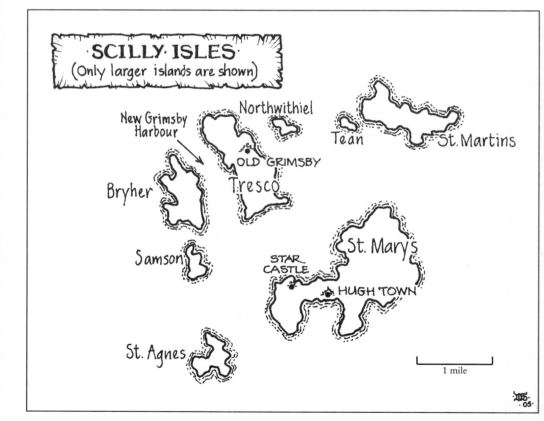

much of a legitimate target as English vessels and, heedless of protest, continued to take Dutch ships, imprison their crews on St Mary's and sell the vessels in France, or even back in Holland! At least one Dutch ship, the *Crowned Lion*, was added to the Royalist privateer squadron.

By 1649, the Scillies were earning the reputation of being 'a second Algiers', and the activities of their privateers required a more or less permanent Parliamentarian naval presence in the Western Approaches. This consisted of 'some of the nimblest frigates' and was most usually formed by the *Mary*, *Constant Warwick*, *Elizabeth*, *Hector* and *Phoenix*, with another smaller vessel hovering off Land's End to intercept any Royalist agents from the Scillies trying to reach the mainland.[3]

By March 1651 the Council of State had decided to take action against the Scillies, and Sir George Ayscue, with his flag aboard the *Rainbow*, was ordered to deal with the Scillies before crossing the Atlantic to attack Royalist-held Barbados. However, before Sir George could leave Plymouth, news reached Weymouth on 28 March that the renowned Dutch admiral Marteen van Tromp, with a squadron of about nineteen ships, was on his way to the Scillies in order to demand satisfaction for the injuries done by Grenville's privateers to Dutch shipping. The Council of State immediately suspected that Tromp was planning to seize the islands for the Dutch, making them in time of war a major threat to English trade through the Western Approaches. On 1 April, Robert Blake, who had been preparing to assume command of the Irish Sea squadron, was ordered instead to take his flagship, *Phoenix*, to join an enlarged force under Ayscue at Weymouth and assume command of the Scillies expedition. He was to demand Tromp's intentions, and if he saw them as prejudicial, to 'use the best ways and means to enforce the rights of the Commonwealth'.[4]

At Plymouth Blake embarked nine companies of foot (900–1,000 men) under Colonel Clarke. These were drawn from several regiments stationed in the West Country and, while they included some experienced soldiers from Sir Hardress Waller's Regiment, many of the others were raw new levies.[5] At 8pm on 12 April, Blake's squadron of 14–22 ships set out for the Scillies.

Tromp, meanwhile, with thirteen ships, had arrived off the islands on 30 March, his objective being rather less sweeping than the English Council of State had feared, but only to secure the release of the captured Dutch ships, with their crews and cargoes. If need be, he was to seize them by force. On 1 April Grenville handed over twelve Dutch prisoners and next day twenty-two more. But the prisoners informed Tromp that the Royalists had no intention of returning the captured ships, possibly for the very good reason that they had already sold them. That evening Tromp recalled the envoy he had sent to negotiate with Grenville, and 'thereupon the rabble in the Scillies treated him very roughly'; Grenville according to one report showing the Dutchman his gallows and threatening to hang him.[6]

It is hard to see why Grenville adopted this confrontational approach, adding another to his already formidable list of foes. The Dutch admiral promptly declared a state of hostilities towards Sir John Grenville, and offered Blake full co-operation in the reduction of the islands.

By 15 April both squadrons were on the scene, some twenty-two English and thirteen Dutch ships. Blake had evidently learned from his diplomatic encounters in Lisbon the previous year, and while obviously having neither the desire, nor, as he saw it, the need for Dutch support, responded tactfully, possibly aided by a pre-war acquaintanceship with Tromp. He suggested that the Dutch should take part in a joint show of strength with the English squadron, before Tromp left the job to Blake. Tromp agreed, though the resulting display off the Scillonian capital of Hughtown did little to impress the Royalists.

Blake and Ayscue quickly appreciated that they faced a difficult task. Grenville had a force of around 1,000 men under his command, a mixture of hardened Royalist professional soldiers, 'reformadoes' (officers without commands), Irish soldiers who faced an uncertain fate if captured, as did the Parliamentarian mutineers, seamen of various nationalities and the probably less than enthusiastic islanders.

Grenville stationed about 600 of his men on St Mary's, where the existing fortifications of Star Castle had been strengthened by other earthworks and mounts, making any landing there distinctly unattractive. Most of the Royalists' remaining 400 men were garrisoning the island of Tresco.

Blake and Ayscue quickly realised that a landing on St Mary's, with its strong defences and several Royalist frigates anchored in the roads, would be a very difficult proposition. It would be necessary to secure a land base from which the attack on St Mary's could proceed at more leisure. Here the troops could recover from the cramped conditions of the voyage, and a sheltered anchorage be found for the supply ships before another of the Scillies' frequent storms struck. The best option seemed to be to secure the islands of Tresco and Bryher, which would give the Commonwealth forces control of the sheltered anchorage at New Grimsby. Ayscue explained:

> . . . the two Islands command the road, as well as St Mary's and the gaining of those Islands would render St Mary's useless to the enemy, besides it would be a speedy means to force St Mary's Island to submission . . . the men-of-war belonging to these piratical rocks, will be like mice that run from a falling house, and must be forced to seek a new rendezvous; neither can St Mary's subsist without them.[7]

However, the entrance to the anchorage of New Grimsby was guarded by two of the Royalists' strongest ships, the *St Michael* with thirty-two guns and the *Peter* (sixteen) as well as 'other helps [possibly booms] so that they could not enter.'[8] So, before attacking New Grimsby itself, it would be necessary to make a landing on the far side of Tresco, in the vicinity of Old Grimsby harbour, 'where it was scarce known any great ship ever ventured to come in, they gained it, being of so great a breadth that it could not be defended.'

After Blake's arrival on 13 April, the wind blew so strongly from the east that, although some ships dropped anchor within musket-shot of the shore, no landing was at first possible. The Royalists, meanwhile, had landed some guns from the two frigates in New Grimsby Harbour, and a few cannon shot were exchanged. Blake reportedly made an attempt to force the entrance to New Grimsby Harbour, but the Royalist ships were still too strong, and the Commonwealth attackers were driven off, after both sides had fired 'an infinite multitude of shot.'[9]

The easterly winds did not die down until the evening of 16 April, when preparations began for a landing next day. Blake's men collected about forty boats and shallops, some with a brass gun loaded with grapeshot mounted in their bows, which in the morning came alongside the ships to load troops. The soldiers, guided by pilots recruited in the West Country, were to make the initial landing with the seamen, who ever since the First Civil War had disliked doing what they regarded as the soldiers' work, kept in reserve.

The landing force was put under the charge of Colonel Clarke, with Blake providing covering fire and transport. At about 6am, the leading boat under Colonel Bawden put off to attempt a landing at St Helens on Tresco. The landing force was formed into two detachments, one of which was to reach the shore in a rocky bay, Green Porth, close to the fort within Old Grimsby Harbour, whilst the other headed for a sandy beach, Cook's Porth, to the west.

As the boats began to pull for the shore, Blake's ships fired some 600 shots to cover them. But it soon became clear that the operation was not going according to plan. The boats were so packed with men that the rowers found it difficult to ply their oars, and they soon became tired with the unaccustomed effort of rowing, and sea-sick with the roughness of the water. As the men flagged, the boats were becoming increasingly scattered as a result of the rocky outcrops jutting into the sea and the effects of the tide, which was driving them eastwards towards Old Grimsby harbour mouth. The pilots, whose loyalty was probably questionable, and who were also afraid of the rocks, also guided the boats in that direction. According to one participant:

> . . . the enemy perceiving our motion, drew their chief strength likewise to oppose us. Our boats being all of them exceedingly crammed with men, and many of them very slenderly accomplished for such service, rowed exceedingly heavily, and could not by any means be brought to row up close one with another, and some were set fast upon the rocks for want of water: whereupon orders were given, that the boats should stop under a rock till they came up altogether, that we might jointly set upon the work. But on the purpose, the pilots and many of the rowers (who were taken up in the West

Country, very backward to the service) misguided our headmost boats to a little island, Northwithiel, standing in the entrance to Old Grimsby Harbour, and within half a musket shot of Tresco, divided by the water, and so situate, as none, save those who were acquainted, should know whether it was part Tresco or no. To this place the timorous pilots directed, affirming once and again that it was Tresco, and when Colonel Bawden replied, that he was doubtful of it in regard he discovered none of the enemy coming down to oppose their landing, one Nants (accounted the most knowing pilot of the place)affirmed resolutely (upon his life) that it was Tresco, whereupon three companies presently landed.[10]

Colonel Bawden forced one of them to admit the truth, and that at low tide there was a feasible crossing place, some half-musket shot (about two hundred yards) between Northwithiel and Tresco. The tide was evidently too high at present to make the crossing possible and, to add to his problems, Bawden now found that his own boat had gone fast aground.

Meanwhile Colonel Clarke and the second landing party now came in an attempt to assist Bawden's men. But once again the pilots went astray, taking the landing party towards a craggy coast where Royalist musketeers were massed to fire down on them.

. . . so that the tide and opportunity might not be lost, orders were given, that the rest of the boats should row on into the bay where we intended to land, but our foremost boats were again misguided, and unadvisedly made to that part of the Island nearest to hand, occasioned the rather, as I suppose, for that the enemy had there drawn down a body of musketeers, and fired much upon our boats, with whom our men desired to be doing; but the shore proved craggy and inaccessible, so that we could not land. Here was hot firing between our men and the Enemy (the rocky shore being the only interponent). They had a sufficient advantage against us, having the Rocks for their shelter, and our men so very crowded in their open Boats as many of them could not make use of their Arms. Indeed it was a miracle of mercy that we lost not many men here, if any of our Boats had been foundered, all the men must needs have been lost, for every Boat was so exceedingly full, that in such an extremity one could not possibly have helped another.

Now to be plain, when the boats drew somewhat near, and the small, great, and case-shot flew about to some purpose, and danger must be looked in the face (for I believe we endured about 70 great shot, besides muskets in abundance) many of the boats, instead of being rowed forward into the bay, turned the helm, and rowed backward, and aside, from the business.[11]

However, one party got ashore:

. . . where the enemys' greatest strength lay, which some of the enemy perceiving began to turn back and run, but Colonel [Edward] Wogan, who commanded them, forced them on again; but was at last shot in the foot, however the enemy did so desperately oppose us in that place, and the place was so rocky, that Captain Smith, who was on the rocks was necessitated to go on board his boat again, and to put off from that place, and then most of the boats rowed off.

Colonel Clarke struggled all he could to draw them on, earnestly calling to one and commanding another to follow him with their boats, yet would neither commands nor threats persuade them to observance; but do what he could, they rowed off. This I must affirm for truth, for that I heard and saw the gentleman above named standing on the head of his boat, midst the thickest of the shot, under this performance. Captain Dover may please to remember that he amongst others was called to, yea and commanded too, upon pain of death, to follow on with his boat; what his answer was, and how carefully observed, cannot be unknown to himself, nor yet to others, for I am sure his boat rowed off and came not near.[12]

Clarke had no option but to rejoin his men, who landed on the small island of Tean to the east of Tresco. Surprisingly, only six men had been lost in the attack, although a boat carrying Bawden's Ensign and some pikemen had been badly damaged and another had lost all but two of its oars.

The Commonwealth troops scrambled ashore with faltering morale. The water on Tean was found to be undrinkable, while rocks and rough weather prevented Blake's ships from landing any supplies. The raw recruits found the succeeding night 'irksome and comfortless' while next morning the Royalists on Tresco opened fire on the makeshift camps of Clarke's men with cannon and musket, although the range was too long for them to do much harm.

With daylight, Clarke had spotted another possible landing site on Tresco, and sent an officer to Robert Blake to request both boats and reliable crews. Blake responded by sending supplies to the men on Northwithiel, and preparing for a new landing attempt on Tresco that night. He also realised that after the previous day's failure the troops would need backing from his more experienced seamen. Captain Morris, a reformado, was sent to Clarke with 200 armed seamen, boats and rowers. Speed was essential if the operation were to be completed before further storms blew up.

On Tean, meanwhile, some of the cold, wet and hungry soldiers were in a state of near-mutiny. Their officers retired to pray, and then returning found their men 'in an alteration even unto admiration, declaring their readiness for a second attempt.' This change in mood probably owed a good deal to the arrival of Morris and his supplies.

In an attempt to deceive the Royalists, eighty men were left on Northwithiel 'to alarm and amuse the enemy', and, as darkness fell, fires were lit on Tean 'as if we had continued there, the smoke whereof was blown towards the enemy, which somewhat obscured our passage'. Nevertheless, the landing party was only halfway to Tresco when its boats were spotted by the Royalists, who opened fire. This time, however, Morris managed to keep the boats close together, and his seamen were first to scramble ashore. The Commonwealth soldier's account relates how:

... we boated our men(being drawn off these 3 companies from Northwithiel) in the dark of the evening, and left there only some 80 men to alarm and amuse the enemy in that quarter as we fell on, and between 11 and 12 of the clock at night set forward (the seamen's boats being headmost), at which time it pleased God that it was very calm, so that the enemies' frigates, whom we doubted might injure us in our passage (being thereunto designed) and do most prejudice, could not come up to do any harm, though they spent some great shot at us. We made fires on Tean as if we had continued there, the smoke whereof was blown towards the enemy, which somewhat obscured our passage; yet the enemy discovered us when we came about half way over, and took an alarm, and ere we attained the shore fired many ordnance upon us, which did no hurt. The boats came up for the most part together, and put to the shore, where the enemy disputed our landing with stout resistance, insomuch as the seamen were forced back into the water. Yet our men charged them resolutely, even to the club musket, and through the blessing of God worsted them, killed upon the place one captain and some 12 or 14 others, took prisoners 167, whereof 4 captains, the rest fled, none had escaped, had we been acquainted with the place.[13]

They managed to hold their ground until the first of Clarke's soldiers reached the beach, but even so a fierce counter-attack for a time drove the attackers back to the water's edge. Meanwhile more troops, some carrying their bandoliers in their mouths to keep their powder charges dry, waded ashore, and a fierce mêlée with clubbed muskets followed until, in the words of a Royalist account, the Commonwealth troops 'overpowered our men with multitudes and strength of their pikes, having the help of 200 seamen, both to lead them on and to drive on their rear.'[14]

After about an hour's fighting the Royalists were routed. Sir John Grenville, who had come over from St Mary's to direct the defence, managed with some of his men to reach their boats, which were hidden nearby, and escape back to his headquarters, though about forty Royalists were drowned in the attempt.

By morning all of Tresco was in Commonwealth hands. Colonel Fleetwood headed northwards to King Charles' Castle, which was situated on high ground to the north of the village of New Grimsby. This was essentially an artillery fort, intended to protect the New Grimsby Channel and the anchorage between Tresco and Bryher. It was poorly sited, particularly on its landward side, and probably surrendered without a fight.

Also captured with little or no resistance were the two Royalist frigates anchored at the mouth of the channel. With most of their guns and crews ashore, they could neither fight nor flee.

Overall, the Royalists seem to have lost up to fifteen dead and 167 prisoners, while the Commonwealth forces admitted to only four men killed, presumably in addition to the casualties of the first attempts to land.

With Tresco and Bryher secured, Blake brought his supply ships and transports into the shelter of the harbour, and sent word of his success to the Council of State in London. Ayscue added his own report, saying that 'the gaining of these two islands will render St Mary's useless to the enemy, for we now have the road, as well as they [the islands] and enjoy a harbour which they have not; so that I perceive they will be forced to a submission.'[15]

Blake proved to have got his ships into shelter barely in time, for next day a storm blew up which drove several vessels from their anchorage and wrecked a number of small boats. This was only a relatively minor setback, however, and on 25 April the Commonwealth commanders summoned Grenville to surrender. The Royalists rejected the call, but two days later, placing little faith in reports that Charles II might mount a relief expedition, Grenville sent an envoy to negotiate and hostages were exchanged for the duration of the talks. On 2 May commissioners from both sides met on Samson Island, but talks were broken off, because, as the Commonwealth commanders reported: 'Their demands [were] too dishonourable to grant.'[16]

Blake resumed operations. Two storehouses were erected on Tresco, a gun platform constructed opposite St Mary's, and a whole and a demi-culverin mounted there. A crowd of soldiers, sailors, and perhaps a few islanders gathered to see the first shot fired, which almost proved fatal to the onlookers, as the whole culverin, which had possibly been over-charged, exploded. The gunner, Ensign Jefferies and eight other men were injured, and Blake and Ayscue narrowly escaped.

Undeterred, Blake mounted another gun, and also sent some warships to bombard St Mary's. In a boost to Commonwealth morale, Captain Parker, in the frigate *Amity*, after a twenty-league chase captured a Royalist ship, which had been attempting to escape to France.

During the next few days events moved quickly. On 10 May the Council of State wrote to Blake with some concern, expressing their fears that some kind of Royalist relief attempt might be mounted, and urging him to reduce St Mary's as quickly as possible. On the previous day, however, a captured seaman had escaped from St Mary's and informed Blake that although there were some 600 Royalists on the island, their morale was dropping rapidly. On the 10th the Royalists' dwindling hopes received another blow when a sudden storm wrecked two of their best frigates, 'which rode under the Hugh Hill near their shore, to prevent our boats coming to land there.'[17]

The Royalists on St Mary's still had their blockhouses and earth 'mounts', but lacked the men to hold them. With the Royalists' will to resist steadily crumbling, Blake felt that renewed negotiations would bring about a speedy surrender. To encourage this, he was prepared to offer lenient terms. A likely sticking point was the fate of Grenville's Irish soldiers, who, as 'native' Irish taken in arms, were theoretically by an Ordnance of Parliament liable to the death penalty. As on similar occasions, the local commanders used their discretion, and it was agreed that the Irish troops should be safely returned to Ireland. The English soldiers among the garrison, of whom it was said that there were 'enough Commissioned and Reformado Officers to have headed an army', could either make their peace with the Commonwealth and go home, or be sent to Scotland to join Charles II. About 100, including Colonel Edward Wogan, chose this latter option. All prisoners were granted an indemnity for previous actions, which was also extended to the crews of fifteen privateers which were still at sea. Sir John Grenville was among those who chose to go to France, and he was paid £1000 for the cannon that he left behind.

Bad weather delayed the surrender, and on 2 June Tromp and his Dutch squadron returned, to be told by Blake, with something complete honesty, that the Royalists were to retain all ~~~ed ships and their cargoes. Thwarted, but unwilling to make ~~~issue of it, Tromp departed in the direction of the Channel Islands. Next day the Royalist surrender duly took place, and a new Commonwealth garrison took over, with Ayscue and his squadron resuming their voyage to Barbados.

By 28 June, having personally landed the Irish troops at Kinsale, Blake was back in Plymouth. Here the victors quarrelled among themselves and, according to a Commonwealth newspaper, a fierce battle took place between soldiers and sailors:

> ... we had that night a great quarrel between the seamen and soldiers, much harm had likely ensued, only it was timely prevented; there were many bloody pates, and one or two dangerously wounded, but none slain; the soldiers with the butt ends of muskets and swords, and the seamen with oars and poles; after a few broken pates the quarrel was taken up and all made friends.

The quarrel was undoubtedly over who deserved the most credit for the victory in the Scillies.

The Channel Islands
Now the Channel Islands were the only remaining Royalist possession on England's south-western approaches, and they would be Blake's next objective. Like the Scillies, the Channel Islands had been an important Royalist privateering base throughout the Civil Wars, although the islanders were predominantly Parliamentarian in sympathy. They had, however, been held down by three main Royalist garrisons, Castle Cornet in Guernsey, and in Jersey Elizabeth Castle, held by Sir George Carteret, and Mount Orgueil Castle, held by Sir George's brother, Phillip.

In Guernsey there was something of an on-going stalemate, with the Royalists largely confined to their stronghold by a small Parliamentarian force. In Jersey, however, Sir George Carteret, as a leading local landowner, enjoyed some support from the islanders.

On 20 September the Council of State wrote to Colonel Hearne in the West Country ordering him to prepare a military expedition for the Channel Islands. The Council also wrote to R... Blake:

> We have given instructions for reducing the Isle of Jersey, and for the better effecting, we desire you, with such ships as you shall think fit, to sail for that place and there give your best advice and assistance for its reduction.[18]

Blake's flagship was the thirty-eight-gun 2nd rate *Happy Entrance*, and his fleet included twelve other warships, with numerous transports and smaller vessels raising it to a total of eighty. At Bridport Hearne was mustering his troops, which included his own regiment and six companies of Sir Hardress Waller's Foot, together with two troops of horse, making in all 2,200 men.

On 17 October the expedition set sail from Weymouth, but,

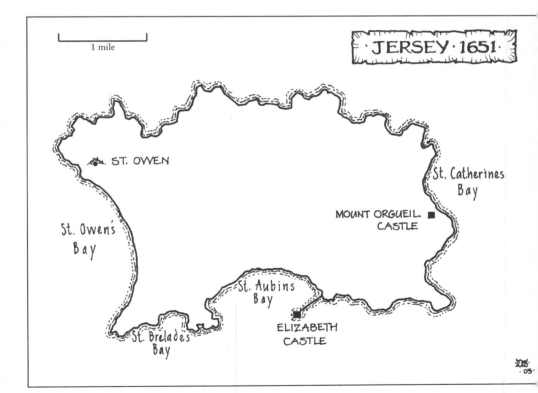

forced back by gales and heavy seas, did not arrive off Jersey until noon on the 20th. They anchored off St Owen's Bay, although the sea was still too rough for the troops to be landed by boat. From his manor house at St Owen, Phillip Carteret saw the enemy armada approaching, and sent word to Sir George at Elizabeth Castle. As the news spread, the bells of twelve parishes across the island pealed to call out the militia.

Sir George Carteret assembled a force consisting of 300 horse and dragoons, his own firelock company of 120 men, 2,000 foot, mostly militia, and six small guns, and brought them down to the shore of St Owen's Bay.

That night Carteret tried to persuade some Flemish sailors to take fire ships into the enemy fleet, but they refused to take the risk. Next morning, 21 October, Blake sent a message by shallop to the islanders, inviting them to surrender. Sir George and his Royalist die-hards opened fire on the boat, forcing it to retire, for as Carteret later admitted, he knew that 'the greater part of his men desired nothing more than to surrender without a fight.'

In response Blake sent some frigates close inshore to fire on the enemy, and the terrified militiamen were thrown into considerable confusion. To spare them from the ordeal, Sir George pulled his men back into the shelter of the sand hills, though in an effort to boost morale Carteret and some of his officers contemptuously remained in the open. Shamed by this example, some of his men left cover and began to fire their muskets at the Commonwealth ships, shouting that their crews were 'traitors, rebels and murderers of their king.'[19] The bombardment continued for about four hours, although most of the 500 cannon-shot fired had their impact deadened by the sand, for only seven or eight of Carteret's men were killed, with a number of others wounded. The response of the Royalist musketeers and Carteret's light guns was equally in-effective, although one of Blake's ships, the *Eagle*, was slightly damaged.

As the seas remained too rough for a landing, Blake decided to sail around to St Brelade's Bay to see if conditions were more favourable there. Carteret and his men followed along the shore, and arrived at the Bay first, as the Commonwealth ships had to detour in order to avoid the Corbière Rocks. In order to retain the initiative, and confuse and exhaust the Royalists, Blake now divided his squadron. Part of his force was sent eastwards to St Aubin's and St Clement's bays, while Blake with the remainder went back to St Owen's Bay, which was now defended only by 300 militia from the St Owen Parish, divided into small bodies to make them appear more numerous.

Observing the beach, Blake and Hearne saw that the enemy defences were reasonably strong, consisting of a line of earthworks defended by two gun batteries. The west side of the bay offered the Commonwealth ships a good anchorage, protected by high ground, but time was running out because of supply shortages aboard the troop transports, especially of fodder for the horses. Kempson Hilliard, a soldier with the expedition, wrote that:

> . . . all this while the wind continued so high that we could not tell what to do, seeing apparent ruin to us all if the wind ceased not. About six at night we considered that though the weather was not seasonable, and sixteen sail of our fleet left at Guernsey, our horse provisions were quite spent, so that they must be lost if we either lay still or returned; and we being willing to do the work we were sent about, resolved to throw ourselves upon the Lord, and tomorrow to endeavour to do it.'[20]

However, during the evening the wind dropped, and: 'within an hour after we had a calm sea and quiet weather'.[21]

A hastily- called Council of War met at 3am, and decided that St Owen's Bay offered the most promising landing place. Two hours later, Blake began shipping troops ashore, using boats manned by Navy seamen, evidently having learnt from the first debacle at the Scillies of the disadvantages of leaving the soldiers, or civilian seamen, to man boats.

Carteret was watching the preparations from the shore, estimating enemy strength at 4,000 men. Though this was an exaggeration, at dawn he found his own force to be dwindling through desertion. Leaving his dragoons and some musketeers to support the militia at St Brelade's, he marched the remainder of his force back to St Owen's, undeterred by a bombardment begun at St Brelade's by some of Blake's ships: 'to amuse and distract the enemy and keep them in alarm, [Blake] left part of the fleet there and by their guns shooting in their boats did so alarm them that the Pastor of a village in that bay with his flock and the forces ran away to Elizabeth Castle.'[22]

However, by the time the remainder of the Commonwealth ships had got back to St Owen's Bay, the tide had ebbed, forcing them to wait for the next full tide before they could begin landing troops. Blake had, however, been reinforced by Major Harrison with 200 troops from Guernsey.

While waiting, Blake decided to confuse and tire the Royalists further by sailing around to L'Etac, as if intending a landing there. Carteret's weary men had to respond by marching along the beach in pursuit, in cold steady rain. Having thus annoyed the enemy, Blake reversed course and sailed back across the bay. The Royalists began trudging back again, and now came under fire from the Commonwealth ships *Elizabeth*, *Phoenix*, a battery ship and the *Eagle*, which threw the Royalist column into confusion, although only one horse and two men appear to have been hit.

Both sides were now fairly uncomfortable; the Commonwealth soldiers were forced to lie in the open boats, 'without bread or beer, until the next tide',[23] while Carteret's militia were wavering and had to be brought back to their duty by their officers at sword point. Three or four of the militia pointed their muskets at Carteret, 'which he pretended not to notice, and did so much with threats and entreaties that he got men into order to receive the foe.'[24]

At nightfall Blake's men were still unable to begin landing, and Carteret ordered his men to try to get some rest, while he himself paced up and down the shore, watching the enemy fleet. At 11pm he noticed one ship hauling on its cable as if attempting to be run aground. Sir George roused his men, and asked a local fisherman whether it was possible for a ship to be beached there at that state of the tide. The man assured him that it was impossible, but 'they had not finished speaking, when two cannon-shot, passing over their heads, showed them plainly to the contrary.'[25] While his wavering militia formed up, Carteret went in search of his cavalry, resting further back from the beach. He discovered that some two-thirds of them had fled, and Colonel Edward Bovill, commanding the remainder, told Carteret that he might as well follow their example, 'unless he would throw his life away in sheer lightness of heart, adding that they were ready to obey him.'[26]

Undeterred, Sir George replied: 'Very well then, in God's name let us go to meet them, that it may not be said that they had us without a fight,' and led them down towards the beach.

In the meantime, Blake's boats had hoisted sails and, cutting their cables to avoid delay, run themselves ashore. Some of them grounded in from three to seven feet of water, but the 'forlorn hope' led by Captain Dover threw themselves into the sea, sometimes up to their necks, and waded ashore. According to the Royalists, some of the attackers had 'in front of their shallops great bridges which gave passage to ten men abreast.'[27] The Commonwealth forces were thus able to land about 1,200 men very quickly. Carteret ordered Colonel Edward Bovill, commanding his horse, to charge the landing party while Sir George drew up his foot. Bovill's attack drove the Commonwealth troops back into the water, with four men killed and Dover, his lieutenant, and sixteen others wounded.

Fierce fighting continued for about half an hour, and if the Royalist foot had seconded their horse the landing might have been repulsed. But only the St Owen militia were still in the field, and they remained only because Carteret was leading them. They fired one volley, and the horse were about to make another charge when Bovill was shot and wounded. This threw the Royalist cavalry into confusion, affording the enemy a breathing space during which Colonel Hearne landed more men, who, firing three rapid volleys, forced the militia into a retreat. Carteret, abandoning all but two of his guns, rode off via St Aubin's, whose governor he ordered to hold out, then returned to Elizabeth Castle.

Hearne had taken twelve guns and some colours, and, to follow up his success, had the horses of his cavalry troopers swum ashore. He marched on without opposition until about three in the afternoon, when the Commonwealth troops occupied a hill overlooking St Aubin's Tower and Elizabeth Castle.

After having a few cannon shot directed at it, the tower surrendered, on condition that its governor could retire to Elizabeth Castle, and a further twelve guns were taken.

Blake's fleet now had a safe anchorage, and it anchored just in time, apart from the transport *Tresco*, commanded by Blake's cousin, William, which struck a rock and sank with the loss of 300 men. The casualties were so high mainly because some of *Tresco*'s crew had gone off in the ship's boats on an unauthorised plundering expedition.

On 26 October, making no mention of this disaster, Blake penned a despatch to the Speaker of the Commons:

> It hath pleased God, that after much conflicting with seas and winds and other difficulties, and a short dispute with the enemy, about 11 at night on Wednesday last, our forces landed on the [west] side of the island in a bay called Porlala Mar, with good resolution and success. The enemy, after a hot charge with their horse flying before them forsaking divers small works and forts; the next day our men took by surrender the tower of St Aubins with fourteen guns in it, which affordeth refuge and safety for our victualling ships and others. Carteret is gone to Elizabeth Castle which is blocked up by a party. The rest of our men are now about the fort of Mount Orgueil, our ships riding before it. We have not above four or five men lost, as far as I can hear; some barques and other vessels are still in that bay aground, and have received some damage since the landing. It hath been such weather, as I could not have intercourse with the shore, so that I cannot give your Honour a perfect narrative.[28]

Hearne, meanwhile, had gone to St Helier with his regiment of foot and Captain West's horse with the object of containing the garrison of Elizabeth Castle, which stood on an island 'about one and a half musket shot off shore.' The castle was believed to be impregnable, as the rocky coastline of the island prevented any ships from coming close, while it was believed to be out of effective artillery range. On 24 October Hearne summoned Carteret to surrender, but received what was described as a 'scurrilous reply.' Hearne left Major Ebzary with six companies from Hardress Waller's Regiment, three companies of Guernsey foot and a troop of horse to maintain a landward blockade of Elizabeth Castle, while Hearne, with his own foot regiment and West's horse, moved against Mount Orgueil. They established their encampment on a nearby rabbit warren and on 25 October offered generous terms, providing that none of the Commonwealth troops were killed. Hearne added that he required an answer 'before I am put to the trouble of bringing up my train of artillery and mortar pieces hither.'[29]

The governor, Sir Phillip Carteret, asked leave to consult with his brother, Sir George, a request which Hearne refused. In response Sir Phillip threatened to starve some prisoners he held in the castle (possibly seamen from captured merchant ships). But his men had no stomach for what they saw to be a hopeless defiance, and threatened to hand Sir Phillip over to the besiegers unless he made terms. As was customary in Blake's operations against the Royalist 'hold-outs', the terms granted were generous. Sir Phillip was allowed to retain his Jersey estates, and an act of oblivion regarding any actions by them during the war was granted to the garrison. About sixty men who so wished were allowed to make their way to Elizabeth Castle, while others were given free passage overseas. Along with Mount Orgueil Castle, Hearne came into possession of forty-two guns, 1,000 arms, and two month's provision for seventy men.[30]

The Commonwealth soldier, Kempton Hilliard, was jubilant:

> Truly, I cannot but wonder to see how the Lord doth strike these people with fear and terror that they should so suddenly deliver up such a stronghold; it is seated very high upon a round rock and many vaults cut in it out of the firm rock, and in my judgement 'tis neither stormable nor to be injured by mortar pieces.

Rather more mundanely, Hilliard ended his letter to his wife: 'my true love to you and my dear sister. I am well, only a little lousy.'[31]

Sir George Carteret, however, still held out resolutely in Elizabeth Castle. He had divided the garrison into three watches, and all had to be at arms at night on occasions when the tide was out, in case Hearne should take the opportunity to make an attack from the landward side.

However, the Commonwealth commanders had no intention of attempting a costly assault. On 29 October Colonel Hearne established an artillery battery mounting six 36-pound cannon on a low hill. They proved fairly ineffective, however, only demolishing a few turf ramparts. Four days later six more guns were emplaced in the same location, and, more threatening for the Royalists, three mortars were hoisted from ships into a nine-foot high emplacement.

Carteret reacted with a night sortie by fifteen horsemen, who returned with a townsman who reported the arrival of 'two cannons as large as barrels' – undoubtedly two of Hearne's mortars.

About a week later 'a huge bomb . . . fell into the midst of the castle, confirming the belief that they were mortars of an extraordinary size, the bomb being actually thirty inches in diameter.' This estimate seems likely to have been an exaggeration; the largest mortar shells normally were no more than 16–18 inches in diameter. A third shell fell on the castle church, which was used as a magazine and powder store, and which promptly blew up, killing five or six men and burying forty others.

Carteret tried to convince his men that the explosion had been caused by an accident in the magazine, not the enemy bombardment, but the effects on morale were severe, with a number of men deserting.

Hoping to take advantage of this faltering resolve, Hearne despatched a summons to surrender. Carteret responded defiantly by opening fire on the besiegers' encampment, but was unable to stem the steady trickle of deserters. Sir George hanged one deserter caught in the act, but 'the fear of the bombs [was] greater than that of the rope.'[32] King Charles II in France could offer no hope of relief, and gave Carteret permission to surrender.

Sir George remained defiant, however, despite the continuing mortar bombardment, which caused him to have his wife and other women in the castle evacuated to France by a Royalist ship which had slipped into the castle's small dock. To try to prevent another major explosion, he had his remaining gunpowder split into small packets and buried at different points within his defences.

Blake was determined to prevent the occasional Royalist vessels despatched from France from communicating with the garrison of Elizabeth Castle, and used his frigates to establish a blockade on the seaward approaches to the Castle. On land, meanwhile, Hearne's continuing bombardment suffered a slight setback when the mortar master, Thomas Wright, over-charged one of his pieces so that 'the middle of them have broken their carriages, and the biggest is in a manner unusable.'[33]

Concealing this setback, on 3 December Hearne sent another summons to the defenders of Elizabeth Castle. By now, provisions within the besieged garrison were almost exhausted, and on the 8th Carteret gave way to the pleas of his officers and agreed to open negotiations, though he pointed out: 'the consideration of any damage we are likely to receive by your Grenades, an advantage which you might imagine to have hitherto gained upon us, be too weak an argument to incline me to harbour your desire, yet I conceive it not amiss to hear what you have to propose unto me.'[34]

This was part of the elaborate bluff and counter-bluff which was customary when the surrender of a garrison was being discussed, and when Hearne sent his commissioners to open talks, Carteret took the game a step further:

> All the officers and soldiers had orders to be under arms on the arrival of the commissioners and to talk to each other as though they were not greatly concerned about the success of the treaty; but the bearer of this order explained it so ill, that instead of this, as soon as the men arrived, the whole garrison gave a shout as though for joy, which made them think that however good a face the governor put on it, he must be in difficulties, and this was the cause, as they afterwards admitted, that they did not get as good terms as they would otherwise have done.[35]

In fact the terms accepted by Carteret closely followed those granted to other garrisons in Blake's operations that year. Elizabeth Castle was to be delivered up by noon on 12 December. Sir George Carteret was given leave to go to St Malo in France with his money, possessions and plate, and his men were also free to depart for the same destination. Along with the castle itself, the victorious Commonwealth forces also took possession of fifty-three guns, 450 muskets, a quantity of powder and shot and eight ships in the harbour.

With Jersey in Commonwealth hands, the remaining Royalists in the Channel Islands quickly submitted. Their last stronghold on

Guernsey surrendered on 19 December on the same terms granted to Elizabeth Castle.

Thanks to Blake's skilful military and political handling of the situation, the Royalists' last remaining strongholds near the English coast were in Commonwealth hands. It only remained for the Council of State to learn the fate of the outposts in the New World.

Barbados

While the English colonies on the American mainland remained divided in their allegiance, they were not the principal concern of Sir George Ayscue in the summer of 1651 as his squadron beat steadily across the Atlantic. More important was the prosperous and relatively densely-settled island of Barbados, which, if un-subdued, might provide another refuge for Rupert's fugitive naval squadron.

The governor of Barbados was Lord Willoughby of Parham, a former Parliamentarian commander in the First Civil War who had defected to the Royalists in 1648 and had briefly held the post of Vice-Admiral in the Royalist fleet before being sent to Barbados.

Ayscue's command was not designed to fight a naval battle, and indeed there was little prospect of one unless Rupert appeared. With Sir George was his flagship, the fifty-gun *Rainbow*, one frigate and five merchant ships, carrying 860 men in all. Ayscue's expedition met with considerable delays, firstly by being diverted to aid Blake in his capture of the Scilly Isles, and then in an unsuccessful search off the Portuguese coast for Rupert's squadron. In fact, this long delay would prove to be to Ayscue's advantage in lulling the Barbados Royalists into a false sense of security. When the Commonwealth squadron finally arrived off Barbados on the evening of 15 October, they came as an unpleasant shock, for, as one of Ayscue's officers, Captain Park, said of the islanders: 'we found the people here like the men of Laish of old; because we had stayed so long they concluded we would not come at all.'[36] Indeed, the Royalist supporters among the islanders had grown dangerously complacent. There had been vague reports circulating that Charles II and his Scottish army were approaching London, and even that Oliver Cromwell had been killed in action.

Ayscue gave the Royalists no chance to recover from the shock of his arrival. On the morning of 16 October he sent Captain Park in the frigate *Amity*, with three merchantmen, to Carhele Bay to attempt to capture the shipping there. The defending forts could only fire ineffectively as the Commonwealth seamen boarded the fourteen ships they found in the harbour. All, however, proved to be Dutch, and when taken aboard Park's ship their captains 'stood in a kind of mazed condition, and suffered themselves all to be taken out of their ships and our men to be put in their place, without any resistance.'[37] Only two of the Dutch ships escaped, by running themselves ashore.

Lord Willoughby 'with a crew of desperadoes, his officers' was at a plantation some miles inland when Ayscue arrived. Park believed that if 1,000 men had been available to form a landing force, they could have taken over all the key points of the island virtually without resistance. As Ayscue moved with the remainder of his squadron to join Park, Willoughby's Marshal, still unclear about what was happening, put out in a small boat to enquire who the newcomers were and was taken prisoner.

Next day, 17 October, Ayscue summoned Willoughby to surrender. By now the governor had mustered a force of 1,000 foot and 400 horse, and rejected Sir George's call, incurring further displeasure by addressing his reply to 'his majesty's ship the *Rainbow*.' For the moment, however, there was not much Ayscue could do beyond instituting a blockade of the island in the hope that the loss of trade would bring the islanders to terms. At the same time a 'Declaration' was carried ashore at night by swimmers offering easy terms. However, encouraged in their belief by Willoughby, the majority of the islanders still thought that Charles II had won a major victory in the battle at Worcester, and on 7 November held a Day of Thanksgiving for the king's success. Two days later, however, a ship brought Ayscue word from the Council of State that the battle had actually resulted in a decisive victory for Cromwell's forces, enclosing a printed relation of the battle, which Ayscue sent ashore by boat to Willoughby.

On 12 November Willoughby replied, acknowledging Cromwell's victory, but continuing: 'if it hath pleased God to add this sad affliction to [the king's] former ones, I will not be a means of increasing it by delivering this place to your keeping.' Ayscue responded briskly: 'if there were such a person as a king you speak of, your keeping this island signifies nothing to his advantage.' He enclosed a letter from Lady Willoughby in London, in which she urged her husband to surrender.

In order to increase pressure further, Ayscue decided to beat up Royalist quarters in 'the Hole', formerly known as Jamestown, where there was a fort mounting four guns. On the night of 22 November 200 seamen, led by Captain Morris, the veteran of the landing on Tresco, came ashore, took the fort, spiked its guns and re-embarked with thirty prisoners, without loss to themselves.

On 1 December Ayscue received a welcome, if temporary, re-inforcement, when the annual Virginia fleet arrived on its way from England. Sir George resolved to take advantage of its assistance by making another attack. He had learnt that there was another lightly held fort at Speight's Bay, which seemed ripe for capture. On 7 December a landing force was prepared, consisting of 400 seamen and 150 of the Scots prisoners taken at Worcester, now being shipped as 'bondsmen' to Virginia. These proved willing to serve in return for 'a gratuity' and the composite force was formed into a temporary unit under Captain Morris and Ensign Adams, and landed under cover of darkness.

However, this time the Royalists were aware of their approach, and a force of 1,200 foot and three troops of horse under a Colonel Gibbs, with the guns of the fort manned and loaded, was ready to meet the landing force. Although Morris and his men were 'notably received' in a confused scuffle in the darkness, the Royalists believed the Commonwealth force to be stronger than was actually the case, and, after a brief encounter, made off, allowing Morris's force to take the fort and its guns. Ayscue admitted to the loss of Ensign Allen and seven or eight men, claiming that the enemy lost 100 dead, eighty prisoners, 500 arms and eleven hundredweight of gunpowder.

As part of his conciliatory policy, Sir George treated the prisoners well and sent them ashore after giving them a full account of the true situation in England. Two unfortunates were later hanged by Willoughby for spreading this information among the population.

Ayscue was no nearer to actually taking the island, and his prospects diminished further on 14 December when the Virginia Fleet left to continue its voyage. He was still faced ashore by an estimated 5,000 armed opponents. Stalemate seemed to have been reached, but Sir George knew that some among the Royalist leadership in Barbados were realists who sought to preserve their own positions and property. Chief among the moderates was a Colonel Modyford who realised that, for the moment at any rate, the king's position was hopeless. He was, said Ayscue, 'master of a good deal of reason and truly sensible of the ruin of the island, if they should be longer obstinate.' Sir George began secret communication with Modyford and an agreement was reached between them. Modyford in turn contacted others whom he felt to hold similar views.

Willoughby and the bulk of the island Royalists were at first ignorant of what was taking place, but in such a small community it was probably inevitable that word would leak out, and while Modyford was still preparing to put pressure on Willoughby to agree to terms he was betrayed on 31 December. Both factions mobilised forces loyal to them, and the result was a stand-off between the Windward Regiment of militia, controlled by Modyford, and about 2,000 foot and 400 horse supporting Willoughby. Modyford's men were supported by the guns of the Commonwealth squadron, and as a result the Royalists hesitated to initiate hostilities. Operations were also prevented by several days of heavy rain, during which time Willoughby began gradually to accept the hopelessness of his situation.

Accepting the inevitable, he sent to Ayscue asking for terms. As in similar situations, these were generous. Barbados was granted what amounted to home rule under a governor appointed by Ayscue, but with the General Assembly retaining considerable powers. In the final agreement, signed on 11 January 1652, Willoughby had to leave the island, although he was allowed to retain his property there.

The end of resistance on Barbados was soon followed by the submission of remaining Royalist-held territories. In Virginia an initial confrontation between the Royalist Governor, Sir William Berkeley, and the provincial assembly ended peacefully on 12 March when the colony submitted to the Commonwealth on similar conditions to those granted to Barbados, and the remaining mainland colony of Maryland and the islands of the Bermudas rapidly followed suit.

The last remaining Royalist outpost of the Isle of Man, for so long the stronghold of the Earl of Derby and his redoubtable wife, surrendered on 31 October 1651 to the Commonwealth Governor of Liverpool, Colonel Robert Duckenfield, when he arrived with a small squadron. The capture and execution of Derby two weeks earlier had demonstrated even to his formidable wife the futility of further resistance faced by islander unrest and Commonwealth forces.

For the moment at least, in a large part thanks to the Navy, the Republic had crushed the Royalist threat. But on the wider scene new storm clouds were gathering.

Chapter 5
The Dutch War 1:
Learning the Lessons

'The English are going to attack a mountain of
gold. We face one of iron.'
Adrian Pau, Dutch envoy in London, 1652)

The war with Scotland
The first foreign nation to feel the full wrath of the new English
Commonwealth was her nearest neighbour, Scotland. With the
Scots unable to put up any significant resistance at sea, Oliver
Cromwell, newly appointed General of the Army in place of Lord
Fairfax, saw the main task of the Navy as providing logistical
support for his advance north of the border. A flotilla of eleven
supply ships and four warships was formed initially, which as the
campaign dragged on indecisively through the summer of 1650
grew to a fleet of 140 vessels, charged with carrying to the port of
Dunbar supplies from London, Lynn, Harwich and Newcastle. For
much of the first part of his campaign, the lack of a major Scottish
port under his control, coupled with bad weather, severely
hindered Cromwell's attempts to keep his forces supplied by sea. A
bombardment of the port of Leith carried out by four warships on
29 July failed to dent its fortifications sufficiently for a land assault
to make progress. Indeed, until his narrow and desperately fought
victory at Dunbar on 3 September, there seemed a real danger of
Cromwell being isolated and forced to surrender.[1]

After Dunbar, although Scottish resistance remained stubborn, the initiative passed to the English, and as Cromwell prepared to send troops north across the Firth of Forth, a fleet of flat-bottomed boats was built in Lynn and Newcastle in order to carry troops, horses and supplies in amphibious landing operations.

The Scots campaign was effectively concluded by Cromwell's decisive victory at Worcester (3 September 1651), and the Navy could look back with reasonable satisfaction on a campaign in which it had performed adequately if unspectacularly.

The Commonwealth had now crushed all of its internal foes, but its position in Europe remained insecure, with foreign recognition grudging at best. There was already a state of low-level, undeclared war with France, and a new conflict was looming.

The Commonwealth and the Dutch

As a result of bad harvests and plague, the English Commonwealth had suffered economic difficulties throughout its existence. By 1651 these problems had also begun to afflict England's influential merchant ship owners. Cromwell and many of his associates had originally seen the Protestant Dutch as natural allies, but this essentially emotional reaction ignored the commercial rivalries of over half a century. Though temporarily diminished by the long war between the Dutch and Spain, and the wider impact of the Thirty Years' War, Dutch merchant ships had been steadily eating into England's share of the 'carrying trade' (the transportation of the goods of other countries). Dutch ship owners grew prosperous on the carriage of highly profitable goods such as spices, whaling products, gold, silks and sugar.

The growing Dutch impact on the carrying trade was regarded with alarm by a number of European rivals, especially the English. English ship owners had benefited from Dutch preoccupation with the Thirty Years' War, but the conclusion in 1648 of a general European peace brought the Dutch back on the scene with a vengeance and threatened the English trade with bankruptcy.

The Dutch capitalised on the use of unarmed, cheaply-built ships, manned by small badly-paid crews, resulting in low shipping costs, backed by the most efficiently run economy in Europe. In 1649 the Dutch reached an agreement with Denmark whereby they obtained a discount on the 'Sound tolls' which all shipping entering or leaving the Baltic had to pay to the Danes. Within a year, instead of thirteen Dutch merchant ships entering the Baltic for every English vessel, the ratio had become fifty to one to England's disadvantage. Dutch commercial agreements with Spain struck another serious blow to England's share of the carrying trade with Spanish possessions and in the Mediterranean. Particularly incensed by these developments were a group of English traders known as the 'New Merchants', mainly Independents in religion and politics, who found what had hitherto been a virtual monopoly of trade with the English colonies of the New World increasingly undermined by the Dutch. They retaliated by pushing through the Act of 1650 which forbade foreign shipping from trading with the English colonies, and the follow-up Navigation Ordinance of 1651, which stipulated that goods carried to or from English colonies should be carried only in English ships, while imports from elsewhere should be transported either under the English flag or by ships of the countries which had produced those goods.

This legislation amounted to only a minor irritant for the Dutch. Much more serious were the frequent incidents during the war between the Commonwealth and the Royalists in which Dutch merchant ships were seized by the English Navy, and, of greater concern, by English privateers of various claimed allegiances, who frequently tortured or killed the Dutch crews. It was estimated that in the course of 1651, 140 Dutch ships had been seized by the English, with a further thirty in the opening weeks of 1652.

There were also festering political disputes. England had traditionally claimed the 'sovereignty of the seas' in a very generously defined area of her coastal waters. Usually this had involved little more than a rather irritating demand that ships of other nations should dip their flags in acknowledgement of this claim when encountering English warships, but the undeclared conflict with France led to a further English claim of a right to search neutral shipping for 'contraband' – in this case French goods. The Dutch retaliated with diplomatic protests, and attacks by their own privateers, but to no avail.

Politically, the early feeling of there being some common ground between the two republics withered. In 1651 the republican Dutch had succeeded in persuading some other European powers to recognise the new regime in England, but whatever goodwill this action brought with it quickly dwindled. The new leaders of

England were influenced in their political actions as much by their conviction of their divinely appointed mission as by more worldly considerations. When the Dutch rejected the proposal of a federation of the two republics in a Protestant league against the Catholic powers of Europe, this refusal was seen in ruling circles in England as a spurning of God's will by Presbyterians, at best imperfectly Protestant, which favoured the power of Rome. It was therefore a religious duty to lead them back into the paths of righteousness, preferably by persuasion, which in this case included the effects of the Navigation Ordinance, by negotiation, and ultimately, if need be, by force.

It is not clear how far the Dutch understood English motivations, and in any case the nature of the Dutch constitution made any political agreement difficult. The seven United Provinces which made up the Dutch Republic were in reality a loose federation of semi-autonomous states. There was no permanent central government. Such national policy as there was was formulated by the States General, with delegates from the different provincial assemblies. Their voting power depended upon the tax revenue of the province they represented, which by virtue of its wealth gave Holland 60 percent of the vote, while Holland's Assembly in turn was heavily influenced by the great mercantile and financial centres of Amsterdam and Rotterdam. As a result, the interests of the Dutch shipping merchants and the rights of their merchant ships occupied a major place in the deliberations of the States General.

Apart from maritime Zeeland, the remaining provinces, agricultural in their economies, were more interested in Continental matters, and for many years, thanks to the princes of the house of Orange-Nassau, whose tenure of the office of 'Stadtholder' (literally 'chief magistrate') carried with it the post of commander-in-chief of the Republic's armed forces, the inland provinces had been able to counter the influence of Holland. However, the ruling mercantile circles in Holland were strongly republican in sentiment. The sudden death, in November 1650, of Prince William II of Orange, and the infancy of his son and heir, allowed the republicans to gain complete control of government. It also placed the Republic on a collision course with England.

The Dutch navy reflected the nature of the Republic's political constitution. There was no single national navy, but instead five provincial admiralties, representing those provinces with a coast-line. Naturally dominant was the Admiralty of Amsterdam, closely followed by those of Rotterdam and Zeeland, which controlled the naval dockyard at Flushing. Each admiralty had its own fleet and naval establishment, financed by its own resources, but to complicate matters further, there were other naval resources outside their control. Both of the major Dutch overseas trading organisations, the West and East India Companies, maintained their own fleets of well-armed ships which might by agreement be placed at the disposal of the Republic.

Even this did not complete the tally. There were a number of 'municipal navies', known as *directieschepen*, which provided convoy escorts for ships of those municipalities, while there were numerous privateering syndicates, especially in Zeeland, each with their own armed vessels. A list of the Dutch fleet compiled in June 1652 comprised twenty-six sections.[2]

The numerous rivalries and disputes of the Dutch provinces were mirrored in naval matters. The men and commanders of Holland and Zeeland, Amsterdam and Rotterdam, Orangeist and Republican, were frequently at bitter odds.

If these factors had not been enough to ensure disunity, they were exacerbated by geography, which divided the Dutch naval forces into three distinct groups. The ships of the so-called 'Northern Quarter', consisting of the squadrons of Amsterdam and Friesland, had no exit to the North Sea except by the Marsdiep, a long and tortuous channel which ran by the island of the Texel. The Rotterdam ships also had a difficult exit on either side of the island of Goree. Although the Zeeland squadrons had fairly easy egress from their base of Flushing at the mouth of the River Scheldt, and could then combine readily with the contingent from Rotterdam, the Texel lay some hundred miles to the north, making it possible for an active opponent to divide the Dutch forces and potentially defeat them in detail.

The Dutch Republic's main experience of naval warfare had been during the Eighty Years' War with Spain. During this the role of the fledgling Dutch navy had been to protect their commerce by escorting convoys, and bottling up the Spanish privateers based on Dunkirk. The task had mainly been carried out by armed merchant ships, supported by a small number of larger warships. Only a few major naval actions had taken place, the most recent being the celebrated Battle of the Downs (11 October 1639), when Admiral van Tromp had destroyed a major Spanish fleet.

The Downs were the broad anchorage off the English coast near Deal, enclosed by the Kentish coast to the west and the treacherous Goodwin Sands to the east. At their northern end the Downs were entered from the North Sea or the Thames Estuary via the Gull Channel, and in the south from the English Channel close to the South Foreland. The Downs were one of the great shipping cross-roads of Western Europe; in the prevailing south-westerly winds, vessels from ports of the southern North Sea and the Baltic waited there for a fair wind to continue their voyages down-Channel. Here too, ships heading up-Channel for London waited to enter the Thames Estuary.

In time of war, the Downs were an excellent anchorage from which a fleet might control the upper Channel and southern North Sea. But they were also in the prevailing wind a potential death trap for any squadron anchored there; the Gull Channel was too narrow for a fleet to negotiate quickly, and it might find itself trapped by an enemy force entering from the southern entrance with the advantage of the wind gauge. This was how Tromp had caught the Spaniards in 1639, and neither the Dutch nor the English had forgotten.

As tensions continued to mount in 1651, the Dutch States General voted to increase their naval strength from 150 to 226 ships. This was intended to deter the English from any hostile acts, but instead convinced them that the Dutch were determined on war.

The Dutch people shared the view of most of Europe that any war would end in a Dutch victory. The reputation of the English Navy had plummeted during the reigns of the first two Stuart kings and the Civil War, while Blake's recent successes against the Royalists, despite giving pause for thought, were not major fleet actions. The Dutch could look back with pride to both Tromp's recent success and Peit Hein's earlier victory over the Spaniards off Rio in 1628. There seemed no reason why the English fleet should fare any better.

There were, however, a number of factors which gave many contemporary observers cause for caution. The Dutch felt that the strategy which had served them well in the war with Spain would continue to fulfil their primary aim of keeping the lifeblood of Dutch trade flowing. But this was to ignore a number of strategic advantages which England possessed. The first, and most obvious, was geographic; an English naval captain, Nicholas Foster of the *Phoenix*, was amazed that the Dutch would risk war 'when (like an eagle's wings extended over her body) our coast surrounded theirs for 120 leagues from Scilly to the Maas in Holland one way, and as many from the Orcades [Orkneys] thither the other way; and the wind blowing above three-quarters of the year westerly on the coast of England, made all our cape-lands and bays very good roads to anchor at.'³

England was self-sufficient in food, and, although she depended heavily on naval stores, such as timber and tar, from the Baltic ports, the need for these would only become pressing in the event of a prolonged conflict, which most English observers thought unlikely. The Dutch would rely entirely on their trade revenues to finance their war effort. Their merchant vessels followed three main routes. One led via the Danish Sound into the Baltic; the second ran through the English Channel to France, Spain, the Mediterranean and the Dutch East Indies, with an alternative passage running north of the coast of Scotland. Both of these vital arteries were vulnerable to English attack, and indeed their protection or disruption would furnish the main reason for most of the major actions of the Anglo-Dutch wars of the 17th century. For if an English fleet blocked one of these lifelines, the Dutch would have to react. This meant that the English could force a battle whenever they wished to by closing a Dutch trade route, and they could also usually fight close to their own coast and ports, giving their damaged ships a better chance of survival than those of their opponents. The Dutch fleet also usually found itself in the disadvantageous position of having to fight a battle while at the same time endeavouring to protect a precious convoy.

The rival fleets
As recently as 1649 the English Navy, with thirty-nine ships, had been outnumbered almost two to one by the Dutch. But in the next three years the Commonwealth built, bought or captured as prizes a considerable number of ships, giving the Navy by early 1651 a

total of eighty-six ships. During the same period only a dozen ships were added by the Dutch, making the two sides approximately numerically equal in warships. In time of war, because of the much greater pool of merchant vessels on which they could draw for auxiliaries, the Dutch would usually have a numerical advantage.

Commanders

Most contemporaries felt that any contest would be settled by the quality of the opposing commanders, and here the Dutch seemed to hold all the advantages. None of the English Generals at Sea had fought in a major fleet action, still less won one. The best-known of them, Robert Blake, had only held command at sea for three years; William Penn had enjoyed little success, and most other English commanders, such as Robert Bourne, were former soldiers with little or no experience of war at sea. The loyalty of many officers and sailors to the regime in England was held in doubt, and exiled Royalists were not the only people who believed that war would lead to dissension, defection and mutiny in the English fleet.

In contrast, the Dutch had a galaxy of proven naval competence available. Their senior commander, Lieutenant Admiral of the United Provinces Marteen Harpertzoon Tromp van Den Briel (usually abbreviated to Marteen Van Tromp), was generally viewed as the foremost naval commander of the age. Born in 1598, Tromp first saw action at the age of nine in his father's ship at the Dutch victory over the Spanish off Gibraltar in 1607. Three years later Marteen's father was killed and the boy captured by English pirates. For the next three years Tromp served as a cabin boy aboard the ship which had captured him. Then, when the corsair's crew was disbanded, he found his way back to Rotterdam, working for a time in the dockyard there before going to sea again in 1617. He distinguished himself in action against the Barbary corsairs before leaving the navy in favour of the merchant service. Tromp was again taken prisoner, this time by Tunisian corsairs. For a year the Dutchman served as a galley slave, until in 1622, having rejected the offer of a command by the Dey of Tunis, he was somewhat surprisingly released and re-enlisted in the Dutch navy. For the next twelve years Tromp served mainly against the privateers of various nationalities who operated out of the Channel port of Dunkirk. In 1624 Tromp obtained his first command, and soon became the best-known of the Dutch commanders in the endless war against the corsairs and privateers. In 1634 Tromp, a deeply religious man, once more resigned his post, this time with the intention of taking up church work. But life ashore proved unsatisfactory, and, re-enlisting in 1638, Tromp was appointed acting Lieutenant Admiral of Holland and West Friesland, winning in the following year his great victory over the Spaniards in the Battle of the Downs.

Henceforward Tromp's reputation as one of the most skilful naval commanders in Europe was assured. A strong supporter of the Orange party, Tromp sympathised with the Royalist cause during the English Civil War and, although he eventually established a close working relationship with the Earl of Warwick when the latter was English Lord Admiral, he had on more than one occasion come close to hostilities with the Parliamentarian Navy.[4]

Tromp was not the only well-known and proven Dutch naval commander. Vice-Admiral of Holland was Witte Cornelius de With. In almost every way deeply dissimilar to Tromp, de With was a staunch republican, foul-tempered and quarrelsome, but, though generally unpopular with his colleagues and the crews who served under him, acknowledged to be a ferocious and able fighter. Jan Evertsen, Vice-Admiral of Zeeland, and his brother Cornelius were disciples of Tromp, while as yet little known, but soon to make a famous name for himself, was Commodore Michael Adrianszoon Ruyter. Ruyter, born in 1607 in Flushing, was the son of a sailor who latterly worked as a brewer's drayman. An adventurous boy, the young Michael first went to sea as a boatswain's boy in 1618, sailing in the Dutch trade with the West Indies. Possibly living for a time in Ireland, over the next few years Ruyter built up a vast store of seafaring experience in voyages to Brazil, the West Indies, North Africa and the Mediterranean, Spain, France and the British Isles. Frequently seeing action against the Spanish and privateers, Ruyter was captured in 1640 by a Basque privateer, but escaped and made his way home. He served with a Dutch squadron sent to support the Portuguese in their fight for independence from Spain, playing a prominent role in a sharp action off Cape St Vincent in November 1641. Following a pattern common to seamen of many nationalities, Ruyter then transferred for a time to merchant shipping. By 1652 Ruyter was showing signs of preferring life ashore, where he enjoyed reading the Bible aloud in the evening or singing psalms. But events were about to compel him to take a different course.[5]

Unfortunately for the Dutch, however able their commanders, their hopes of political disunity among their opponents would prove to be ill-founded. Not for the first or last time, the officers and men of the English Navy would largely subordinate their own differences in the face of an external foe. It would, in fact, be the Dutch who would face such problems, divided by the political disputes between republicans and supporters of the House of Orange. Tromp and the Evertsens were pro-Orange, de With strongly republican, while only Ruyter seems to have been politically neutral.

Ships and tactics
Dutch seamen had taken a keen interest in naval developments of the previous half century. In 1588 they had noted the apparent failure of either English or Spanish gunnery to achieve decisive results during the Armada campaign. This convinced Dutch commanders that the gun was not by itself a decisive battle-winner, and over the next half-century they favoured a system in which ships were built for speed, in order to counter the major ongoing threat of Flemish-based privateers, mounting light guns and carrying large crews. Dutch tactics involved using speed to catch up with an opponent, then gunnery to disable his masts and rigging, followed with boarding a by now disabled enemy.

In pursuance of these tactics, the Dutch copied from the Spaniards the type of ship known generally as the 'frigate', which frequently differed widely in individual detail, but whose essential features, in comparison with existing types, were an increase in length relative to breadth, the cutting down in height of previously unwieldy superstructures, and the construction of continuous flush decks running from stem to stern. The *Amelia*, launched in 1632, was the prototype of most Dutch ships built in the following years. In 1652, out of 100 Dutch ships sent to sea, only the fleet flagship, *Brederode*, carried as many as fifty-four guns, and the majority only twenty-one to thirty.

The contrast with English practice was stark. Although they had not succeeded in all of their objectives, English commanders felt that the Armada campaign had proved the value of gunnery, and continued to build larger and heavier ships. The *Prince Royal*, launched in 1610, had 102 guns, making her the largest and most heavily armed warship in Western Europe. She was followed by *Sovereign of the Seas*, a three-decker with space for 120 guns. Though not on the scale of these two leviathans, between 1618 and 1623 a series of large, heavily-gunned ships followed: *George*, *Andrew*, *Victory*, *Constant Reformation*, *Triumph* and *Happy Entrance*. Most of these were still in service, and had been followed during the 1630s by the so-called 'Ship Money' fleet, at the heavier end of which were the 2nd rates, *Charles*, *James*, *Henrietta Maria*, *Unicorn* and *Garland*. They were supplemented by the excellent 3rd rates, *Bonaventure*, *Lion*, *Leopard* and *Swallow*.

The main weakness of the English Navy was that its 'great ships' were entirely unsuitable to deal with fast commerce raiders of the kind which operated out of Dunkirk and Ireland, and only a handful of smaller ships had been added to the fleet in the decades preceding the Civil War. The result was that every suitable prize was bought up and added to the Navy, and a new construction programme put in place after the war to add a class of ships known as convoy frigates. But these 4th rates, as they were also known, remained heavily-gunned. The *Tiger*, for example, built in 1647, was able to carry up to forty-four guns, though she rarely did so. All of the English 4th rates were potentially more heavily armed than all but one of the Dutch ships in 1652. The largest English ship had sixty-two guns, six had between fifty-one and sixty, ten forty-one to fifty, twenty-four thirty-one to forty, fifteen eleven to twenty, and seven less than ten. In other words, seventeen of the English ships out-gunned any vessel in the Dutch fleet with the exception of the *Brederode*. And this list does not include the two great 1st rates, with 100 and over eighty guns respectively, and three 2nd rates with fifty-one to sixty guns.

The English mainly used iron guns. In 1655, out of eighty-eight pieces carried by one 1st rate, five sakers were made of bronze (generally known by contemporaries as 'brass'), while the remainder, including nineteen cannon, nine demi-cannon, twenty-eight culverins and thirty demi-cannon, were iron. A 2nd rate had sixty-four guns, including four 'brass' sakers. A 3rd rate vessel had sixty guns, including eight sakers. A 6th rate carried eight brass guns. Guns ordered at Woolwich in March 1652 for the new frigate *Foresight* included twenty demi-cannon, four culverins, twenty demi-culverins and two sakers, making a total of forty-six.[6]

A full cannon fired a ball of 60lb weight, a demi-cannon one of 30.5lb, while a culverin was loaded with a shot of 17.5lb in weight. By contrast, the heaviest Dutch gun fired a shot of 24lb, and in 1655 there were only forty-four of them in the entire Dutch fleet. The most common Dutch guns were eighteen-pounders, of which there were only 157, regarded by the English as only sufficient to arm seven English 4th rates.

So the Commonwealth fleet had a clear superiority in weight of ordnance, but could this be utilised effectively? The answer was the truck gun carriage, which at least as early as 1588 English warships were employing, allowing English guns to be loaded inboard, with much greater speed, safety and efficiency.

In 1618 a Naval Inquiry had decided that all new warships should be built with flush decks. This was similar to the Continental frigate-building programme, but with the aim of building a stable floating gun platform. Ships would be low in the water, to avoid the danger of capsizing, and as solid as possible, in order to provide massive gun batteries, and be capable of absorbing considerable battle damage while remaining fit to fight. In contrast, most Continental navies did not adopt the truck gun carriage until some time later.

However, the disappointing performance of English gunnery against the Armada had demonstrated the need for new tactics, by which all the guns on one side of a ship were fired together. It is not entirely clear when the broadside was first employed, but a likely first exponent was Captain Richard Swanley, later a leading Parliamentarian naval commander, who in 1625 appears to have fired broadsides in an engagement between East Indiamen and the Portuguese.

The main effect of this reliance by the English on gunnery was that boarding by them, if it happened at all, would only take place after an opponent had been thoroughly smashed by gunfire. Generals at Sea such as Richard Deane, who had commanded the artillery of the New Model Army, and Robert Blake, with his first-hand experience of siege warfare, were quick to understand the implications of gunnery.

Outbreak of war

By the spring of 1652 war between England and the United
Provinces was inevitable. The Commonwealth was committed to
the non-negotiable demands that England's 'sovereignty of the
seas' should be unconditionally recognised, that the Dutch should
pay a tribute for being allowed to fish in widely defined 'British
seas', and that they should relinquish their claim to be allowed to
carry the goods of belligerent nations under a neutral flag.

There was no realistic chance of averting a conflict that one of
the Dutch delegation in London, Adrian Pau, felt that his country
had no chance of winning: 'The English are going to attack a
mountain of gold; we have to face one of iron.'[7] Indeed, the
slightest spark would now be enough to trigger war, and it came
on 19 May.

That morning a Dutch fleet of over forty sail was reported in the
Channel, heading for Dover, near where a detached English
squadron of nine ships under Rear-Admiral Bourne lay at anchor
in the Downs. Robert Blake, with another thirteen ships, was
several miles away to the west. The Dutch ships lay to on the outer
side of the Goodwin Sands, and two small vessels approached
Bourne's ship with their flags dipped in recognition of the
'sovereignty of the seas' claim. After a brief discussion, in which
the Dutch captains assured Bourne that Tromp and his squadron
were merely seeking shelter from rough weather, the Dutch fleet
dropped anchor off Dover. However, Tromp's flagship *Brederode*
failed to dip her flag in the expected salute, and Dover Castle fired
a warning shot as a reminder. Bourne readied his ships to raise
anchor in case of emergency.

Tromp had been instructed by the States General not to dip his
flag to English ships, and to be ready to defend Dutch convoys in
the Channel against attempts to stop and search them. Though he
had not actually been ordered to commence hostilities, Tromp
knew that his orders, if fully complied with, were likely to have that
effect, and he seems to have been reluctant to be the man responsible for war. He repeated to Bourne that the Dutch were merely
sheltering from blustery weather at sea, and the rest of the day
passed in uneasy stand-off. Blake, meanwhile, was working his way
up the coast against contrary winds towards Dover, ordering
Bourne to join him.

Next morning found the Dutch still at anchor off Dover, though Tromp rather provocatively ordered his men to carry out musketry practice. At noon the Dutch raised anchor and stood off towards the French coast, in plain sight of Blake's squadron, which was tacking up towards them. Then, as Tromp approached mid-Channel, he met two battle-damaged Dutch warships which reported that, while escorting a convoy from Genoa, an acrimonious argument with a small English squadron over acknowledging the 'sovereignty of the seas' had ended in an exchange of fire. Soon afterwards Tromp sighted another Dutch convoy apparently surrounded by Blake's ships, and turned back and headed towards them.

In fact Blake had ignored the convoy. Seeing Tromp's squadron bearing down on him, Blake also altered course downwind, in the direction of the Dutch fleet. Blake's flagship, *James*, as a result now at the rear of the English line, took in sail, so that both Bourne and the Dutch could catch up. The Dutch, straggling in some disorder behind Tromp's flagship, arrived first. By 4.30pm the *Brederode* was within musket range of Blake's flagship, which fired three shots, the third one through Tromp's flag in a final demand for acknowledgement. Tromp replied with a broadside, and action quickly became general, with Bourne's squadron steering for the rear of the Dutch and opening fire.

The English had the better of the short and confused engagement which followed. Three Dutch ships were taken and their crews made prisoner, with another abandoned apparently in a sinking condition, though she was later salvaged by the Dutch. Blake's flagship, the *James*, was hit by seventy shots, with her master and mate and a number of other crew members killed.

There would later be some dispute concerning which side had been responsible for commencing hostilities. On 23 May Tromp wrote to Blake, telling him that: 'my intention was to greet you, but seeing that I was attacked, and not knowing your intention, as I was not spoken to by any of you, either before or at that time, yet by no means expecting that we were other than friends and good allies . . . I was forced, as a man of Honour, to defend myself.' Blake replied uncompromisingly that 'the only answer that I can return is that I presume Parliament will keenly resent this great insult, and the spilling of the blood of their unoffending subjects, and that you will find the undersigned one ever ready to carry out their commands.'[8]

By now war was inevitable, though Dutch envoys remained in England until 6 July in a fruitless attempt to find some compromise. Two days later Cromwell declared war on the United Provinces.

The first campaign

Neither side had any very clear strategy. With no intention of fighting a war on land, for the English the main aim was to destroy Dutch trade at sea, and the Dutch to defend it. The English Navy found its resources stretched by the onset of war. Delays were caused by shortages of provisions, of prime seamen and of guns. As a result the Dutch were ready first. Jan Evertsen, on convoy escort duties in the Channel, was reinforced, and other ships were despatched to strengthen Dutch squadrons in the Baltic and to protect overseas convoys and the fishing fleet in the North Sea.

The English Council of State decided to concentrate on intercepting Dutch convoys returning from the East and West Indies. With their captains already aware of the growing tensions between England and the Netherlands, the Council of State reasoned that the convoys were more likely to head for home by the longer route around the north of Scotland rather than risk the voyage up the English Channel. On 7 June, well before the official start of war, Blake was ordered to intercept the Dutch East Indies convoy in the vicinity of the Orkney Islands. It appears that the Council of State assumed that Blake would assign the task to Sir George Ayscue, newly returned with his squadron from the capture of Barbados, while retaining the bulk of the fleet in the Channel to counter Tromp. But, apparently discounting intelligence that Tromp was building up the strength of his own fleet, Blake chose to leave the defence of the English Channel to Sir George Ayscue and his squadron of ten ships, now anchored in the Downs, awaiting reinforcements from the Thames, including the two recently refitted 1st rates.

The dangerous situation in which Ayscue now found himself was partly Blake's fault, for the Council of State had left it to him to decide how many ships to send north. In the event, the squadron left with Ayscue was too weak to do more than present a tempting target for Tromp, whom Blake apparently assumed would make the protection of the convoy from the East Indies his first objective, and so would pursue him northwards, and that a decisive fleet action would follow.

As Blake made his way steadily northwards, with eighty-three ships, it became clear that he had dangerously miscalculated. Ayscue sortied from the Downs with nine ships on 2 July in order to attack a Dutch convoy of thirty to forty ships in the Channel. With only four escorts, the Dutch lost five ships captured, three burnt and twenty-six others ran themselves aground on Calais Sands, in French waters, to avoid the same fates. Even so, despite French efforts to prevent him, Ayscue was able to refloat two.

It appeared that retribution would quickly follow. Tromp appeared off the Downs with eighty-two warships and nine fire-ships.[9] Ayscue, who had been ashore undergoing a course of physick, hurried back to his flagship, *Rainbow*. Hopelessly outnumbered, Ayscue prepared for a 'last stand', placing his ships in line to afford each other mutual defence, and hastily erected shore batteries. However, Tromp made unduly ponderous prepa-rations for an attack, and on 11 July, the day before his planned assault, the wind changed to the south-east, preventing the Dutch from entering the Downs. In fact Tromp's clear orders from the States General had been to pursue Blake, and he was in all proba-bility merely filling in time by threatening Ayscue until on 12 July the winds were favourable for him to head up the North Sea.

On the same day a detachment from Blake's fleet in the North Sea sighted the Dutch fishing fleet and engaged its escorts. It was a one-sided battle in which eleven out of twelve escorts, along with 900 prisoners, were taken by the English. It has been noted that the English attack was delayed long enough for most of the fishing boats to escape, and uncharacteristically Blake did not punish the captains concerned. Blake was always reluctant to inflict damage on fishermen, and both he and Tromp seem to have spared them whenever possible.[10]

With the Dutch East Indies fleet his main objective, Blake took up position off Fair Isle, a widely recognised rendezvous point where he could be confident of encountering either the convoy or Tromp's fleet on its way to join it.

At 4pm on 24 July, after being delayed by bad weather, Tromp sighted the topsails of Blake's fleet. Action seemed imminent when, an hour later, a fierce gale blew up, apparently one of the worst any fleet in the age of sail encountered:

> The [Dutch] fleet being as it were buried by the sea in the most horrible abysses, rose out of them, only to be tossed up to the clouds; here the masts were beaten down into the sea, the deck was overflowed with the prevailing waves, the tempest was so much mistress of the ships they could be governed no longer, and on every side appeared all the forerunners of a dismal wreck.[11]

The Dutch were being driven straight towards the rocks of Sumburgh Head, the southernmost point of the Shetland Isles, and spent all night desperately clawing out to sea. At dawn on 27 July, as the storm finally eased, Tromp found only thirty-four ships still with him.

It would be six weeks before the Dutch admiralty had any clear idea of the fates of the rest. The East Indies convoy had been hit by the same gale which broke over Tromp's fleet. According to one of those who endured it:

> . . . the wind was making such a din that it was terrible to hear it, but what was far more awful was to see the boiling sea foaming and dashing up to the height of a house upon the rocky cliffs of Shetland. Everyone thus seeing his graveyard before his eyes did his best to save life and ship by keeping off the danger, whilst many of the Dutch ships had these rocks to leeward, they all, except four or five (amongst which were some fireships which though destined to perish by fire, were now consumed by another element), were preserved, though many ships appeared rather to sink than to drive through the great troughs of the sea, which boiled as if they would swallow up each ship. In the morning were seen two ships, almost uninjured, lying between the rocks, upon which they had been driven, and the hulls of three others, and the corpses of their crews being dashed about.[12]

Two of the convoy ended up on the coast of Norway, while most of the others sheltered in the fjords and inlets of the west coast of Shetland. English estimates were that ten Dutch vessels were wrecked on the Shetlands and six more lost at sea. Blake's fleet had taken shelter in Brassey Sound in East Shetland, and none of them were lost, although every ship suffered some damage.

As the gales dropped, both admirals decided to head for home. The two fleets sighted each other briefly, but neither had any desire for battle, and the English ships were in any case mostly too damaged to be able to catch up with the Dutch.

Eventually, as the last stragglers limped into port, the Dutch were able to calculate that they had lost sixteen ships, while most of Tromp's fleet reached home too late, or too battered, to be of any further use that year. The result had been the equivalent of a major defeat, and the Dutch republican government required a scapegoat. The obvious choice was the Orangeist Tromp, who was compelled to resign and was replaced by the politically reliable de With.

Ayscue versus Ruyter
The departure from the Channel of Tromp and his fleet had meanwhile left the way clear for Sir George Ayscue to resume operations. With twenty ships now available, and more on the way, Sir George was eager for action. His squadron included two sixty-gun ships, the *George* and *Vanguard*, and eight of thirty-six to forty guns. His instructions were to proceed to the western English Channel to escort into port an English convoy from the East Indies, and to do all possible damage to Dutch and French shipping.

By 21 July the first part of Ayscue's task had been successfully completed, and he was lying off Plymouth, flying his flag in *George*. Meanwhile the Dutch had despatched Ruyter to escort a convoy outward-bound from the Texel, and then to pick up in the western English Channel the vitally important West Indies silver fleet. Because of various delays, Ruyter was not able to begin his mission until the middle of August. By the time that he sailed, the Dutch commander knew of the uncertainty regarding the fate of Tromp's fleet in the north, and how vital his own task was. Although he successfully accomplished the first part of his mission, Ruyter then had to pick up the silver fleet off the coast of Spain. He would, he knew, almost certainly have to fight Ayscue while at the same time protecting the convoy, and after that he might have to face Blake's returning fleet in the Straits of Dover.

Ruyter rendezvoused with the Dutch convoy off the coast of Brittany, and began his return voyage. On 16 August, between 1 and 2pm, he was intercepted by Ayscue's squadron, which had left Plymouth on the previous day and headed out into mid-Channel in search of the Dutch. The English squadron consisted of about thirty-eight warships and four fireships. Ruyter had about thirty men-of-war, and was further disadvantaged by the need to safe-guard the sixty vessels in his convoy, though several of the latter joined in the fighting. However, as was usually the case, the English squadron had a clear advantage in terms of ordnance carried. While Ruyter had only two ships of forty guns, the remainder carrying from twenty to thirty-four, Ayscue had two ships of sixty guns and eight of thirty-six to forty.[13]

When Ayscue sighted the Dutch they were lying to leeward, giving the English squadron the benefit of the wind gauge. Ruyter's squadron was deployed in three divisions, the most westerly under Rear-Admiral Verhaeft, the centre one led by Ruyter himself, and the easterly division under Vice-Admiral den Broucke. The English

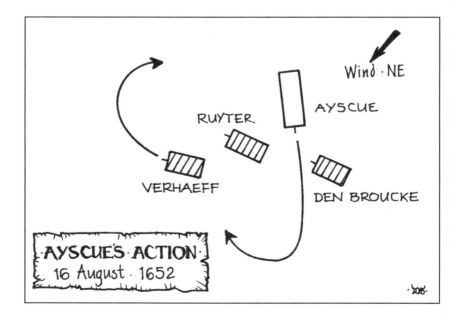

Wind · NE

RUYTER

AYSCUE

VERHAEFF

DEN BROUCKE

·AYSCUE'S·ACTION·
16 August · 1652

attack was concentrated against the latter two squadrons, meaning that Verhaeft would have to tack back before he could engage. Like most commanders of the time, Ayscue adopted 'charge' tactics, in which groups of ships bore down on the enemy, possibly to break in among them, but more often turning away after firing their guns in order to reload.

A desperate battle centred around one of the largest of the Dutch ships, *De Struisvogel*, commanded by Captain Dovwe Aukes. As they seemed to be getting the worst of the encounter, the Dutch crew attempted to surrender, but their captain forced them to fight on by threatening to blow up the ship. After a hard fight Ayscue's flagship, *George*, broke through the enemy line, followed by half a dozen other English ships. However, the remainder failed to follow, and with Dutch gunfire concentrated against their masts and rigging, Ayscue and the ships with him appeared trapped in the midst of the enemy. They were saved by the firepower of the largest English ships. In the words of a contemporary report: 'Sir George tacked about and weathered them, and charged them all again, and so continued still engaged in the body of their fleet until it was dark night.' Particularly hard fighting took place around the English ship *Bonaventure* (thirty-eight) which was only saved from capture when Captain Smithson's fireship was set ablaze and drifted among the Dutch ships, disrupting them sufficiently for *Bonaventure* to be towed clear.

Darkness ended a battle in which each side claimed to have sunk several of the enemy, although the only vessel actually lost appears to have been Smithson's fireship. The Dutch lost fifty to sixty dead and forty to fifty wounded, while English casualties totalled ninety-one, including Ayscue's flag captain, Thomas Lisle, who died from his wounds.

Both sides claimed victory, though in fact the advantage lay with Ruyter, who had not only preserved his convoy, but had damaged his opponent sufficiently to cause Asyscue to return to Plymouth, where Ruyter briefly considered attacking him. However, his primary responsibility was for the safety of his convoy, and this, together with a change in wind direction, caused him to abandon the idea and concentrate on gathering his scattered convoy, continuing his voyage up-Channel and passing through the Straits of Dover without encountering Blake.

While most attention was now concentrated on the Dutch, the undeclared war between the English Commonwealth and France was still in progress. In September Blake struck a telling blow. French-held Dunkirk was under attack by the Spanish, and early in September the Duc de Vendome ordered a convoy to carry supplies from Calais to the French forces at Dunkirk. On 4 September, as it lay at anchor off Calais, the French squadron found itself surrounded by Blake's fleet. The French were both outnumbered and outfought. The pride of the English Navy, the 1st rate *Sovereign*, engaged the French frigates, blasting them with her massive armament. One was sunk, and the remainder dismasted and captured. The remnants of the French squadron were chased onto Dunkirk Sands, with Blake claiming to have sunk fourteen and captured seven of them.

Whatever the exact tally, the engagement struck a fatal blow at French hopes of holding Dunkirk, which fell soon afterwards, while France acknowledged the realities of naval power in the English Channel by recognising the Commonwealth by the end of the year.[14]

Blake versus Ruyter

With the main Dutch fleet still recovering from its ill-fated voyage to the Shetlands, a relative lull followed in operations in the North Sea and English Channel. Blake intended to stay at sea until the end of October, instead of reducing the active fleet to a 'Winter Guard' a month earlier, as had hitherto been the usual practice. The most immediate threat seemed to be presented by Ruyter, who was again hovering in the Western Approaches. Blake considered trying to intercept him in the Straits of Dover when Ruyter eventually headed for home, but this idea was fraught with difficulties. The English fleet might, if the tides were not favourable, be hindered by shoals as it left the anchorage in the Downs, and Ruyter would probably have the advantage of the wind gauge, given the generally prevailing south-westerly winds. There was also the risk of the main Dutch fleet making a sortie and trapping Blake between itself and Ruyter. On balance, Blake decided, it would be preferable to take his own fleet westwards down the Channel to try to meet Ruyter as far from his home ports and reinforcements as possible. This would also have the advantage of taking the English fleet into

Robert Rich, 2nd Earl of Warwick (1587–1658). Involved in colonizing and privateering ventures before the Civil War, Warwick was appointed Lord Admiral by Parliament in 1643. Commanded the Parliamentarian Navy at Lyme and during the Lostwithiel campaign of 1644. He retained the loyalty of part of the fleet in 1648, but was removed from command in the following year.

Prince Rupert (1619–82). Best known as a Royalist cavalry commander during the First Civil War, the nephew of Charles I proved to be an equally daring if somewhat less successful commander at sea.

Robert Blake (1599–1657). A Somerset merchant and MP for Bridgwater, Blake gained his military reputation in the defence of Lyme and Taunton during the Civil War. Quick-tempered and domineering, though popular with ordinary seamen, if not always with his officers. By the end of his career Blake could be ranked among England's leading naval commanders. Buried in Westminster Abbey, his body was exhumed after the Restoration and thrown into a common burial pit.

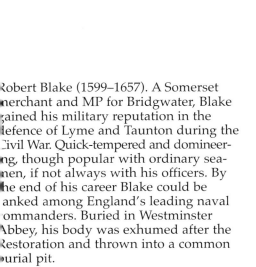

Sir William Penn (1621–70). A generally competent if uninspired commander, hindered by his own suspicious nature. He failed to contain Rupert in the Mediterranean, though he performed creditably in the Dutch War. A Navy Commissioner in 1653, Penn was dismissed following the failure of the 'Western Design'.

Sir George Ayscue (d.1671). Knighted by Charles I, Ayscue served as a captain in the Parliamentarian Navy during the First Civil War. Commanding the Irish Sea squadron in 1649, he played an important part in the defence of Dublin. Discontented with political developments, Ayscue left the State's Navy after the Dutch War and commanded the Swedish fleet in 1658. He served with the Royal Navy during the Second Dutch War.

Lisbon.

Richard Deane (1610–52). Deane commanded the Parliamentarian artillery during the Lostwithiel campaign of 1644 and at Naseby. He fought at Preston (1648) and Worcester (1651). An enthusiastic republican and efficient administrator.

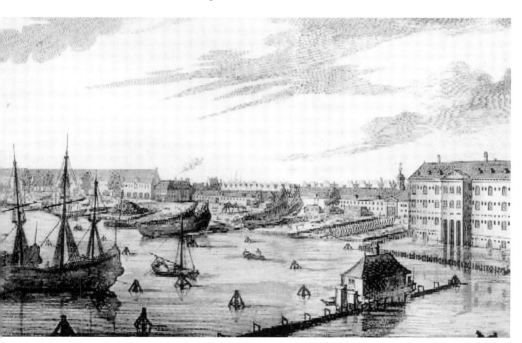

Dutch dockyard. Note the ships under construction on the slipways. Rapid shipbuilding enabled the Dutch to make speedy partial recoveries from some of their defeats.

The *Amelia*, built in 1632, was the model for most Dutch warships at the start of the First Dutch War.

Maarten Haperteszoon van Tromp (1598–1653). One of the most experienced and able officers of his era, Tromp, a tough fighting commander, was loved by his men.

Michiel Arianenszoon Ruyter (1607–76). Though relatively unknown at the start of the Dutch War, Ruyter quickly proved himself to be an outstanding commander

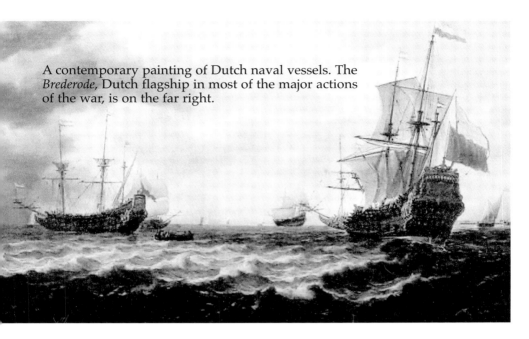

A contemporary painting of Dutch naval vessels. The *Brederode,* Dutch flagship in most of the major actions of the war, is on the far right.

The battle off Dover.

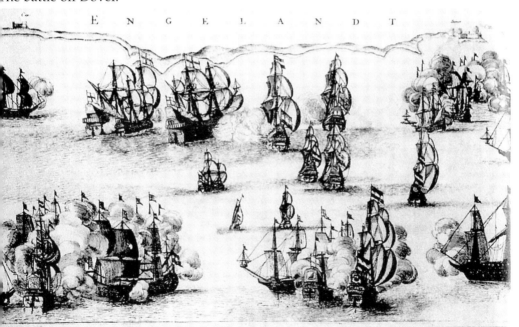

Battle of the Kentish Knock (8 October 1652).

Battle of Leghorn (4 March 1653). The ship blowing up is the English *Bonaventure*.

Battle of Scheveningen (8–10 August 1653).

Porto Farina.

Oliver Cromwell (1599–1658). During Cromwell's time as Lord Protector he viewed the Navy as a major instrument by which to expand the influence of the Protectorate in European affairs. But he never fully understood the uses and limitations of naval power.

Charles II (1630–85). Whilst in exile Charles's fleet and off-shore garrisons proved a serious annoyance to the State's Navy. In 1660 the ships of that same Navy brought Charles back to England as its restored monarch.

George Monck (1608–70). A professional soldier with no discernibly strong religious or political beliefs, Monck was originally Royalist but became commander in chief of the Commonwealth forces in Scotland in 1651–2, and a General at Sea in the following year. He was probably one of the main originators of the 'Fighting Instructions'. Commanding again in Scotland, Monck played a leading role in events leading to the Restoration. He served in joint command with Rupert in the Second Dutch War, with mixed success.

deeper and more easily navigable waters, but in the wider area of the Western Approaches Ruyter would find it easier to evade Blake.

However, for the English commander anything was better than continued inaction. Blake spent the next ten days beating slowly down-Channel against the prevailing winds. Ruyter, meanwhile, had taken on stores in Brittany and was now lurking in the Western Approaches, awaiting another expected convoy to escort home. It was customary for homeward-bound Dutch convoys to stay close to the English coast. Ruyter knew that this was likely to take him straight into the arms of Blake's waiting fleet, while hugging the French shore might entangle him with the rocks of the Brittany coast.

Ruyter called his captains together in a council of war, which decided on the latter plan. Rendezvous points were fixed on the French coast at Cape Barfleur and near the port of Harfleur. If Blake came west and the Dutch were forced back, a rendezvous near the French coast seemed preferable to being on the enemy shore. If Blake remained in the Downs, the French port of Havre was a suitable place to await news of the main Dutch fleet.

Blake had sent a squadron under William Penn ahead of his main force to seek out Ruyter. Just before noon on 15 September Penn's scouts sighted two sail, one of which was identified as a Dutch flyboat, and soon afterwards the English lookouts spotted the main Dutch fleet. Penn immediately called a council of war, telling his captains that 'I was resolved to use all means I could to bring them to engage us, it being their choice, they having the wind, to which our commanders showed a great deal of willingness.'[15] A ketch was sent to inform Blake of events.

Ruyter had between thirty-six and forty ships, of which probably thirty-six were men-of-war, supported by some armed merchant ships. Penn had eighteen ships, including his flagship, *James, Andrew, Speaker, Triumph, Garland, Assistance, Foresight, President, Nonsuch, Ruby, Constant Warwick* and *Vanguard*, organised into six divisions. With only half Ruyter's numbers, Penn, not the most daring of the Commonwealth's commanders, may have thought it rash to engage. Indeed, according to Ruyter's version of events, he spent most of the day 'chasing' Penn. Quite possibly Penn was hoping to draw Ruyter on to Blake's main force, but the weather steadily worsened. With the wind direction switching from west by north to south-west and increasing to gale force, Penn lost sight of the Dutch at around 5pm.

At dawn on 16 September Penn's lookouts spotted twelve ships anchored under Start Point on the Cornish coast. They were re-inforcements sent to join him by Blake, and with renewed confidence Penn began casting around to regain contact with the enemy. But Blake's orders barred Penn from going to the east of Portland Bill, and Ruyter was now far away off the coast of Guernsey. He had decided against any further attempt to seek action, and by 22 September had made his way safely up-Channel and rendezvoused with the main Dutch fleet off Nieuport.

Ruyter had good cause for satisfaction; during a summer of campaigning he had bested Ayscue and got his vital convoys home intact.

Kentish Knock

Blake now took his fleet to Portsmouth to resupply and then by 25 September he was back at his old anchorage in the Downs. He knew that although the Dutch had brought their homeward-bound convoys safely into port, some 200 outward-bound Dutch merchant ships were waiting to pass through the Straits of Dover, and he was confident that the Dutch fleet would risk battle in order to get them through. Action was made more probable with the fiery-tempered Cornelius de With now in command of the Dutch fleet. However, a number of Dutch ships had not yet returned from the Shetlands expedition or were still undergoing repairs. At present the Dutch had about sixty-four ships fit for action, compared with Blake's sixty-eight, among the latter the big 1st rates, *Sovereign* and *Resolution*. This was a slim English numerical superiority, but Blake had a clear advantage in firepower, and, their mood worsened by de With's unpopular leadership, many of the Dutch seamen were unpaid and mutinous.

De With did not leave the port of Schoonveld until after Blake had left the Downs in his unsuccessful quest for Ruyter. De With was rejoined on 29 September by Ruyter, bringing his strength up to forty-five ships, but ten of Ruyter's squadron, including his flagship, *Neptune*, were in urgent need of repair and had to be sent into port. Though reinforcements brought de With's fleet back to sixty-four ships, his underlying disadvantages remained.

The first months of war had highlighted many of the problems which continued to dog the Dutch navy. There was still no effective central direction of the Dutch naval war effort. Each of the five admiralties continued to take many independent decisions. Some would send their ships promptly to an agreed rendezvous while others delayed. Some would provision their vessels for eight months, some for six and some for less. Each admiralty had to supply its own equipment, and damaged ships had to return to their home port for repairs. The crews of the India Company ships were better paid than the remainder, but all of the regular warships met with strong competition for recruits from the privateers, whose men were better paid and operated under looser discipline than those of the navy. Even within the fleet, there were differences in the treatment afforded to the crews. The men of the Zeeland ships were allowed shore leave when in port; those of Amsterdam remained confined to their ships. This was mainly because the latter were paid less, and therefore thought more likely to desert. In September some 2,000 of the Amsterdam seamen had rioted over their pay grievances, and had to be dispersed by the army.[16]

Effective discipline was made more difficult because captains were appointed by the different admiralties, and could only be dismissed by the fleet commander with the agreement of that admiralty. This was frequently almost impossible to obtain, particularly if the Lieutenant Admiral, as was the case with de With, a violent-tempered republican in a largely Orangeist fleet, was unpopular and divisive. Indeed, so disliked was de With that he even feared assassination by his own men.

De With had yet to experience the effects of English firepower and, even though all his officers called to a council of war opposed the idea of seeking battle, de With was fearful of the economic and political consequences of a prolonged closure of the Channel to Dutch trade, and overruled his commanders. On 25 September he put to sea with the object of clearing the English fleet out of the Straits of Dover, telling his officers that he would take the fleet into the presence of the enemy, and the Devil might bring it off.

That afternoon Blake's lookouts in the Downs sighted the Dutch topsails, but, although eager for the fight, Blake and his council of war reluctantly decided that action must be postponed until the next morning, as darkness was approaching and the weather was rough and blustery. Next day the wind was favourable, but the seas were too rough for the English ships to be able to open their lower gunports, and conditions remained so on the 27th.

On 28 September both the wind and the sea moderated, and an engagement was possible. By noon the whole English fleet was heading northwards out of the Downs, in such haste that they were in considerable disorder. The Dutch had suffered most from

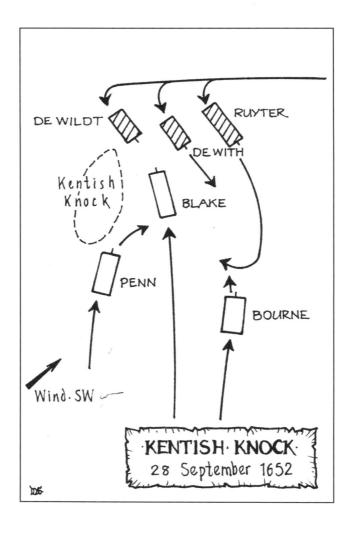

the stormy weather, as they had been riding at anchor in the open sea, and were considerably scattered as a result. When the English were sighted emerging from the northern exit from the Downs, there was no time for the Dutch fleet to hold a council of war before battle was joined, though de With sent a galliot around his ships with orders for their captains, and managed to form three squadrons commanded by himself, Ruyter and Rear-Admiral de Wildt.

Once in the open sea, Blake ordered those vessels which had got ahead of the flagship to halt until the rest of the fleet caught up with them. The Dutch fleet was in sight, sailing in a westerly direction, roughly eighteen miles to the east of the North Foreland, near a shoal known as the Kentish Knock. It was now about noon, and so far Blake had only been joined by Captain John Mildmay in *Nonsuch* (forty). Many of the ships of Blake's and Penn's divisions had become intermingled in their passage through the Gull, and Penn brought his flagship, the *James*, under Blake's stern and suggested that Penn should begin the attack with his division, and that Blake should join in as soon as his own division closed up. Blake replied that 'as soon as some more of our fleet come up we should bear in amongst them.'[17] The rear-most English division, under Bourne, had been delayed in leaving the Gull, and was some two leagues behind the rest of the fleet.

However, with only a few hours of daylight remaining, Blake concluded that he could not afford to wait for the laggards, but would launch a 'charge' with what he had. In retrospect, it is clear that Blake had underestimated his opponent when he made this decision, and de With was quick to take advantage. He waited until Penn and Blake's divisions, with the prevailing south-westerly wind behind them, were almost upon him, then ordered the whole Dutch fleet to tack from its westerly course to face south-east with the wind abeam. This brought de With's own squadron into contact with Blake, while the rest of the Dutch fleet came down onto Bourne's isolated division. De With related how:

> . . . we were within gunshot of General Blake and we began to exchange fire, and both fired heavily, being nearest the enemy we stood the first onset of their greatest force, nor were we idle meanwhile, so that from

about 3 o'clock in the afternoon, we saw nothing but smoke, fire and the English, until the sun went down.[18]

Meanwhile Bourne's division was involved in a ferocious battle, with the brunt of the Dutch attack falling on the ship commanded by Captain William Badiley:

First Major Bourne with the *Andrew* led on and charged the Hollanders stoutly and got off again without much harm. Captain Badiley with his ship also, he charged exceeding gallantly; but was in very great danger to have lost his ship, for the Hollanders were so close on both sides of him charging against him, that one might have thrown biscuits out of his ship into the Dutch ships. All his sails were so torn and shattered that he could not sail to or fro any more but as the tide drove him and there were about 60 men killed in that frigate and she had near a 100 shot in her hull and was in danger of sinking or taking; but blessed be God they got her safe to harbour the fighting being not above six leagues from the shore.[19]

There were two main reasons for Bourne surviving the onslaught. The Dutch, their manoeuvrability affected by previous storm damage, had difficulty in tacking quickly in the presence of the enemy, as a result of which some of them fell away to leeward, and could only fire less effectively over the tops of friendly ships. Others, mainly because of the disputes and personal animosities raging within the Dutch fleet, took advantage of the ordered change in course to stay out of the battle.

The weight of English fire was lessened when both the great *Sovereign* and Penn's flagship *James* ran aground for a time on the Kentish Knock while attempting to make room for Blake's division on their starboard side. But Blake's ships were soon in action against de With's division, and Captain Mildmay of the *Nonsuch* reported that 'it was most hot service, our General giving and receiving broadsides and so ranged the length of Holland's fleet.'

With its initial advantage fast disappearing, the bulk of the Dutch fleet found itself trapped between Bourne's squadron to the south and Blake and Penn to the north. De With admitted that the weight of English gunnery, which he was experiencing for the first time, was having an increasing effect: 'we found the guns on their smallest frigates carrying further than our heaviest cannon: and the English, I am sure, fired smarter and quicker than did many of ours.'[20] De With suffered personal humiliation when, his own ship badly damaged, he attempted to transfer by boat to Tromp's old flagship, the *Brederode*, only for her staunchly Orangeist crew to refuse to allow him aboard. The Dutch Lieutenant-Admiral was forced to make a shame-faced journey from one ship to another until he eventually got aboard the small *Princess Louisa*, where, de With complained: 'I found a captain seventy years old, a sick crew, the pilot and several officers drunk.'[21] De With, as a result of his difficulties, had lost overall control at a critical stage of the battle.

With the *Sovereign* and *James* pulled clear of the shoals by boats, and at last able to make their presence felt, the danger for Bourne's squadron had begun to recede. Penn felt that 'indeed it fell out better for doing execution on the enemy than we could have cast it ourselves, for as the Dutch fleet cleared themselves of our General, he standing to the northward and they to the southward, we fell pat to receive them and so stayed by them until night caused our separation.'[22]

Penn's 'charge' was all the more effective because the Dutch ships were already partly scattered, so the English attack was able to penetrate their formation more easily. Now at last in action, the massive *Sovereign* took on no less than twenty enemy ships at once, and inflicted considerable damage: 'Blessed be the Lord she hath sustained no very great loss but in some of her backstays and some shot in her, which her great bigness is not much prejudiced with'.[23] By 6pm, after the fight had lasted some two hours, the Dutch were in considerable difficulty. De With's own flagship, the East Indiaman *Prinz Wilhelm*, had lost her main and foremasts, and was out of action; another ship had exploded as a result of a shot penetrating her magazine, and the gunner of the *Gorcum* had only saved his ship by threatening to blow her up if English boarders did not withdraw. The main brunt of the English attack was now falling on Rear-Admiral de Wildt's division. The English 3rd rate *Garland*, on its third attempt, seems to have captured de Wildt's dismasted flagship, but the Rear-Admiral had escaped to another ship commanded by Captain Seppe Fokkes. However, both this and another vessel had also been dismasted by nightfall, and around 7pm Captain Mildmay's *Nonsuch* emerged from the smoke of battle and encountered Fokkes, who had apparently been trying to tow the second cripple. Mildmay forced Fokkes to surrender, and sent a prize crew aboard his ship, but assumed the other Dutch ship was sinking and left her to her fate. She was eventually salvaged by the Dutch.

Next morning de With called a council of war and urged that the battle should be resumed. Though on both that day and the 30th it was theoretically possible for the Dutch to re-engage, there was no prospect of the captains heeding the demands of their unpopular and increasingly furious commander. For their part most of the English ships had been too badly battered to make a renewal of the action either possible or desirable, though Penn claimed they had done their best to harass the enemy; on the evening of the second day (29 July) he wrote that:

> . . . our General perceiving that their [the Dutch] spirits declined, by their making no great haste in their way towards us, commanded our frigates to ply so near them as they could, and keep firing at them, while the rest of us did our best to get near them. About 3am some of our frigates got within shot, and much powder and shot was spent on both sides, it continuing till night, but I think to little purpose. At which time, three in the afternoon, the Dutch set their mainsails to get away from us towards their own shore.[24]

Captain Mildmay of the *Nonsuch* rather unfairly commented that the Dutch 'most poorly and sneakingly stole away.'[25]

De With by this time was almost incandescent with fury. Both of his senior surviving commanders, Ruyter and Cornelius Evertsen, refused to renew the action, and de With had no option but to order his battered fleet back home, where he accused a large number of his captains, the list headed by Ruyter and Evertsen, of cowardice: 'never in my life have I seen such cowardice among sea captains as these have shown.'[26] De With's discomfiture caused a good deal of not very quiet satisfaction to his enemies in the Netherlands. A popular joke referring to his boast before the start of the battle ran that 'he had saved the Devil the trouble, having brought off the fleet himself.'27

De With had at least learnt at first hand the power of the English guns, and by October, although a full switch to English gunnery tactics was impossible, he was urging that the English practice of preparing gunpowder charges in paper cartridges should be adopted.

Some in the English government believed that the Dutch had received such a pounding at the Kentish Knock that they would speedily sue for peace, but this over-estimated the extent of English success. Cromwell's Navy had done well, but, with its degree of superiority, should have done better. Blake's decision to begin the action without waiting for Bourne had given de With a potentially dangerous opportunity. Though Blake did not yet realise it, he had missed the best chance he would have of destroying the enemy.

War in the Mediterranean

If the State's Navy was narrowly holding its own in home waters, in the other theatre of war, the Mediterranean, it had met with near-disaster.

On the outbreak of war there were two small English squadrons in the Mediterranean; the first was commanded by Captain Henry Appleton, a former merchant captain from Hull, who after many years at sea had been nominated for naval command in 1650 and by the following summer was captain of the *Leopard* (forty-eight). The other squadron was led by Richard Badiley, another veteran sailor, who had traded and fought corsairs in the Mediterranean from 1637 to 1645 before returning home and in February 1649 being given command of the warship *Happy Entrance*. A few months later Badiley came to notice by a daring exploit in which he made a night raid on the Dutch port of Helvoetsluys and burnt the decrepit Royalist ship *Antelope*. Next year Badiley was Blake's Vice-Admiral off Lisbon, and was regarded as one of the Commonwealth's more promising commanders.

Each of the English squadrons consisted of three men-of-war, together with the merchantmen which they were escorting on the outbreak of war.

Dutch ships had been sent to the Mediterranean to protect Dutch trade from attacks by the French, who were using their ongoing war with Spain as a pretext to seize shipping of other nationalities as well. With Tromp unavailable through illness, command went to Joris van Cats, who spent the opening months of 1652 cruising off the French ports of Toulon and Marseilles, waiting on events. On 29 June he received news of the imminent hostilities with England, and had already taken up station with fourteen ships off the Tuscan port of Leghorn, where Appleton and his squadron of two ships were berthed, having been given rather reluctant refuge by the Duke of Tuscany.

Cats proved unwilling to apply pressure on the Grand Duke to expel Appleton, and he was replaced by Johan van Galen, who arrived in late August. Both of the Dutchmen had been in the service of the Admiralty of Amsterdam for many years, seeing action at the Battle of the Downs in 1639, and against the Dunkirkers and the 'Turks'. With the Dutch squadron temporarily absent to meet Galen, Appleton took the opportunity to send *Constant Warwick* in search of Badiley to inform him of the situation.

Another month passed, with both sides vying for the support of the Grand Duke of Tuscany. Van Galen was able to send most of his squadron in search of Badiley. Leaving four ships to watch Appleton, van Galen took the remainder after Badiley, and on 27 August encountered his squadron off Monte Cristo, eighty miles south of Leghorn, towards which Badiley had been heading.

The English squadron consisted of four men of war and four merchant ships. Badiley was still flying his flag in *Paragon*.[52]

Though only van Galen's flagship, *Jaarsveld*, with forty-four guns, matched the larger English vessels, his total of ten ships carried 364 guns, giving the Dutch a significant advantage in firepower. Badiley's only possible edge lay in the fact that his flagship was the heaviest-gunned ship on either side, and that his men-of-war were probably faster sailers than their opponents. Whether this would be enough was doubtful.

At around noon on 27 August the Dutch spotted *Constant Warwick*, scouting in advance of the rest of Badiley's squadron. Following her retreat, van Galen sighted the rest of the English squadron at about 4pm, too late in the day for any serious fighting. Next morning, with the wind light and blowing from the southeast, Badiley saw the Dutch about four miles to windward. Van Galen ordered those of his captains who lay nearest to concentrate on attacking *Paragon*, while Badiley, instructing his merchant ships to try to escape northwards, formed his men-of-war into what was intended to be line ahead and awaited attack.

As the Dutch came within range, the English ships opened an accurate fire. The Dutch flagship *Jaarsveld* was too badly hit aloft to close with the enemy, but *Maan* (forty) and *Zeven Provincien* (forty) managed to run aboard *Paragon*, but were driven off with heavy loss, including the captains of both ships. The crew of the *Maan* actually tried to surrender, but Badiley was too heavily engaged to have time to take possession. Van Galen in the meantime made another attempt to close with the English flagship, but Badiley drew ahead out of reach. The remainder of the Dutch squadron was also suffering heavily; Captain t'Hoen of the *Prinses Royal* (thirty-four) was killed, the *Waipen van Zeeland* (thirty-two) lost her foremast, and the *Maagd van Enilchvysea* (thirty-four) both main and foremasts. The *Paragon*, *Constant Warwick* and *Elizabeth* broke clear of their opponents, but the *Phoenix* was 'lost in a most sudden and strange manner'. While trying to come to the support of *Paragon*, the *Phoenix* ran across the bows of the enemy ship *Eenchacht* (forty) and was boarded and taken, although some of the crew managed to escape by boat to Badiley's flagship.

Losses on both sides had been heavy with at least two Dutch ships entirely disabled.

At dawn on 29 August Badiley's position seemed desperate; the crew of *Paragon* had been infected with panic by the survivors from *Phoenix*, the flagship's main mast had fallen, while the captains of the merchant ships had come aboard to demand that their crews should be evacuated to the men-of-war and their ships sunk to avoid capture. Badiley refused, and attempted to tow his flagship to safety using boats. Fortunately a light breeze then sprang up and the English ships were able to outpace their pursuers, taking refuge in the neutral Spanish port of Porto Longone on the island of Elba. A stalemate followed, as van Galen established a blockade of the port; the English were too weak to assail the Dutch, while van Galen was unable to attack the former in a neutral port.

Van Galen considered disregarding the legalities by making a surprise attack on Badiley, but his council of war dissuaded him on the grounds that the harbour was too small, the shore defences too close, and that the Dutch might be excluded from all Spanish ports as a consequence. The ensuing deadlock continued for two months. The Dutch had a number of armed merchant ships in other parts of the Mediterranean, and eleven of these were ordered to join van Galen, who was also reinforced by two more warships. The English were able to take over a couple of their own merchant ships in the port.

Throughout this period Badiley and Appleton were able to communicate through messages sent via neutral merchant ships. The lethargic Appleton was meanwhile quarrelling with some of his officers, who wanted to try to capture or destroy the *Phoenix*, which had been brought into Leghorn by her Dutch prize crew. The main supporter of this scheme was Captain Cox of the *Constant Warwick*, who had been sent in a neutral ship by Badiley to replace the dead captain of *Bonaventure*. Cox was a regular naval officer, who seems to have held Appleton in some contempt, so that the latter attempted to dismiss him. Badiley had now received orders from home putting him in command of both squadrons, and made his own way to Leghorn, where he reinstated Cox.

Badiley was strongly in favour of the plan to retake *Phoenix*, and believed that provided it was done with the minimum of fuss, the Duke of Tuscany would not strongly object. William Blackthorne, the Secretary of the Navy, had given a strong hint that some such action should be taken, writing to Badiley that he 'longed to hear of the regaining or destruction of the *Phoenix*.'

Van Galen had now departed with part of his squadron on a commerce-raiding expedition, leaving his second in command, van Salingen, with seven ships to keep watch on Appleton. On 20 November (St Andrew's Day), most of the Dutch officers went ashore to celebrate, and then continued their festivities aboard *Phoenix*. Many of the forty-strong prize crew were also the worse for wear. When most of the Dutch captains had tipsily returned to their own ships, the English took advantage of their long-awaited opportunity. After some confusion in the darkness, three boatloads of men under Cox and Lieutenants Young and Lyme of the *Leopard* and *Bonaventure*, stole up to *Phoenix* with the first glimmer of dawn. The Dutch commander, Captain Tromp, opened his cabin door to find the English in possession of his upper deck. He shot Young (one of three Englishmen killed) and leapt through his cabin window to be rescued from the harbour by a boat from a Dutch merchant ship. With fighting still going on below decks, the *Phoenix* put to sea under her new prize crew and, evading two Dutch ships, reached Naples on 30 November.

The Dutch placed the main blame for the debacle on van Salingen, who reportedly was ashore with a woman at the time of the incident, but he died before any action could be taken against him.

A few weeks later, both *Constant Warwick* and *Elizabeth* slipped out of Porto Longone and joined *Phoenix* and the armed merchant ship *Harry Bonaventure* at Naples.

Meanwhile, on hearing of the English defeat off Dungeness,[28] van Galen knew that there was no immediate danger of Badiley receiving reinforcements, and felt it safe to divide his own forces. He sent seven ships to watch for Cox's squadron at Naples, and two other ships to observe some merchant ships being fitted out in Genoa. The Dutch detachment, under Captain Blok, sent to Naples, found the English ships there apparently immobilised by a dispute with the local authorities, and sailed on to meet a Dutch merchant convoy. However, on 24 January 1652 Cox sortied and encountered Blok and his convoy in the Straits of Messina. An indecisive action followed in which *Phoenix* was hit in the hull seventy times and had eight men killed and twenty-two wounded, with Dutch casualties reportedly higher.

In response van Galen himself put to sea to try and find Cox, but on 29 January two of his ships went aground, and Galen's flagship, *Jaarsveld*, became a total loss.

By the middle of February, however, Badiley's relations with the Duke of Tuscany had almost completely broken down. The English were informed that they could no longer use Leghorn; the Duke gave Badiley until 8 March to remove his ships from the port.

At dawn that day Badiley was off Piombino, fifty miles from Leghorn, where Appleton received his superior's instructions. Badiley's squadron comprised the same vessels as in his previous engagement, except that the merchantman *Richard and William* had been replaced by the *Lewis* (thirty). In Leghorn, Appleton had *Leopard* (forty-eight), *Bonaventure* (forty-four) and four merchant ships. In all the English had fourteen ships, of which six were regular men-of-war, carrying a total of 496–520 guns. Van Galen had eight men-of-war and eight merchant ships, with roughly the same number of guns as the English. Although the opposing forces appeared roughly equal, the Dutch had the advantage of united forces, under a single commander.

Badiley's instructions to Appleton were that if the wind were blowing onshore, he himself would try and break through the enemy and join the Leghorn ships, as soon as he saw that they were under sail. If the wind were offshore he would accept action and expect Appleton to join him. In this case, Badiley warned: 'Haste for your life to follow with all the sail you can, that we may not be too much oppressed before you come', and added a rather laboured pun inspired by the name of the commander of the Dutch blockading force: 'I suppose you and the Dutch vice-admiral will try a pluck for it, and although he is a great boar, yet he is but a Boer, and . . . may be hunted as well as others.' The inference was that Appleton should deal with Jacob de Boer aboard the *Eendracht.*

On the morning of 2 March the wind was blowing from the west (onshore) and Badiley sailed up and down within sight of the Dutch, but van Galen remained at anchor at the mouth of the harbour, and there was no sign of activity by Appleton. Next morning Badiley sent a second message to Appleton suggesting that he should try to break out under cover of darkness that night if the wind served. Appleton replied: 'If you can draw near in the night within the Malora [entrance to the harbour], the wind being off shore, we shall, with God's assistance and your approbation, break through the enemy.'

But that night Appleby's council of war decided that as they had made no preparations it was too late to move. Next day (4 March), the wind was still offshore, but this time van Galen got under way as Badiley approached. Everything now depended on timing; if Appleton was too slow, Badiley would have to face the full strength of the Dutch squadron, at odds of two to one. But if Appleton came out too soon, when the Dutch were well to leeward, he might himself be overwhelmed. Sadly for the English, this was exactly what now happened.

Captain Lyme in *Bonaventure* led out and was hit by a broadside from *Zeven Provincien*. A shot penetrated the English ship's magazine, and she blew up. Only five men of her crew of 980 survived. However, in an act of posthumous vengeance, a shot from the doomed ship hit van Galen, shattering his leg, a wound from which the Dutch commander died nine days later. In the mêlée, the remainder of Appleton's ships were generally grappled by two or more opponents, boarded and captured. Appleton's *Leopard* put up a fierce fight against the *Zon* and *Julius Caesar*; Tromp, in *Main*, came close to taking *Sampson*, but then the latter was rammed by a Dutch fireship and blew up and sank; forty-two of her 130 men were saved.

The *Peregrine* and *Levant Merchant* were also taken, although the latter inflicted enough damage on a Dutch ship to force her to beach. The *Mary* managed to break through and join Badiley. This left the *Leopard*, with Appleby aboard, and she was engaged by *Eendericht* in a duel which lasted for up to six hours, during which the English ship lost around seventy dead and fifty-four wounded, before being forced to surrender.

Badiley, meanwhile, was attempting to join in the action. But his efforts seem to have been half-hearted and certainly ineffectual, and he left the scene as the defeat of Appleton became certain. Three English ships had been sunk and two taken, with two-thirds of their crews casualties, while the Dutch lost one ship.

The Dutch had won the battle for the Mediterranean; Badiley headed back to England, reaching the Downs early in May. The last English vessel in the Mediterranean, *Harry Bonaventure*, was taken by the Dutch on 25 June.[29]

Dungeness

Meanwhile, in the main theatre of war, the English success in the action off the Kentish Knock had left many dangerously complacent. Their confidence was heightened by the reaction in the Netherlands. The immediate impact of the defeat was summed up by the Swedish minister in the Hague, who reported: 'Until now people claimed that the Dutch could sail, tack and fire faster than the English, but de With writes that they have found otherwise.'[30] All the animosities simmering among the men of the Dutch fleet burst out with renewed fury. De With's anger was directed against his subordinates, though he claimed that the English had lost their best opportunity by failing to pursue after the battle.

It was obvious to the States General that the current situation could not be allowed to continue, and, bowing to the inevitable,

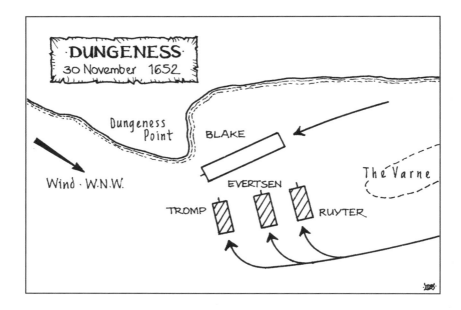

they reinstated van Tromp, with Jan Evertsen as his second-in-command. Deeper problems remained, however, as the politicians failed to address the defects which had left the fleet crippled by mutiny and desertion. In addition, Ruyter's success against Ayscue had led them to believe that they could continue to run convoys through the English Channel.

Tromp eventually took his own measures to deal with his more urgent problems. When the next convoy was assembled he took the opportunity to press men from among their crews. During his period of unemployment Tromp had drawn up a far-reaching ship-building proposal designed to enable the Dutch fleet to meet the English on equal terms. This involved the construction of thirty new ships corresponding to those of the first three rates of English ships. But Tromp's opponents said that the type of ship proposed would draw too much water to enter Dutch ports. The main opposition came from the Amsterdam Admiralty, which put forward its own plan for fifteen ships of the already employed *Amelia* pattern. The rival plans were discussed by a Board of Deputies from the States General, assisted by de With. The latter had absorbed the lessons of the Kentish Knock, and basically favoured the Tromp plan. However, the opposition was such that the programme eventually adopted in February 1653 was basically the Amsterdam proposal.

In England, the result of Kentish Knock had induced a state of over-confidence. A number of new 'frigates', including the *Kent*, *Essex*, *Sussex* and *Hampshire* had been launched, but political in-fighting was causing problems. There was a clear difference of opinion between those favouring a vigorous prosecution of the war, and those, including the immensely influential Sir Henry Vane, who sought a peaceful solution. The fleet had been supplied until the end of October, and the intention was to send first into port those vessels which had either been badly damaged at Kentish Knock or which were earmarked to form part of the Winter Guard. Once these were ready for sea Blake could bring in the rest. But the necessary supplies were not ready as a result of lack of money, and several seamen's strikes over pay took place. In the meantime Blake rode at anchor in the Downs with a skeleton fleet, short of both equipment and men, but unable to leave his station as the exchange of his ships with those intended for the Winter Guard was taking place in piecemeal fashion.

Blake seems not to have been particularly alarmed by the news of Tromp's return to command, and indeed proved complacent in the face of reports that the Dutch were almost ready for sea. On 24 November Blake had just completed a despatch in which he reported that the Dutch fleet was still in port when eighty enemy sail were sighted off the North Foreland. By nightfall Dutch strength, including the merchant convoy being escorted, was esti-mated at 400 ships. However, adverse weather conditions delayed contact, and Blake decided to wait for dawn before making a move. Day broke stormy, with drizzling rain. With the wind against them, the Dutch were making slow progress down-Channel. By evening conditions had worsened to the point that most of the merchant ships had returned to the Goree, and the men-of-war took refuge in the anchorage known as the Wielings or off the Flanders coast between Ostend and Blankenburgh. Tromp was burning for action, writing on 26 November: 'I could wish to be so fortunate as to have only one of two duties, to seek out the enemy, or to give convoy.'[31]

Next day, Saturday 27 November, the weather had moderated enough for the Dutch to make a new attempt to carry out their mission. By midnight Tromp's fleet was between the North and

South Forelands, with the convoy some distance behind. On Monday Blake called a council of war aboard his flagship, *Triumph*. The odds were not favourable; the Dutch had between eighty and ninety-five men-of-war compared with Blake's forty-two, and, not surprisingly, Blake and his commanders agreed to avoid action if possible. The English ships therefore left the Downs by way of its southern entrance; Tromp went in pursuit, but with the wind still blowing from the south-west, that is against him, found it difficult to get within range. With the weather once more deteriorating, both fleets anchored for the night, with Blake in the Dover Roads and Tromp about five or six miles to seaward. Though there were gales during the night, by dawn the wind had shifted to the west-north-west and the sea had moderated.

Tromp, determined to bring on an action in his current situation of numerical superiority, ordered his fleet to make all possible sail westwards. His aim was to get far enough to the windward of the English to be able to tack down on them. Blake imitated the Dutch move, so that the opposing fleets headed on down-Channel on parallel courses, separated by the Varne and Rip-Rap Shoals. Both commanders knew, however, that once these ended and Dungeness Point came in sight, Blake would be forced to alter course seaward towards the Dutch.

As that moment approached, Tromp hoisted the red battle flag; he had caught the English at a disadvantage, as the latter were too close to the shore to be able to manoeuvre effectively. Tromp's flagship, *Brederode*, was the most weatherly ship in the Dutch fleet, and rapidly drew ahead, making for Blake's *Triumph*. Tromp was thwarted by the intervention of *Garland*, the second ship in the English line, and responded by grappling her. A fierce action began between the two ships, the balance being tipped in the English favour by the arrival of the *Anthony Bonaventure*, an armed merchant ship, which attacked *Brederode* on her unengaged side. She in turn was grappled by Evertsen's *Hollandia*, her captain, Walter Hoxton, killed and his ship taken. Both the Dutch ships now turned on *Garland*, which in a desperate attempt to deter boarders blew up her own decks. But, with her captain, Robert Batten, dead, *Garland* was also captured.

Blake himself had drifted to the west of the fighting and turned to try to assist the two stricken English ships: 'but immediately our fore-mast was shot away, our main-mast being shot before, and our rigging much torn, so that we could not work our ship to go to their relief, and by occasion thereof, and night coming on, we saved ourselves, who were then left almost alone.'[32]

Triumph suffered most of her damage from the fire of the Dutch ships following Tromp and Evertsen. The *Victory* tried to support Blake, but was engaged in turn by Ruyter. Though other ships also endeavoured to come up, it was clear that many English captains were making no attempt to take part in the battle. An English account admitted that 'not twenty came to the engagement, the rest pretending want of men, and that they had not enough men to ply their tackle. Among these were some frigates as well as merchantmen that were backward, and among them that did engage, not eight stood it to any purpose.'[33]

The onset of night prevented a major Dutch victory. The English fleet drew off towards Dover. One Dutch ship had accidently exploded, but the Dutch had taken two warships and a rich merchant ship. Three English frigates on their way to join Blake also ran into the Dutch, and one of them, *Hercules*, ran aground and was later floated off and taken by the enemy.

Having seen his convoy safely clear, Tromp returned in the hope of finishing off Blake, but the English fleet had taken refuge behind the shoal known as Long Sands Head. Tromp seriously considered entering the Thames, but was dissuaded by his pilots, and sailed off down-Channel to pick up an inbound convoy. As a result the Dutch had missed their best opportunity to inflict a decisive defeat on the English. But, however they might try to minimise it, the English Navy had suffered its greatest humiliation in over a century.

If it was to be avenged, radical and far-reaching changes would be needed.

Chapter 6

The Dutch War 2: Winning the War

'. . . the English are now our masters and
command the sea.'   (With de Witt)

Dungeness had been Robert Blake's first serious reverse as a
commander, and he reacted angrily, writing to the Navy
Commissioners in London: 'I presume your Honours' longing for
an account of what hath passed between us and the Dutch fleet and
I hope you have hearts prepared to receive evil as well as good
from the hands of God.'[1] Blake went on to offer his resignation,
asking to be relieved 'from this employment, so far too great for
me, especially since your Honours have added two such able
gentlemen [Richard Deane and George Monck] for the under-
taking of that charge, so that I may spend the remainder of my
days in private retirement and prayers for a blessing on you and
the Nation.'[2]

But there was an element of calculation in Blake's plea. While
admitting to the loss of *Garland*, he made no mention of the
Anthony Bonaventure, and put much of the blame for his reverse
on the alleged cowardice of some of his commanders, asking for
commissioners to be sent to the fleet to investigate. Eventually six
captains would be removed from their posts, and four of them were
charged with failing to support Blake during the action. One of
them, Captain John Taylor, had performed well during the Scillies
operation of 1650, and another, Anthony Young, had been
regarded as one of the most active commanders in the State's Navy,
with an excellent fighting record. It seems unlikely that such men

should have been guilty of the faint-heartedness which Blake alleged, and it is more probable that they simply regarded the odds against the English fleet as being too great.

Blake's purge did not spare even those closest to him. His brother, Benjamin, flag captain aboard *Triumph*, lost his command, and Robert Blake's secretary, Francis Harvey, was also dismissed. In neither case are the reasons clear, but both of the Blakes were noted for their ferocious tempers, so a rift between them was not unexpected. Robert Blake had certainly been impetuous in his decision to fight in a situation where retreat might have been more judicious, and some of his captains did not share the official enthusiasm for war against the Dutch, feeling that nothing vital to the nation's welfare was actually at stake. The real reason for the removal of battle-hardened officers was probably that they had used their own initiative in following what they felt had been the decision of the council of war and ignored Blake's orders.

This attitude was unacceptable to Blake, who, as his self-confidence as a naval commander grew, increasingly felt that the admiral in charge should make key decisions and his captains obey unquestioningly. The role of the council of war was merely to advise on the best way of carrying out the admiral's decision. In practice, Blake generally only hearkened to a council of war when he was himself uncertain of what course of action to follow.

Significantly, four of the dismissed captains, including Benjamin Blake, were quietly reinstated shortly afterwards. Robert Blake had in effect given the Council of State an ultimatum to either back him or sack him, probably well aware that he was indispensable.

Dungeness had nevertheless demonstrated that wide-ranging reforms were needed if the war was to be prosecuted successfully. It had been clear for some time that commanders of hired merchant ships were sometimes reluctant to take them into close action. In future, it was decided, armed merchant ships would be commanded by a captain appointed by the state, not by their owners.

New Articles of War were drawn up,[3] and, partly to ensure closer political control of the fleet, a new Committee of Admiralty was set up, headed by the veteran Sir Henry Vane. This was a clear victory for the Independent party within the Government, who were the most active supporters of the war. Blake's views on these changes are unrecorded, but the new naval leadership had expressed confidence in him.

Blake's immediate concerns were for the welfare and morale of his seamen. The relatively heavy casualties suffered in the opening battles of the war had led to the introduction of new measures for the care of the sick and wounded,[4] but Blake also felt strongly that the needs of the rest of his men should be improved. He felt so strongly that this was essential that he reportedly threatened not to put to sea until measures were taken.

The immediate step was a long-overdue increase in pay. On 20 December new rates were announced. The biggest rise was for captains of ships, with the commander of a 1st rate being paid £21 a month. The organisation of ordinary seamen was reformed, three ranks being introduced. The most senior and experienced, termed 'yeomen of the sheets, tackles and haliyards' was to be paid 21s a month; next in rank were 'able seamen', to be paid 24s, while the ordinary seamen were to receive 19s. Boys were to be given 14s 3d. A longstanding grievance of the seamen was tackled with the promised payment of all arrears due to them. Nevertheless, in 1653 Dutch seamen were still paid at roughly double the rate of their English counterparts.[5]

These measures would not solve the shortage of seamen at a stroke, and soldiers were drafted aboard ships to fill out their complements. As army pay had been lowered to compensate for the increases given to seamen, and soldiers were already widely disliked in the fleet because of their past deployment to suppress naval mutinies, relations between the men of these mixed companies were understandably frequently fraught. During the course of the war about 12,000 soldiers served in the fleet, mainly drawn from raw recruits rather than seasoned veterans.

It was common practice in most European navies to fill out ships' companies with troops. In March 1653, when the States General decreed that 150 ships should be fitted out as men-of-war for the coming year, it was decided that most should be of twenty-eight to thirty guns, and be manned by an average of eighty-five sailors and twenty-five soldiers (twenty-four musketeers and an NCO). Unlike in the English fleet, pressing was not formally resorted to.[6]

In England a major effort was also planned for 1653, and on 16 December warrants were issued for the supply of victuals for the

Summer Guard for the coming year, with each man allowed 8d (soon increased to 9d) a day when at sea and a penny less when in port. In order to provide for this increased expenditure, taxation was raised to £120,000 per month, of which £40,000 was to be allocated to the Navy.

Increased funding did not in itself end supply difficulties; naval victuallers had considerable problems in meeting the increased demand, which included an annual amount of 7,500,000lb of bread, a similar quantity of beef and pork, and 10,000 butts of beer, together with large quantities of cheese, butter and fish. Blame for earlier supply difficulties had been assigned to the Surveyor of the Navy, John Holland, who now resigned. He was not replaced, and instead the number of Admiralty Commissioners was raised to seven.

Feverish activities were meanwhile underway to repair and prepare the ships themselves for the coming campaign. Vast quantities of naval stores were required, and, in case difficulties arose in obtaining them from traditional sources in the Baltic States and Scandinavia, steps were taken to ensure supplies from Scotland and the colony of New England.

As the time approached to put to sea, Commissioners Hutchinson and Bourne were despatched to Portsmouth with £25,000 to pay the seamen. By 19 January the worst of the usual unrest over pay had died down, and Commissioner Bourne, after paying off the crews of a large number of ships and discussing the grievances of their crews, was able to report that:

> I find them in a hopeful condition and spirit of temper
> . . . [but] some few of them expecting a complete paying
> off, at the first a few were a little distempered, but are
> since better satisfied, and the most ungenerous among
> them are sensible that the rudeness of some among them
> hath justly merited and occasioned the abatement and
> stop upon their pay for the present, which may be a good
> caution for the future.[7]

Despite this Blake was still undermanned when he sailed on 11 February, his aim to intercept Tromp, homeward-bound with a convoy.

Dutch attempts to exploit their success at Dungeness had proved disappointing. The legend of Tromp mounting a broom at his mast-head in a boast that he had swept the English from the seas is almost certainly untrue.[8] Tromp had landed raiding parties on the coast of Sussex and Kent. The first party safely re-embarked with some captured sheep and cattle, but the second group was cut off by troops under Colonel Nathaniel Rich, and sixty of them were captured.

On 6 January Tromp arrived at St Martin, Isle de Rhé. He had been unable to take aboard provisions or ammunition before setting out, and was anxious to get home with his convoy before the English fleet could get back to sea. Tromp had with him seventy-five warships and 150 merchant vessels, including half a dozen fireships and five store ships. When his return voyage up-Channel began on 30 January, the Dutch commander's main worry was over the discipline of some of his crews.

The Dutch convoy sailed round to the west of the Scilly Isles, which would give them the weather gauge, and, as the enemy would be to leeward, would also provide room to manoeuvre.

Action off Portland Bill
As on previous occasions the English fleet was divided into three squadrons, Red, Blue and White. Each was led by one of the Generals at Sea, and each squadron would have its own vice and rear admirals, making control more flexible, and establishing for the first time a clear command hierarchy. As a result, from then on councils of war usually consisted of flag officers, excluding captains, who were expected to execute their seniors' orders. The Red Squadron was led by Blake, the Blue by Deane and the White by Monck. Vice-Admiral Lawson, whose political views remained suspect, and who may not have been thought reliable enough to lead a squadron, was with Blake. It is sometimes suggested that there may have been friction between Blake, the idealistic republican, and George Monck, the calculating professional soldier, but there was little evidence of this as the fleet moved down-Channel.[9]

The English plan was to engage the enemy in the deeper waters of the western Channel, where the Dutch would be far from home and less able to salvage any damaged ships. The disadvantage of this was that the greater width of the Channel in this area might give Tromp the opportunity to slip past them. In an attempt to avoid this happening, the English fleet zig-zagged its way westwards, somewhat surprisingly making no attempt to station scouting vessels in the Western Approaches.

It was not until 17 February that Blake obtained firm news of his quarry, when the English captain of a Spanish merchant ship reported having sighted the Dutch twenty leagues to the west, between Lands End and Start Point. With the wind blowing from the north-west, it seemed likely that Tromp would stay close to the English coast in order to avoid the danger of being trapped on a lee shore on the French side of the Channel. As Blake was off Alderney in the Channel Isles when he received the news, he had now to tack back across the Channel in order to intercept Tromp.

The Dutch commander had been delayed by latecomers and bad weather, so that he did not reach the mouth of the Channel until 16 February, and in an effort to make up lost time, decided to continue sailing through the night.

It was dawn on the 18th when lookouts on board Tromp's flagship, *Brederode*, sighted the English fleet off Portland Bill. The Dutch were surprised, but Tromp had kept his fleet well in hand, while the English squadrons were scattered all over the Channel. To the south the Dutch could see a dozen or so ships of Penn's squadron, and another similar-sized group some two miles to the east. In between, caught in the eye of the wind, was Blake's *Triumph*, with half a dozen other ships. The remainder of the English fleet was five or six miles to leeward. If Tromp acted quickly, he had an opportunity to destroy the English in detail. Hoisting his red battle flag the Dutch admiral bore down on the enemy.

Ruyter aimed for Penn's squadron, while Floriszoon's division headed for the gap between Penn and Blake and Evertsen, Larsen and Tromp set a course directly for *Triumph* and her group. The English had been caught badly off-balance, and a contemporary account could only rather lamely claim that 'as we ordered the matter we could hardly have missed them [the Dutch] for we stretched the Channel over as far as the Isle of Alderney and were close aboard Cape de Hogue.'[10] Rather than being a deliberate tactic, however, it is more likely that the mixed bunch of English captains, some of them soldiers with little experience of the sea, had lost touch with each other during the night. In his anxiety not to miss the enemy, Blake had placed his fleet in grave danger for the third time during the war. During the night he had stood as close to the wind as possible, and as a result his more weatherly ships had forged ahead of the remainder of the fleet.

Despite his disadvantage, however, Blake was unwilling to retreat and allow the enemy to escape. The wisest course might have been to attempt to draw Tromp on towards Monck's approaching ships, but instead *Triumph* hauled to the wind and hove to, and the other ships in her group followed suit, keeping as close together as possible. Richard Deane explained that if he and Blake failed to make a stand until the rest of the English fleet came up, 'the Dutch Admiral might possibly (if he had been pleased to keep his wind) have gone away with his whole fleet, and we had not been able to have reached him with our whole body, only with our few frigates – which had not been likely to have done very much upon them.'[11] Penn also drew together his ships with the aim of going about in order to support Blake, a manoeuvre which took some time, and his subsequent movements remain rather unclear.

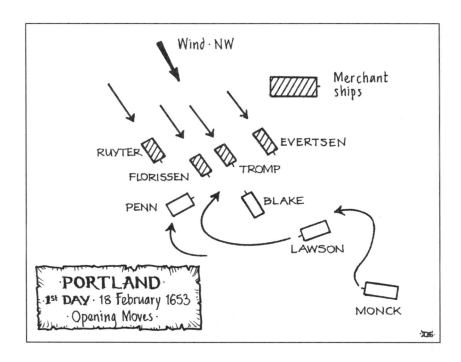

Vice-Admiral Lawson, aboard *Fairfax*, was to windward of Blake's flagship, and so in a better position to bring speedy assistance to his commander by putting his ships on the starboard tack. But by doing so he would also face a grave risk of being overwhelmed. In order to minimise this risk, Lawson had to put the Dutch to leeward, so that only part of their force could engage him. He tacked his group so as to pass south of Blake's ships. Once he had cleared them to the west, Lawson would come round on the port tack and join in the fight from the south-west. It was, however, a high-risk move which initially left Blake and Deane alone to face the full Dutch attack for about an hour, for Floriszoon had thrust between Blake and Penn before the latter could join forces. As Floriszoon explained:

> When we came up to them, several English frigates that were close together opened a fearful fire on me from their five or six ships all at once. Nevertheless I was not behindhand in answering them, but as I had run to leeward of our fleet and received no assistance from our squadron I suffered heavy damage. The English followed us with their five or six ships, shot our mainyard to pieces so that it fell on the deck, and our mizzenyard also together with the sails, ropes, courses and brails, so that we had nothing left standing.[12]

Tromp came under heavy fire from Blake and his group, with both sides sustaining severe damage. The gunfire was clearly heard as far away as Portsmouth and the Isle of Wight, and even claimed to have been audible aboard a privateer some 150 miles away. Ruyter was also heavily engaged with Penn, gaining some initial success, as Penn's formation was somewhat scattered, allowing the Dutch to get among them.

The second phase of the battle now opened, with both fleets struggling for possession of the weather gauge. Evertsen's Dutch squadron tried to outflank Lawson from the south, but failed, mainly because all of the English ships were now withdrawing slowly in a westerly direction. The Dutch followed, trying unsuccessfully to grapple and board.

Meanwhile, the remainder of the English fleet was at last

approaching. Monck had been slowly beating up all day with a succession of tacking movements, and having eventually gained enough ground to the north, headed westwards in a bid to thwart Florizoon's attempt to outflank Lawson from the south.

Ruyter engaged the *Prosperous* (forty-four), an armed merchantman, but was met with heavy fire. The Dutch attempted to board, but were beaten back, then driven on again by Ruyter, and the ship taken. Unwounded members of the English crew were removed, and a prize crew put aboard. But Monck now counter-attacked, and Ruyter was himself in difficulties until extricated by Evertsen and some of his squadron, while the *Prosperous* was retaken.

Some of the fiercest fighting centred around Captain John Day's *Advice* (forty-four), which was attacked by five Dutch ships. Although three of Day's attackers were driven off by the fire of other English ships, the remaining two grappled *Advice* on both sides. Day's men continued to fire their cannon into the enemy at point-blank range. One Dutch ship, her wounded captain still defiantly flourishing his sword, drifted away and sank. Another, commanded by Captain Swers, was caught by two English ships and sunk so quickly that only Swers himself and half a dozen of his men were saved.

For Tromp the sight of Monck's approaching squadron was a bitter disappointment. He had failed to secure or sink a single English ship, and Monck was now attempting to break through the Dutch warships in order to attack the convoy, which was now heading westwards, further away from home. Tromp ordered his fleet to break off the action, heading northwards in order to keep his warships between the English fleet and his convoy. He would comment later that 'divers of our captains were not as staunch as they ought to be, they did not second myself and their other honest comrades as the English did.' When he attacked *Triumph*, Tromp noted that Blake's captains rallied to their commander and 'I had such a welcome from three or four ships that everything on board was on fire and Blake still unhurt.'[13]

In the confusion several badly damaged Dutch ships had to be abandoned before the onset of darkness brought the action to a close. Jan Evertsen estimated that the Dutch had lost eight ships, including four sunk, three captured and one destroyed in an explosion. Commodore Balck and twelve captains had been killed. The English lost only one ship, the *Sampson*, though they suffered a high number of casualties, including John Mildmay, the courageous captain of *Vanguard*. Blake's *Triumph*, as might be expected, suffered particularly heavily, with eighty casualties, including Blake himself, who was wounded in the thigh.[14]

That night Tromp held a council of war. Evertsen and Ruyter declared that the convoy could not be exposed to further action, particularly as the ships of their squadron were running short of powder and shot, the majority of their captains agreeing. Further debate took place after daylight next morning, when it was agreed the Dutch warships would form a half-moon formation similar to that adopted by the Spanish Armada in 1588 in order to protect the rear of the convoy. Those ships most short of ammunition were placed amid the convoy in an attempt to stiffen the morale of its crews. Tromp put his own flagship in the centre of the rearguard, with Evertsen commanding the left 'horn' of the half-moon and Ruyter the right.

Fortunately for the Dutch, the English fleet had been slowed down sufficiently by the damage which it had suffered in the previous day's fighting for Tromp to complete his deployments without interference. Blake spent some time arranging for his prizes and more badly damaged ships to be sent into port, and effecting hasty repairs to the rest, so that it was not until about 1pm that Blake's faster frigates began their attack, which continued until nightfall. In the course of the action the Dutch seem to have lost a further four ships, with others severely damaged. Writing up the log of his flagship, *Monnedam*, Florizoon admitted that: 'In the fight my main topmast and mizzen yard were shot down again, after having been previously repaired. We also received several shots under water, so that it was with difficulty we kept afloat.' Ruyter had lost his mainmast, and had to be towed to safety.[15]

To add to Tromp's desperate situation, many of his captains failed to support those ships which were bearing the brunt of the English attack. Florizoon was furious at this dereliction of duty:

> I also called Captain Gabriel Theunassen to remain with me in accordance with the written instructions specially given him. In reply, I was informed from his ship that he

took little account of that. I then called to him that if it pleased God to bring me home again, I would take care to settle with such rascals.[16]

Among the warships, two of Evertsen's squadron were taken, and Floriszoon saw one of his division captured.

Captain Mert van Nes of Rotterdam, known familiarly as 'Farmer Jim', was in the thick of the action that day:

About noon the admiral signalled for me with a blue pennant at the mizzen peak . . . but I couldn't get astern of him. Then the admiral hailed: 'Farmer Jim, Farmer Jim, run down to the merchantmen and tell them to escape E by N and ENE . . . then go to Commodore Ruyter and tell him to take station ahead of me. I said 'Aye Aye, Sir'. Then I went to de Ruyter and told him, from him I went after the merchantmen.[17]

Tromp managed to protect most of the convoy during the long hours of skirmishing, although some were taken, mainly ships which had panicked and broken formation in an attempt to reach French ports, because of their crews' fear of falling into Spanish hands if they were driven ashore in Flanders.

In the course of the day the fighting had moved steadily eastwards up-Channel, as the Dutch tried desperately to reach home. Darkness brought a brief respite for Tromp's weary and faltering men, but it seemed certain that the next day would see the destruction of the Dutch fleet.

Next morning (20 February) action resumed at about 9am. Organised Dutch resistance collapsed after about two hours, with one broadside from the heavier English ships proving enough to put the enemy to flight. Throughout the day a running fight continued, as the English frigates tried to get to leeward of the Dutch convoy in order to cut off its retreat through the Straits of Dover. A Dutch participant related:

After this the English got to the leeward of the fleet; seeing this I tried to get on the lee of the fleet. I got up to them and fired; on this, two more of our ships also bore down on them, and they moved on with the wind. Then

I sighted an Englishman on their lee so I turned and sailed towards them upon which he veered round with the wind and made off. Then I sailed close among the merchantmen; then hoisted the topsails upon the topmasts and tacked again to the rear of them, which I succeeded in doing. Then I did my best again in firing on the enemy, whenever I could. The merchantmen closed up, some with the ships of war and some with one another athwart them, so that they all lay together. God knows, if they had only made sail at first, when I told them, there would be no need for this, but they would not do it at the time.[18]

As night fell, only about thirty-five of Tromp's warships were still able and willing to fight. The veteran Dutch admiral decided on a desperate bid to avoid total destruction. After dark he led his fleet into the lee shore of Cape Griz Nez, on the French side of the Straits of Dover. The English vessels, with their deeper draught and battered rigging, dared not follow. In any case, they believed the Dutch to be trapped by a north-westerly wind and an ebbing tide. They could be finished off at daylight.

However, Tromp, with his expert knowledge of these waters, knew that there was just sufficient deep water around Cape Griz Nez for him to make his escape. Under cover of darkness the Dutch slipped clear of the jaws of Blake's trap, and by dawn were anchored off Dunkirk.

Blake and Deane had understandable difficulty in explaining Tromp's escape:

Also as we supped this night they stole away from us notwithstanding our Pilots and Seamen best acquainted with the coast said that as the wind rose they could not weather the French shore to get home, and for us in the condition we were it was not possible to have done it, or if we had been in a better condition it being night without extreme hazard to the whole Fleet.

Even so, they claimed that with another two or three hours of daylight the English fleet could have got between the Dutch and home:

So that they must have been forced to have made their way through us with their men of war, which were at that time not above thirty-five, as we could count, the rest being destroyed or dispersed. The merchantmen also must have been necessitated to have run ashore, or fallen into our hands, which, as we conceive the Dutch Admiral being sensible of it, just as it was dark, bore directly in upon the shore, where it is supposed he anchored, the tide of ebb being come, which was a leewardly tide, so near that we durst not follow them; it being nigh a lee shore, and most of the great ships had their masts, yards and sails in such a condition as they were ready to fall down every hour, we thought it best to come to an anchor, the tide being leewardly, and the Dutch fleet between the French shore and us at anchor.[19]

Although Tromp had avoided total destruction, the running battle which had commenced off Portland Bill had been a major Dutch reverse. Only seventy out of a total of 220 ships were still with Tromp, although by no means of all of the others had actually been lost. The English claimed to have sunk or taken seventeen enemy warships, and about sixty merchant ships. They estimated that the Dutch had suffered 3,000 casualties. For his part Blake had lost only one ship, although many others had been badly damaged, and about 600 men were casualties.

The English commanders had grounds for at least partial satisfaction. But they had been in serious trouble during the first day of fighting, and at the end of the battle had allowed Tromp to escape from a seemingly hopeless situation.

For the moment, however, the English fleet was in control of the Channel, and Dutch convoys would be forced to revert to the longer northerly route around the tip of Scotland.

However, the Dutch navy recovered with its customary resilience, and by early May more than a hundred ships were ready for sea. But the battle had a dire effect on Dutch trade, which slumped so much that grass was said to be growing in the deserted streets of Amsterdam's mercantile district. In an attempted riposte for the Dutch defeat, in March de With, his crews as discontented as ever with his leadership, sortied into the North Sea with a small squadron of eighteen ships and two galliots. His target was the large coal fleet which carried the products of the mines of north-east England south to London. But the colliers took shelter beneath the guns of Scarborough Castle, and without pressing home an attack, de With returned to the Dutch port of Schoonveldt, complaining that without heavy ships to counter those of the English, the Dutch fleet was doomed to destruction.

In the days following Portland English shipyards worked frantically to repair the damaged warships. On 25 April seven Swedish ships reached port with desperately needed naval supplies, while men were pressed energetically in order to fill out depleted crews.

Blake himself would be out of action for most of the summer as a result of the wound which he had suffered at Portland, and it is unclear whether he played any part in devising the new tactics which were now introduced, probably compiled mainly by Deane and Monck, and based on the experiences of Portland. On 20 March the 'Fighting Instructions for the Better Ordering of the Fleet' were published. One of the most significant developments in the history of the English Navy, the 'Instructions' would have a major influence on its tactics for over a century. Included were an elaborate series of flag signals and instructions for the conduct of the fleet in high winds, stormy weather and at night, with penalties laid down for those captains who failed to conform.

Of greater immediate significance were the instructions for conduct in battle. Captains were no longer to act on the free-for-all basis which had proved such a problem in battle. Instead, when the General commanding hoisted the red flag as a signal to engage 'then each squadron shall take the best advantage they can to engage with the enemy next unto them, and in order hereunto all ships of every squadron shall endeavour to keep in line with their chief.' Lines were to be formed from the ships of individual squadrons, not by the whole fleet, so this was not the 'line of battle' as it would be understood in the eighteenth century. Instead, if the fleet were to windward of the enemy, each squadron would proceed in line ahead until it saw the signal to engage, upon which ships would turn towards the enemy so that they were in line abreast. No captain was to get to windward of the commander-in-chief until the action began, but after that there is no indication that, when at close quarters, the ships of a squadron were to form into line again. Indeed the opposite is inferred when the 'Instructions' state that if the flagship of a squadron were to be disabled, 'then every ship of the squadron shall endeavour to get in line with the Admiral, or he that commandeth next in chief to him and nearest the enemy.' In other words, if the squadron commander should be disabled in the midst of battle, his subordinates should assume that he had fallen out of the action, and should form on the nearest senior officer. The tactics were designed to exploit the proven English superiority in gunnery.

Though still a long way from the sometimes over-rigidity of the later years of the age of sail, the 'Instructions' were a serious attempt to impose some degree of order on conduct in battle. Monck had witnessed the lost opportunities in the Portland action which had been due to lack of discipline, and the 'Instructions' were intended to minimise similar failings in the future. They were also intended to maximise the effects of English gunnery and to prevent the Dutch from coming to close quarters. They would quickly experience their first test.[20]

Gibbard Shoal

On 5 May Tromp, with Ruyter and de With as his squadron commanders, sortied from the Texel with eighty warships and five fireships. The Dutch fleet headed northwards, escorting a convoy of 200 merchant ships towards the Shetlands. The Dutch admiral knew that it was vital to get seaborne trade moving again, and was eager to bring on a fleet action.

On 29 April Monck and Deane were off the Isle of Wight with eighty-eight warships and 105 armed merchant ships, and hoped to receive further reinforcement from a squadron under the convalescent Blake.

Having seen his convoy off safely, Tromp returned to the Narrow Seas, where he was joined on 20 May by Floriszoon with sixteen warships. Tromp was confident of success, for he now commanded a force of ninety-two warships, five fireships and six smaller vessels. The English fleet had been unable to locate Tromp during the earlier part of his voyage, and after going as far as the Texel had returned to pick up reinforcements from Yarmouth. An equally frustrated Tromp had vented some of his spite in a bombardment of Dover, before at last locating the English fleet and moving west to engage them.

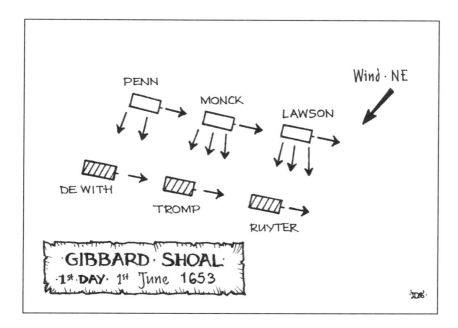

The English commanders had ordered all available ships between Sands Head and Orfordness to join them. Blake, though far from fit, had assembled a squadron of ships in the Thames and was now near the anchorage at Gunfleet. This was a deep channel to the south of Harwich and north-east of the mouth of the Thames, protected by the Gunfleet Shoal.

At 6am on 1 June Monck and Deane sortied from Sole Bay with 105 ships carrying a total of 3,817 guns. Deane and Monck, aboard *Resolution*, led the Red Squadron in the centre of the English fleet. Penn in the *James* (sixty-six) led the White Squadron, while Vice-Admiral Lawson, aboard the *George* (fifty-six), commanded the White Squadron.

At around noon the frigates which had been sent to scout ahead of the main body of the fleet lowered their topsails as a signal that the enemy were in sight.

Tromp and his fleet were about four leagues to leeward, as the English steered towards him. At about 4pm, Lawson, whose White Squadron was closest to the enemy, slowed in order to allow the remainder of the English fleet to close up with him. The English ships were now just south of the Gibbard Shoal, about forty miles east of Harwich, and in fading misty light dropped anchor for the night. The Dutch lay to several miles to the south.

Monck and Deane were still hoping that Blake's reinforcements would arrive in time to take part in the battle which now seemed inevitable next day. But Blake had not yet left the Gunfleet anchorage with his squadron of thirteen ships, including his flagship, the fifty-six-gun *Essex*. He raised anchor on the morning of 2 May using what light wind there was to try and join his fellow generals.

Monck and Deane had decided to give the new 'Instructions' their first test. In continuing light winds, the English fleet, its squadrons forming three roughly parallel lines, bore down on the enemy. Just as the English ships got within gunshot range, the wind dropped entirely. With no prospect of closing, the English ships remained in line-ahead formation, bombarding the enemy. Lawson's squadron formed the van, followed by Monck and Deane's Red Squadron, with Penn in the rear. Strict orders had been given that no enemy ship was to be boarded until it had been effectively shattered by gunfire, the English seamen being assured that they would not lose out on prize money as a result.

Owing to the light winds it was not until about 11am that the English fleet was close enough to the enemy to open fire. The situation was already unfavourable for the Dutch, who would not be able to endure the superior English gunnery at a range of 500 yards for long. Ruyter, leading the Dutch line, tried to get ahead of Lawson, with the English van, so that he could turn across his bows and rake him before forcing a mêlée. However, in the light breeze he had no success.

Heavy firing continued for several hours, the Dutch ships showing signs of edging away from their more powerful opponents. But at about 3pm the wind veered to the north-east and freshened, and Lawson's course began to converge with the Dutch. Ruyter, eager for action, tacked up towards Lawson, while at the same time Tromp saw that a gap had opened up between the English van and Monck's squadron, and steered towards it with his flagship, with boats towing round his other ships until they faced the gap and could follow.

Lawson was soon suffering considerable damage, as Monck

strove to break through to his support. Monck's flagship, *Resolution*, came under fire from no fewer than sixteen enemy ships, and Richard Deane was killed by a roundshot. Monck, standing close by, was covered with Deane's blood. In order to conceal Deane's death from the crew, Monck ordered his body to be shrouded with a cloak and carried below.

The Dutch advantage proved fleeting as the weight of English gunnery made itself felt. Monck was rapidly supported by Penn, and as the English ships gained the advantage of the wind, the Dutch were steadily forced to leeward. By dusk Tromp's fleet was in full retreat, and his ships were swept along the Dutch coast past their objective of the Weilings anchorage and on towards the mouth of the Maas. In another demonstration of poor morale, some Dutch captains deserted under cover of darkness.

By midnight the opposing fleets were off Dunkirk. So far the Dutch had lost one or two ships in the action with Lawson, and another blown up, while the English had not lost any.

At dawn a council of war was held aboard *Resolution*. It was resolved that the English squadrons would sail towards the Dutch line in three parallel columns, break through it and disperse Tromp's ships, and then pursue them as far as they could while avoiding the shoals which lay off the Flanders coast in this area.

The Dutch were also holding a council of war. As well as being concerned by a shortage of ammunition, Tromp was also angered by the open defeatism of some of his captains. Though the Dutch admiral accused them of lack of courage, it had by now been amply demonstrated even to the bravest of the Dutch seamen that their lighter ships were unable to withstand their heavier English opponents. Unwilling to retreat without at least striking a blow, Tromp ordered 'one more sharp attack' before a general retirement.

Fighting did not begin until noon, and the Dutch attack quickly faltered. Finding that Monck had the weather gauge, Tromp set course for the Scheldt estuary. He was almost too late. As the Dutch fought a desperate rearguard action, many badly damaged ships straggled behind and were captured by the English. By evening the Dutch fleet had been routed, and Tromp's flagship, *Brederode*, was only saved by the desperate efforts of her crew. One entire group of four or five Dutch ships became entangled together in their panic, and all were captured. By the time Tromp reached the safety of the Scheldt only seventy-four of his 103 ships were still with him. Eight had been sunk and eleven taken.

As Monck, joined by Blake's squadron, took up blockading station off the Scheldt, the Dutch faced a grim prospect. De With, reporting the disaster to the States General, was outspoken: 'What use is it to equivocate, standing here before my sovereigns? I can and must say that the English are now our masters and command the sea.'[21]

Sending home his prizes and damaged ships, Monck maintained his blockade for a month. The effects on the trade and economy of the Netherlands were disastrous. As the English fleet rode off the Scheldt, clearly visible from Dutch church steeples, the seaborne trade which was the lifeblood of the Netherlands was at a standstill. In some of the great coastal cities people faced famine, and there were growing fears of an Orangeist coup.

Yet the States General knew that, although they faced financial ruin, any peace which they were likely to obtain in their current situation would be still more ruinous. The only hope lay in a naval victory which would break the English blockade and allow the Dutch to seek better terms.

The last battle

After a month Monck was forced to return to port in order to resupply, but by 16 July he was back on station off the Scheldt. Meanwhile, as a result of a last frantic effort, the Dutch fleet, with its crews suffering badly from the effects of the blockade, was again reorganised and ready for a final bid for victory. Unfortunately it began its campaign divided, with Tromp's survivors from the Gibbard Shoal action still in the Scheldt, and the squadron commanded by de With at Helder at the entrance to the Zuider Zee. Before they could fight the English with any prospect of success the Dutch would need to unite their forces.

While absent resupplying his heavy ships, Monck had left a number of light vessels off the Dutch coast, in order to maintain the appearance of a blockade. It is unclear if Tromp was deceived by this, but he was probably not ready for sea before Monck resumed his station off the Scheldt, still in overall command, as Blake was too ill for active service.

In early August Tromp ordered de With, whose base at Helder

was not under blockade, to take station just outside the port. From there he could retire to safety if attacked or move to take the English fleet in the rear if they attacked Tromp as he came northwards up the coast from the Scheldt.

On 25 July Tromp put to sea. Though he had a good idea of the likely Dutch strategy, Monck decided to ignore de With and go after Tromp, and when the wind shifted to the north the English gained the advantage of the weather gauge. Tromp turned south with the intention of drawing Monck away from the Texel to allow de With to join in the action.

Some sharp fighting occurred, with Monck's flagship, *Resolution*, losing seventeen dead and twenty-five wounded before the onset of darkness brought fighting to a close. The advantage now shifted to Tromp, who, with his customary skilful seamanship, managed to slip past Monck under cover of night, and head northwards, while the English fleet continued to drift south. At dawn Tromp and de With were in sight of each other and had also gained the weather gauge.

Holding his ships as close to the wind as possible, Monck beat back northwards to engage the enemy, but high winds and a severe swell prevented any action that day.

What would prove to be the final battle of the war took place on 31 July off Scheveningen. The Dutch had 107 warships and nine fireships, against Monck's 104 warships and sixteen smaller vessels, and Monck also expected to be reinforced by Blake's old squadron.

Tromp had formed his fleet into a ragged line and turned downwind to meet the enemy. Monck, in accordance with the 'Fighting Instructions', had formed his fleet into squadron lines, and headed for the Dutch fleet. Led by *Resolution* and *Worcester*, the English made as many as four 'desperate charges' through the Dutch fleet, breaking it up section by section. Each time they passed through the Dutch line, the English ships poured in heavy broadsides, with the Dutch, as usual, suffering severely. Captain Cubitt, of the English ship *Tulip*, described how:

> In passing through we lamed several ships and sank some, as soon as we had passed them we tacked again upon them and they on us, passed by each other very

near, we did very good execution . . . Some of their ships which had all their masts gone put out a white handkerchief upon a staff and hauled in all their guns.[22]

There was no time, however, to take possession of any prizes, as the opposing ships continued to pass each other 'almost at push of pike' and doing 'great execution'. Cubitt wrote that the 'very heavens were obscured by smoke, the air rent with the thundering noise, the sea all in a breach with the shot that fell, the ships even trembling and we hearing everywhere messengers of death flying.'[23]

The journal of the *Vanguard* reported 'many of their ships' masts were shot by the board, others sunk to the number of twenty. At last God gave us the wind.'

Having lost the weather gauge, the Dutch fled for the Helder, with the English in hot pursuit. Marteen van Tromp had been mortally wounded early in the action by a marksman aboard *Tulip*. As he was carried below, Tromp told his officers: 'I have run my course. Have good courage.'[24]

The death of Tromp was a shattering blow for the Dutch. He has good claim to be regarded as the greatest naval commander of the first half of the seventeenth century, and was capable of inspiring his seamen to greater feats than any of his contemporaries could. Both as a naval innovator, with his proposed ship designs, and as a tactician, Tromp had been outstanding, and although rising stars such as Ruyter would soon demonstrate equal skills and build on Tromp's legacy, for the moment he was irreplaceable.

The action had been another decisive defeat for the Dutch, who lost at least fifteen to twenty ships, together with 3–4,000 men. The English lost one ship, the thirty-two-gun *Oak*, and about 500 men.

The victory won, Monck did not wish to risk remaining on a dangerous lee shore and retired to Southwold Bay, where he took on stores, including 1,000 barrels of powder and eighty tons of shot. He then resumed a partial blockade of the Dutch coast, although in the interim de With was able to get a large convoy of 340 merchant ships safely to sea and return with a convoy of Baltic traders.

The last battle of the war had been fought. While Blake, Monck and their leading officers received gold chains and a variety of medals and the thanks of Parliament, both Cromwell and the Dutch government were seeking peace. Cromwell had never really been in favour of the war. He was aware, however, that many of the more radical elements within the country had seen a conquered Holland as the first step in a march on Rome, so he had to tread carefully. The Dutch remained unwilling to enter into a military alliance with the Protectorate, but in September 1654 a treaty was agreed by which the Dutch acknowledged the English flag in territorial waters and accepted the Navigation Acts. Compensation was to be paid to English merchants, and the Dutch agreed to expel all Royalist exiles from Dutch territory.

Some of the more extreme religious sects would never forgive Cromwell either for becoming Protector, or negotiating a settlement with the Dutch. But the great majority of naval officers were relieved by the end of a war with which they had never felt entirely comfortable. Cromwell's Navy, after an uncertain start, had refined its tactics and administration and won a crushing victory. The State's Navy was now the dominant maritime force in Europe, and its influence was far-reaching. As Cromwell told Parliament: 'There is not a nation in Europe but is willing to ask a good understanding from you.'

Chapter 7
War with Spain

'. . . his [Cromwell's] greatness at home was but a
shadow of the glory he had abroad. It was hard
to discover which feared him more, France,
Spain, or the Low Countries . . .'

Edward, Earl of Clarendon

Road to war

The end of the Dutch War brought only a brief respite for the
Protectorate. The close of hostilities left Cromwell with a Navy of
160 ships and an Army of twelve horse and eighteen foot regiments.
With much of Europe still potentially hostile, and the ever-present
threat of Royalist insurrection at home, Oliver Cromwell dare not
take the risk of reducing his forces, but neither could he afford to
maintain them at this strength for long without some additional
source of finance.

To add to the Lord Protector's concerns, there was continued
disquiet among some sections of the Navy at political developments
in England. In December 1653 the plural form of 'Generals at Sea'
was used for the first time, implying that the officers holding that
title were now regarded as independent commanders rather than a
collective decision-making body. In the spring of 1654 the Generals
were Cromwell's brother-in-law, John Desborowe, Robert Blake
and William Penn, the latter the first professional sailor to be
appointed to the post rather than the army officers who had always
held command previously. A previous General at Sea, George
Monck, had been transferred to head the army in Scotland.

Desborowe was mainly occupied ashore with administrative matters, and his role at sea would be carried out by Vice-Admiral John Lawson. Although Lawson's fighting record was second to none, politically his appointment carried some risks. He was a noted Anabaptist, and suspected on good grounds of being connected with the radical Leveller movement, active plotters against the Cromwellian regime. Lawson was widely popular among the seamen, and in October 1654 he and his captains backed a petition from their crews complaining about continued impressments and the inevitable pay arrears.

It was clear to the Government that, while the ever-present threat from European powers such as France and the Dutch, simmering over their recent defeat, persisted, the Navy could not be safely reduced, but that some means would have to be found to keep it occupied, preferably well away from home waters, where dissent or mutiny could be immediately threatening. As so often in such circumstances, war was the obvious solution. With the Dutch for the moment subdued, the choice lay between England's traditional foes, France and Spain.

Blake in the Mediterranean

While Cromwell and his Government weighed the options, the long-running undeclared conflict with France continued. Blake was sent to the Mediterranean with a naval squadron, with instructions to thwart French ambitions in the area by deterring a rumoured French attack on the Spanish possession of Naples. This was intended as a practical demonstration of English naval strength, aimed at pressurizing France into making an alliance with England against Spain. If time allowed, Blake was to take action against the Barbary pirates before, assuming a French alliance was concluded, turning his attention to the returning Spanish Plate fleet.

Blake's squadron consisted of three 2nd rate ships. He flew his flag in the *George*; Vice-Admiral Richard Badiley commanded the *Andrew*, while Rear-Admiral Joseph Jordan was aboard the *Union*. All of these vessels pre-dated the Civil Wars, for the Commonwealth was fortunate in having inherited a sound core of capital ships, which only needed periodic updating and refitting, allowing them to concentrate resources on the construction of smaller vessels. Blake had four 3rd rate ships, *Langport*, *Bridgewater*,

Worcester and *Plymouth*, all built after 1649, while six of his nine smaller vessels were former prizes.

Blake arrived off Cadiz on 30 October, to receive a cool reception from the Spaniards. He proceeded into the Mediterranean to his first objective of Naples. Blake was in poor health, and this in part may have explained the unfavourable impression which he made on observers. The Venetian envoy in Naples said of Blake that he was:

> A deep sombre man of few words. Owing to his advanced age, he never shows himself even on his own ship except when the sun shines, and although invited, he would never go ashore on a single occasion to see the place and his countrymen.[1]

The envoy's colleague in Florence added that the Grand Duke of Tuscany, who had played such an ambivalent role in the Dutch War, was 'trying to keep Blake friendly, the more so because he seems to be a very touchy and particular old man. His Highness has talked to me about the extreme severity with which he treats the captains of his ships.'[2]

Blake had, of course, always been a notably autocratic naval commander, and this tendency seems to have been deepened by his poor health. He was also uneasy when having to attempt diplomacy in Catholic states of which he disapproved, and was probably glad when events gave him reason to turn his attention to the Barbary pirates.

Tunis, along with Tripoli and Algiers, was nominally part of the Ottoman Empire, although its ruler, the Dey, followed a fairly independent course. The North African coastal rulers were engaged in more or less continuous warfare, which in their case normally took the form of the *corso*, raids against Western shipping, and occasionally their territories, with the object of carrying off booty and slaves, who, if sufficiently valuable, could sometimes be ransomed. The corsairs, unlike their victims, did not see their actions as piracy as such. Although most of the Western nations affected had been trying for decades to curb their activities, they found the strongly fortified cities of the North African coast formidable challenges.

The spark which ignited conflict between Blake and Tunis came when the Dey reacted violently after an English merchant ship captain sold some of his Tunisian passengers as slaves to the Knights of Malta. On arrival off Tunis, Blake received an 'insolent' response from the Dey, who was confident of the strength of his defences. This in turn gave Blake an excuse to attack 'these pirates', as he termed them.[3]

On 22 February Blake arrived off the Tunisian port of Porto Farina. Watching him from the shore was a considerable army led by the Dey, but of more interest to the English commander were eight Turkish men-of-war and a captured English merchant ship which were anchored in the harbour. At the ensuing council of war the English commanders were reluctant to attack the Turkish vessels, as the Ottoman government was believed to be attempting to persuade the Dey to agree to call off his hostile activities.

So Blake played for time. Six ships were left to maintain a blockade of Porto Farina, while the remainder of the English squadron returned to Spanish and Italian ports to take on supplies. Blake was back off Porto Farina on 20 March, but it was 4 April before weather and wind conditions were suitable for mounting an attack.

Then, led by Captain Nathaniel Cobham in *Newcastle*, the English 4th rates entered the harbour in line ahead via the El Bakira entrance. Following *Newcastle* came *Kent*, *Foresight*, *Amity*, *Princess Mary*, *Pearl*, *Mermaid* and *Merlin*. The larger ships, led by the *Andrew*, were to tackle the harbour's fortifications.

The attack began at 4am, and the shore defences were quickly overwhelmed by the brutally effective fire of Blake's ships. The crews of the Turkish vessels abandoned ship when they saw the longboats of the English boarding parties approaching, and their ships, together with the English prize, were set ablaze. By 8am the main action was over, and the last of the English ships had safely withdrawn three hours later. English casualties totalled twenty-five dead and about eighty wounded.

The operation had been a striking success against shore defences, and had been planned with particular care. This was a sign of Blake's growing maturity as a naval commander. A few years earlier he would probably have simply stormed into the enemy port with little regard for the circumstances. But now he recognised the value of careful planning and consideration before rushing into action.[4]

The attack on Porto Farina had little long-term significance. Indeed, as the Dey of Tunis pointed out with scarcely concealed satisfaction, the destroyed ships had actually belonged to his nominal Ottoman overlords. Blake, however, saw the operation has having had a significant punitive effect: 'We found them [the Tunisians] more wilful and intractable than before, adding to their obstinacy much insolence and contumely, denying us all commerce of civility, and hindering all others as much as they could from the same. These barbarous provocations did so far work upon our spirits, that we judged it necessary for the honour of our fleet, our nation and religion, seeing they would not deal with us as friends, to make them feel us as enemies.'[5]

That the action had had some moral effect seemed to be demonstrated a few days later when the squadron anchored off Algiers. It was true that its Dey had already reached a treaty with England prior to Blake's arrival, but the English ships received a warmer welcome than they had at Tunis, and all English and Irish slaves held in the port were promptly handed over. Some Dutch slaves swam out to the English ships, and in a demonstration of the brotherhood of the sea and the bonds of religion transcending old enmities, Blake's seamen clubbed together in order to buy their freedom.

Blockading Cadiz

Arriving back off Cadiz, Blake, aware of the poor condition of many of his ships after months at sea, wrote to the Council of State suggesting that the large 2nd rates should be replaced by frigates. He suggested that one of the most unserviceable ships should be sent home with each of his despatches, and replaced by a fresh vessel bringing orders from home. Blake's frustration was increased by his ignorance of the current political situation. He was unsure whether war with Spain had actually begun, and lacked clear orders on what to do in the interim. It appears that the English commander had initially been given leave to defend himself if attacked, but not to initiate any action, but on 13 June the Council of State had amended Blake's instructions, telling him to attack any Spanish ships bound for the West Indies, but ignoring the question of how

Blake was to determine the destination of any Spanish ships which he sighted.[6]

The confusion in orders reflected the slow process by which the Council of State determined its policy towards Spain. A major factor in the eventual decision to go to war with Spain rather than France was that the former was seen as militarily weaker, and less likely than France to retaliate by mounting a military expedition in support of the exiled Charles II. In fact the possibility of any European power lending such support to the exiled Stuarts was remote. There was also the practical consideration that Spain to many eyes was the more Catholic of the two countries, and therefore to popular opinion and the religious radicals the more acceptable enemy. Cromwell was able to claim with some credibility that Spain was England's 'natural enemy', and invoke the always potent memory of Queen Elizabeth. General John Fleetwood and his officers voiced the predominant radical viewpoint when they demanded: 'What peace can we rejoice in, when the whoredom, murders and witchcrafts of Jezebel are so many?'[7]

Although the details of his thinking remain unclear, Cromwell possibly hoped to avoid full-scale war in Europe with Spain, and to confine action to the West Indies. The Lord Protector made two demands of Spanish Ambassador Carderas. These were that Spain should allow unhindered access to the English colonies in the New World, and that English merchants living in Spain should be afforded full religious toleration. The Spanish ambassador retorted angrily that this would be asking his monarch 'to give up his two eyes', a defiant response possibly founded on an over-estimation of Cromwell's desire for peace.

Cromwell indeed had hopes for gains at Spain's expense, and this resulted in the project known as 'the Western Design'. This was an ambitious scheme for a major amphibious operation in the Spanish Caribbean, involving a naval squadron and 3,600 regular troops from England supported by forces raised locally in the English colonies, notably in Barbados. It was designed to capture Santo Domingo, Puerto Rico, Havana or Cartagena in the Panama Isthmus, or, in more optimistic moments, all four. Equally attractive, given Cromwell's parlous economic state, was the hope that the expedition would pay for itself.

With hindsight, it is difficult to understand how, considering the vast distances and huge logistical difficulties involved, Cromwell could have hoped for such sweeping successes. But there was a widespread tendency to belittle Spanish military ability. A principal proponent of the Western Design was a former Dominican friar, Thomas Gage, who assured the Council of State that 'the Spaniards cannot oppose much, being a lazy, sinful people, feeding like beasts upon their lusts, and upon the fat of the land, and never trained up to war.'[8] As an intelligence appreciation for a major military operation this left something to be desired.

News of the proposed Western Design led Spain to withdraw her ambassador from London, and to follow up with a declaration of war. This in turn brought England and France together in an alliance which at first was defensive only, although clearly more was intended to follow.

The war with Spain would bring with it none of the great naval actions which had been a feature of the conflict with the Dutch. The greatest days of Spanish naval power were over, and knowing that they could not face the new English Navy on the open seas, the Spaniards chose instead to mount privateering operations against English merchant ships and to place an embargo on English trade.

Blake, meanwhile, was still hovering discontentedly off Cadiz, awaiting clear orders. Throughout the early summer of 1655 the true state of Anglo-Spanish relations remained obscure to him. In June the Spaniards assisted Blake in salvaging some guns from the wrecked ships of Rupert's squadron in Cartagena Bay, but the Spaniards were aware that Blake had stationed the bulk of his squadron between Cape St Mary and Cape Spartel in order to watch out for the returning Plate Fleet, and it was also noted that Blake had begun using supply ships to provision his fleet rather than enter Cadiz harbour. Not unnaturally, Blake commented that 'They of Cadiz are very distrustful of us.'[9]

Although bearing little other fruit, Blake's *de facto* blockade of Cadiz at least prevented any warships being sent to the Caribbean to oppose the Western Design, and reduced the danger to English merchant shipping entering and leaving the Mediterranean. However, the ambiguous nature of his orders, leading Blake to believe that he was only to attack Spanish warships heading westwards, cost him the chance of a major victory when, on 16 August, a Spanish fleet of thirty-one sail was sighted in Lagos Bay. It was correctly deduced that this was the escort for the Plate Fleet, whose arrival was imminent. At one point the rival fleets were steering parallel courses, and Blake actually ordered an attack, only to be told that the seas were too heavy for the lower gunports to be opened. Reluctantly, Blake decided both that conditions were unfavourable and his orders too ambiguous to risk an engagement, and on the following night the Spanish ships slipped into Cadiz.

It was not until 13 September that a letter from the Council of State made it clear that Blake had misinterpreted his instructions, and should in fact have engaged. However, it was by then too late. Increasingly short of supplies, on 24 August Blake abandoned the blockade of Cadiz and went into Cascaris Roads. Six days later, Blake wrote to Cromwell that he would not trouble the Lord Protector with 'any complaints of myself, of the indisposition of my body, or troubles of mind, but rather of the firm purpose of my heart, with all faithfulness and sincerity to discharge the trust while reposed in me.[10] By 22 September the fleet was on its way home, and dropped anchor in the Downs on 6 October. Significantly, Blake's return met with no reproaches from Cromwell.

The Western Design

By now attention had switched to the Western Design, news of which was eagerly awaited. However, there were reasons for concern even before the expedition set sail. Its naval contingent was under the command of General at Sea William Penn, but Penn was made subordinate to the army commander, the un-distinguished General Robert Venables. Both were hindered by the presence of two civilian commissioners, who were secretly reporting on their actions to Cromwell. Co-operation between the commanders was minimal from the start. William Penn was by nature suspicious and ill-tempered, and quickly on bad terms with Robert Venables. He was not informed by Venables of their objective until after the expedition was at sea. If these were not sufficient reasons for concern, Venables was accompanied on the expedition by his domineering wife, who regularly interfered in his conduct of operations.

The calibre of the troops was also mixed. While most of the officers were capable enough, the ranks had been filled out with undesirables of various kinds, whose military value was limited.

They were reinforced by 4,300 plunder-seeking colonists from Barbados, and 1,200 from other English-held islands in the Caribbean, although the expedition was unpopular with the merchants of Barbados, where it was seen as disrupting profitable trade with the Spanish possessions. And both supplies and equipment were lacking, thanks to the incompetence of the committee, headed by Desborowe, responsible for logistical matters.

In April 1655 the expedition at last arrived off the Spanish island of Hispaniola. The troops had considerable difficulty in making a landing on the rocky coastline, but on 14 April got ashore about thirty miles from the island's capital of Santo Domingo. The men were soon suffering considerably from the effects of heat and thirst, having no water bottles and in any case little fresh water with which to fill them. Four days later, as they struggled through thick brush on the approaches to the town, the English troops were ambushed by a small force of 200 local *vaqueros* (cowboys). Panic ensued. Some of the officers fought and died bravely, and the 'sea regiment' formed from sailors of the fleet retained its order, but the outcome of the skirmish was the total rout of the remainder of the English force.

Penn's ships, which had meanwhile been ineffectively bombarding Santo Domingo, re-embarked the surviving troops. Penn urged that another attack be made, but the army officers were too disheartened. In order to salvage some small credit from the humiliation, the council of war decided instead to attack the island of Jamaica.

This island seemed to have little apparent value, and consequently it had been only lightly fortified by the Spanish. On 11 May English troops and sailors under Penn's command went ashore. He had told the civilian commissioners that 'he would not trust the army with the attempt, if he could come near with his ships.' To provide covering fire, the galley *Martin* was run aground in front of the Spanish coastal defences.

Formal Spanish resistance ended after six days, but a prolonged guerrilla campaign followed, with many of the English troops suffering from sickness and starvation.

Penn and Venables did not wait for the conclusion of the campaign but, with the fleet, returned to England in an attempt to make their peace with Cromwell. They arrived home on 31 August, and both commanders were committed to the Tower for a short time. In the end Penn was made principal scapegoat, and was never re-employed by Cromwell, although he in fact deserved little blame, apart from failing to attack the Plate Fleet at Havana.

For some time there would be grave doubts about whether the new English colony in Jamaica could survive. It was saved by its suitability as a base for buccaneers and privateers operating against Spanish shipping in the region. Some of the State's Navy joined in these legally dubious activities, notably Captain Christopher Mynget of the frigate *Marston Moor*, who in the spring of 1659 took booty worth between £2–300,000 in a raid, much of which was never declared to the Governor of Jamaica's prize court.

Blake and Mountagu

Even before news of the failure of the Western Design reached him, Cromwell had begun to realise that the war with Spain was likely to be both tougher and less profitable than he had expected. He still clung to the belief that 'six nimble frigates' would suffice to blockade the coast of Spain and cut off the supplies of bullion from the New World which were its economic lifeblood. The immediate problem lay in the selection of a commander for an expedition on whose success so much rested.

Robert Blake remained the obvious choice, but he was by now seriously ill. He remained, however, the only senior naval commander whom Cromwell felt that he could trust. As second-in-command, Cromwell perforce appointed the vastly experienced John Lawson, but although the expedition to Spain would thus serve the purpose of getting a noted dissident out of the way, Cromwell feared the consequences if Blake should die at sea and Lawson take over command. His solution was to appoint a new General at Sea to share joint command with Blake.

Edward Mountagu came from a distinguished Parliamentarian family, and had first seen action at the age of eighteen at the battle of Marston Moor. He became colonel of a regiment of foot in the New Model Army, and as well as gaining a reputation as a competent soldier, Mountagu also won friends as a result of his approachable and amiable nature. A cultured man of scientific interests, Mountagu was 'a gentleman of so excellent a temper and behaviour that he could make himself no enemies.'[11]

Liked and trusted by Cromwell, Edward Mountagu's rise was rapid. Penn's failure opened further doors for the new favourite. He became a member of the Council of State, and in October 1655 was appointed to the Admiralty Committee. On 22 January 1656 he was named as a General at Sea, in joint command with Blake of the forthcoming Spanish expedition.

It has been suggested that Blake was opposed to Mountagu's appointment, but there is some evidence that it was in fact Blake's idea. The veteran commander was aware that his own days were numbered, and that he had no obvious successor. Penn was in disgrace, Monck was needed in Scotland. Of the vice-admirals, Richard Badiley was also in poor health, while Lawson was politically suspect. Mountagu, in fact, was eminently suitable. He had no discernible political views, other than loyalty to Cromwell, and could be relied upon to squash political dissent while acting as a tactful and agreeable colleague for the sick old Blake.

The immediate consequence of Mountagu's appointment was the resignation of John Lawson and three captains of similar views, which suited Cromwell's purposes very well. In practice any potential friction between Blake and Mountagu quickly disappeared, as the younger man proved to be supportive of his older colleague and eager to learn from him.

In the spring of 1656 the blockade of Cadiz was resumed when on 20 April the English squadron appeared off the Spanish port. Blake and Mountagu's fleet consisted of thirty-seven men-of-war and a fireship, divided into three squadrons. Mountagu and Blake led the first squadron, with the second under Richard Badiley, flying his flag aboard *Resolution* (eighty-four). The third squadron was under Rear-Admiral Robert Bourne, in *Swiftsure* (fifty-six). The first two squadrons each had five or six ships, each mounting at least fifty guns, and only two out of the total of thirty-seven carried less than thirty guns.

It soon became clear, however, that there was little prospect of a fleet action. As the blockade dragged on, the English ambassador in Lisbon wrote home in frustration: 'The Spaniard uses his buckler more than his sword. In the Dutch war we were sure of an enemy that would fight, besides good prizes to help pay charges: but the Spaniard will neither fight nor trade.'[12]

The previous year's Plate Fleet had reached port safely during

Blake's absence, and it was clear that the defences of Cadiz were too strong to attack. Mountagu sailed on into the Mediterranean to look at the possibilities of capturing Gibraltar. However, he reported home that the project would require 4–5,000 regular troops, and the idea was quietly shelved.

In May the fleet was sent to Lisbon to pressurise the Portuguese government into ratifying a treaty which had been imposed by the English Navy in 1654, and to establish a supply base in the port.

The blockade of Cadiz was maintained throughout the summer of 1656, though with no prospect of the Spanish fleet, which included 20 galleons but was crippled through lack of naval stores, coming out to fight, Blake's captains could only relieve the monotony with small-scale actions. On 12 June Captain Edward Blagg was sent with a squadron of eight ships, headed by the *Fairfax* (fifty-six), to raid the Galician and Biscayan ports on the northern coast of Spain. Early on 24 June, *Fairfax*, *Centurion* and the frigate *Beaver*, towed by boats in a light breeze, entered the port of Vigo, taking the Spaniards by surprise. Two Ostend privateers and an English prize tried, too late, to retreat upriver. All three were boarded, the privateers blown up with gunpowder and the prize set ablaze.

In the Mediterranean a second detachment bombarded Malaga, and burnt five ships anchored in its roads. Spanish shore battery crews fled under the weight of the English bombardment, and landing parties went ashore to spike their guns.

Late in the summer Blake withdrew the bulk of his squadron to Lisbon in order to take on water, though some accounts suggest that he deliberately drew off the majority of his ships in order to lure the Spaniards to sea. However, he left a detachment of eight ships under the command of Captain Richard Stayner to maintain the watch on Cadiz. On 8 September Stayner was forced off-station by a gale, and his lookouts spotted eight Spanish ships between five and six leagues to the west of Cadiz. They were part of the long-awaited Plate Fleet, which, knowing the desperate need of the Spanish government for its cargo, had taken the risk of sailing without an escort.

The Spanish squadron included two large galleons, two store-ships, three merchantmen and a Portuguese prize. The Spaniards expected no danger, as they had been told by the captain of the

Portuguese ship that Blake's squadron had been driven away from
Cadiz by the Spanish fleet a month earlier. They initially mistook
Stayner's ships for large fishing vessels, and remained unsuspecting
as darkness fell.

During the night the Spanish vessels, believing themselves to be
safe so near to home, maintained touch with each other with
lanterns and signal guns, so enabling the English squadron to keep
track of them.

As dawn broke, the English ships closed in for the kill. Stayner,
aboard his flagship, *Speaker*, gave the Spanish 'vice-admiral' a
broadside and then went on to attack the 'rear-admiral', whose ship
was taken after a sharp fight. The *Bridgwater* then took up the
attack on the Spanish 'vice-admiral', which, after a six-hour
engagement, was set ablaze by her own crew as they took to their
boats. Only about ninety of them survived. The Governor of Peru,
who was on board, refused to leave his unconscious wife and
daughter, and died with them, although his two young sons were
rescued by the English. *Bridgwater* herself narrowly escaped being
caught up in the inferno.

The frigate *Plymouth* engaged a large merchant ship, which
caught fire and sank with 600,000 pieces of eight still on board.
However, the *Tredagh* provided some compensation for the
English by taking a richly laden merchant ship. Only two of
the Spanish ships escaped by running themselves aground. Taking
his prizes into Lagos Bay, Stayner found that the Spanish 'rear-
admiral' was carrying a cargo of forty-five tons of silver, 700 chests
of indigo and 700 chests of sugar.[13]

Though inevitably some of the booty stuck to the fingers of
Stayner and his men, (out of goods and money worth an estimated
£200,000, only about £45,000 actually reached England) the prizes
gave the English Government a much-needed boost in morale.
Cromwell's Secretary and intelligence chief, John Thurloe, was
angry at the amount of treasure which had been misappropriated:
'a private captain, they say, had got to his share £60,000 and many
private mariners £10,000 a man, and this is so universal amongst
seamen, and taken in the heat of fight, that it is not possible to get
it again, nor any part of it.'[14] Thurloe, although undoubtedly
correct in his accusations, probably exaggerated the amount of
treasure captured and indeed the quantity siphoned off by the

seamen. More importantly, the two young sons of the Governor of Peru had been placed in Mountagu's charge, and one of them innocently informed his amiable guardian that the remainder of the Plate Fleet, including galleons carrying several million pounds of bullion, intended to make the voyage home in December via the Canary Islands.

Santa Cruz

News of the Spanish intentions galvanised Cromwell, who rescinded earlier orders that the larger ships of the blockading squadron should return home for the winter. 'There can be nothing of more consequence than to intercept the Spanish fleet going to and coming from the West Indies, for which end our purpose is to keep a fleet in those seas, which may be able to fight with any fleet the Spaniards can set forth, as the most effectual means to prosecute that war.'[15] Capturing the Plate Fleet would be a huge political boost for the Lord Protector; not only would its cargo pay off many of the Commonwealth's debts, but some of the international prestige lost as a result of the debacle of the Western Design would be restored.

Cromwell was never particularly knowledgeable about naval matters, and undoubtedly took an over-optimistic view of the profits which the war with Spain might still bring. He failed, for example, to understand that most of Spain's overseas trade was now carried in foreign-owned ships, so that, as Mountagu pointed out: 'we cannot hinder unless we should fight with all the world.'

Although Cromwell now ordered Blake to be reinforced with two 2nd rates, *George* and *Unicorn*, and four 4th rate ships, Mountagu, with the 3rd rates *Naseby*, *Andrew*, *Resolution* and *Rainbow*, together with seven damaged ships and prizes, was ordered back to England, where renewed Leveller plotting with which Lawson was involved, and a brief clash with the Dutch, made the presence of a reliable senior naval officer imperative. The sick Badiley accompanied Mountagu, and was replaced as Vice-Admiral by Nehemiah Bourne, Stayner stepping up as Rear-Admiral.

Throughout the winter Blake maintained the blockade of Cadiz. The old admiral was by now seriously ill, suffering from 'the stone' and an eruption of his old thigh wound suffered at Portland against the Dutch, and was clinging to life on a diet of broth and jellies. By the beginning of 1657, his ships were suffering increasing damage from the weather. Blake waited with increasing urgency for news of the Plate Fleet. It seemed overwhelmingly likely that the Canary Islands, with their fine natural and strongly defended harbour of Santa Cruz, would be the refuge of the Plate Fleet while it waited for definite intelligence of the situation off the Spanish coast.

Blake knew that in those circumstances he would have to move quickly if he were to deal with the Plate Fleet at Santa Cruz before his absence from Cadiz allowed the main Spanish fleet to put to sea.

On 11 March 1657 he warned Cromwell that his ships were ill-supplied and becoming increasingly unseaworthy, and of the dangers of keeping them on station for so long in what was for the period a very rare example of a winter blockade, 'wherein though the Lord hath most wonderfully and mercifully preserved us hitherto, I know no rule to tempt Him.'[16]

On 19 February Blake had been told by a former English naval officer who had entered the merchant service after losing a hand in the war against the Dutch that he had sighted the Plate Fleet heading for Tenerife and the harbour of Santa Cruz. Bourne and Stayner urged Blake to fit out eight ships with six months' supplies by stripping the remainder of the fleet, and send them after the Plate Fleet. However, Blake rejected the idea of splitting his force in the face of the Spanish fleet in Cadiz. He was also concerned that a Dutch squadron under his old opponent Ruyter, which had appeared in the area, might be persuaded or hired by the Spaniards to escort home the Plate ships. In fact Ruyter's presence was coincidental, as he was actually on his way to the Mediterranean to negotiate with the rulers of the Barbary Coast.

More to the point, Blake also feared that a detached squadron might fail to intercept the Plate Fleet or might not be strong enough to tackle it successfully.

For a further six weeks the English squadron remained on station off Cadiz. On 28 March a resupply convoy at last reached Blake, and a fortnight later an English privateer confirmed that the Plate Fleet was still at anchor in the harbour of Santa Cruz. Blake had also learned that the Spanish squadron in Cadiz remained unfit for sea because of a lack of naval stores, and he decided to take the risk of immediate action.

On 14 April, leaving only two ships on watch off the Spanish coast, Blake set sail for the Canaries with his remaining twenty-three ships. Blake was by now exhausted, and in constant pain, none of which improved his always abrasive personality, and his relations with his captains were even worse than normal. Stayner once again proposed that a squadron of picked frigates should make an immediate surprise attack. Possibly because he feared Stayner would place the chance of booty above the greater good, Blake angrily rejected this plan. Instead he proposed an attack plan which was basically a repeat of that employed successfully at Porto Farina. His sullen captains, possibly realising that their views would be rejected anyway, had no suggestions to make at the council of war, other than to request that Stayner should lead the assault.

Arriving off Santa Cruz on Saturday 20 April, Blake decided that he would attack the harbour two days later on Monday 28 April. The assault, whose details may have been devised by Stayner, would be made by twelve ships, four from each of Blake's divisions, under Stayner's overall command. The vessels which were to take part, all 3rd or 4th rates, were: *Speaker, Lyme, Lambert, Nonsuch, Bridgwater, Plymouth, Worcester, Centurion, Winceby, Newcastle, Foresight* and *Madeline*.

The Spaniards had sighted Blake's fleet on the day he arrived off the Canaries, but, confident in the defences of the harbour, were unconcerned. An English prisoner reported that they 'laughed our intentions to scorn, and were for Spaniards very jolly.' A Flemish captain who had served against Blake during the Dutch war was much less confident of success, and decided to put to sea in an attempt to escape. The Spanish admiral, Don Diego de Diagues, commented scornfully: 'Begone if you will, and let Blake come in if he dares.'[17]

The Spaniards had some grounds to feel confident. The bay formed a shallow semi-circle, with the town of Santa Cruz in the middle. A rocky shoreline would make any landing attempt highly dangerous, and the roadstead in front of the town was partly protected by a mole. The shore defences appeared formidable, consisting of a line of seven forts running northwards from the port, linked by a triple line of entrenchments joining them to the forty-gun St Phillip Castle on the north side of the town of Santa Cruz. Nine of Diagues's smaller galleons were anchored in a line parallel but at right angles to the shore, with their bows pointing outwards. They were covered on one side by the guns of the forts, and by seven larger galleons of between 1–1,200 tons, which were anchored further out in the harbour just within the five-fathom line, and which were deployed in line ahead, with their broadsides facing out to sea. All of the treasure was safely ashore, and the Spanish commander was confident that he could not only withstand Blake's attack, but probably inflict a serious defeat on him in the process.

Blake's plan was for Stayner's squadron to enter the harbour and engage the galleons while he and the larger ships of the English squadron remained off-shore to act as a reserve.

The winds proved unfavourable for the attack to be made as planned on Monday, but next morning the English assault began. Stayner ordered all of his ships to hold their stations, and not to open fire until they had dropped anchor in line. But the captains of *Plymouth* and *Nantwich*, who had apparently not been present at the council of war, misunderstood or were ignorant of Stayner's orders. *Plymouth* opened fire prematurely, while *Nantwich*, which had not even been intended to take part in the attack, caused confusion by forcing its way into the English line.

Stayner, meanwhile, was leading his squadron down the outside of the main Spanish line, leaving two of the largest enemy ships for the moment unmolested, as they were shielding the English ships from the fire of St Phillip Fort. He described later how:

> I stood upon the forecastle of our ship to seek a good berth for the better doing of our work; I perceived I could get in between the Admiral and the Vice Admiral, to our great advantage, which I did – we went as near as we could with safety, and were within pistol-shot of the Admiral and the Vice Admiral, and a little more of the Rear, they were all great ships that rode near the Castle – the Spaniards firing so thick from the ships and shore put us into some confusion for want of due care in the commanders to prevent it.[18]

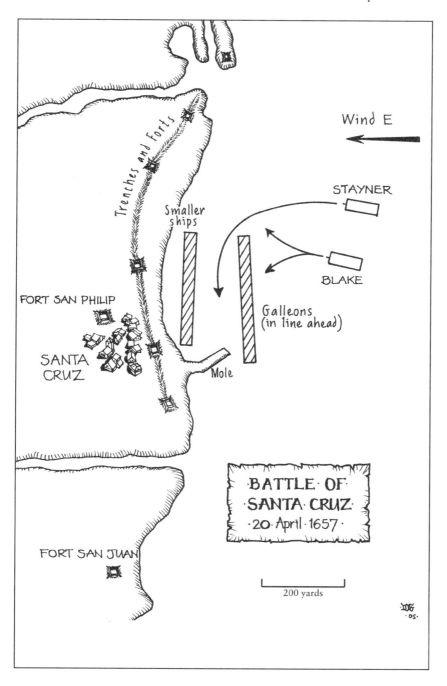

Wind E

STAYNER

BLAKE

Trenches and Forts

Smaller ships

FORT SAN PHILIP

SANTA CRUZ

Mole

Galleons (in line ahead)

FORT SAN JUAN

BATTLE OF SANTA CRUZ
·20·April·1657·

200 yards

The lack of any surviving contemporary chart makes the action at Santa Cruz particularly difficult to reconstruct, and there are considerable differences in some of the modern attempts to do so. In outline, however, a furious cannonade took place, in which the Spanish shore batteries were hindered firstly by the line of small galleons anchored close in shore, and then by the dense clouds of black powder smoke blown inshore by the wind. At about noon Blake and his heavier ships, fearing that the destruction of some of the Spanish ships was exposing Stayner's squadron to increased enemy fire, closed in to engage the shore defences.

Stayner described how he fired repeated broadsides into the Spanish 'admiral' and 'vice-admiral', causing them to blow up, then warped his ships back out to sea under heavy fire. However, Thomas Lurting, boatswain of the *Bristol*, gave a different version of events. His ship joined in the later stages of the action, and either Blake or Stayning ordered *Bristol*'s captain to squeeze into the English firing line wherever he could find space, and his ship found herself ' a half cable-length' (about 300 feet) from the Spanish 'vice-admiral' and a similar distance from the 'admiral'. His captain ordered Lurting to steer *Bristol* closer to the 'vice-admiral' with a view to boarding, but the Spaniard in his turn veered away, having slipped her stern anchor. *Bristol* now moored with a spring to her anchor, allowing her to be held steady in the current while she fired into the 'vice-admiral'. Her twenty-eight guns fired two broadsides and one shot penetrated the magazine of the Spanish vessel, which blew up, 'not a man escaping.' A third broadside was directed against the 'admiral', which also took fire, her crew leaping overboard before the ship blew up, leaving only her elaborately decorated stern drifting forlornly towards the shore.

Lurting now had a moment to look about him:

> I saw three galleons on shore, all on board one another,
> one of them along the shore, and one across her hawse,
> and the other cross her stern, about a musket shot from
> our ships, and there was a castle on one side of them and
> a breastwork on the other, with about fifty or sixty men
> in it, as was supposed, and the galleons lay about half a
> cable's length from the castle, and the same distance

from the breastwork, about fifty yards from the shore. Then I took the pinnace and two men with me, and was going to set them on fire; but the captain saw me, and called me back, and sent five men more with me, and on our setting forward our ship fired a gun, and in the smoke thereof we got on board the galleon, receiving no harm (the Spaniards having left them), and I instantly set one of them on fire, which burnt the other two galleons. And when we could stay no longer by reason of the fire, and our ship's crew not being, as formerly, mindful of us to fire some guns, that in the smoke thereof we had retired from the galleons without the discovery of any from the breastwork . . . the breastwork having full sight of us, discharged a volley of about fifty or sixty small shot, and killed two of our men, and shot a third in the back, and I sat close to one that was killed between him and the shore, and received no harm.[19]

Despite their instructions, Stayning and his captains lingered in the hopes of salvaging some plunder, and an increasingly furious Blake had to repeat his signal to withdraw before it was reluctantly heeded at about 2pm. Lurting remembered:

It remained to complete this Mercy, that our own ships should come off well, wherein the greatest hazard and difficulty lay; for some riding near into the Shore, and being sorely maimed did require to be warped off, others when we came to weigh, drove with the wind, all the while blowing right into the Bay, and one of our best Frigates struck. The Enemy in the meantime supplied fresh men into his Forts for those we had killed and beaten out, in the heat of the Action, and from them and the Castle continued playing upon us, till about seven of the clock at night every Ship and Vessel belonging to the Fleet, were by the good hand of God got safely out of command.[20]

The badly damaged frigate mentioned by Lurting was Stayner's flagship, the *Speaker*, and her commander described how:

> We had holes between wind and water four or five foot
> long and three or five foot broad, that we had no shift to
> keep her from sinking but by nailing hides over the holes,
> and nail butt staves along the sides of the holes, for we
> had eight or nine foot water in the ship, that our pumps
> and bailing would hardly keep her free.[21]

Speaker was taken in tow by Robert Bourne's *Swiftsure*, which
for some unknown reason then cast off Stayner's ship while still
within range of the enemy guns. Stayner complained that: 'They
paid us extremely; so we rid till the sun went down, then the wind
came off shore, and we set those pieces of sail we had, and cut away
her anchor.'[22] Scarcely had Stayner rejoined the rest of the fleet than
his battered masts fell down.

Although once again Cromwell's hopes of capturing treasure had
proved fruitless, the action at Santa Cruz was regarded as a major
victory, as well as being Blake's greatest exploit. For the loss of fifty
dead and 120 wounded, he had penetrated one of Spain's most
strongly defended harbours, burnt twelve enemy ships and taken
five others which Blake eventually had destroyed.

The victory boosted the image of Cromwell's Navy throughout
Europe. Even that arch-Royalist, Edward, Earl of Clarendon, paid
tribute, writing:

> The whole action was so miraculous that all men who
> knew the place concluded that no sober men, with what
> courage soever endowed, would ever undertake it; and
> they could hardly persuade themselves to believe what
> they had done; whilst the Spaniards comforted them-
> selves with the belief that they were devils, not men who
> had destroyed them in such a manner.[23]

In England Parliament called a Day of Thanksgiving; Blake was
voted a jewel worth £500 and Stayner promised a knighthood.
Although the hoped-for treasure had not materialised, some of the
Santa Cruz plate was captured later when a Dutch ship attempting
to run it into Cadiz was wrecked. In any event, with fourteen
English ships under Captain John Stokes still lurking off Cadiz,
the bulk of the plate remained marooned at Santa Cruz, and

the Spanish war effort was crippled as a result. The most immediate consequence was that the Spanish government was unable to pay the troops who had just commenced an invasion of Portugal. The invasion collapsed, and the Portuguese independence was for the moment secured.

Blake and his squadron resumed their blockade of Cadiz, but with the destruction of the Plate Fleet and the end of the Western Design its main purpose was at an end, and on 22 June Blake was ordered to return to England.

Robert Blake was now dying, and on 7 August, as his flagship entered Plymouth Sound, he breathed his last. Although Cromwell had always regarded Blake with some unease, he recognised the debt owed to him by the English Republic, and afforded the old sailor a state funeral in Westminster Abbey. John Thurloe said of Blake: 'a very worthy and brave man is gone and a faithful servant of his Highness.'[24]

Though Blake is often ranked alongside Nelson, the comparison is not entirely accurate. Blake, unlike Nelson, did not become involved in naval warfare until middle age, and had to learn as he went along. He was fortunate that his early encounters, against the Royalists and their Portuguese allies, did not pit him against opponents of the first quality who would have ruthlessly exploited his mistakes.

Blake's limitations and lack of experience were more evident during the Dutch War, when he faced some of the finest fighting seamen of the age. He never learnt very much about naval tactics, and repeatedly found himself surprised, or with his fleet divided, and close to disaster. While it is true that Blake was unfit for action during the closing stages of the war, it would be fair to comment that the lion's share of credit for England's eventual victory rested with George Monck and his development of new and effective tactics to capitalise on English superiority in gunnery.

Blake reached the pinnacle of his naval career during the war with Spain. He was the first English naval commander to demonstrate the possibility of maintaining a long-distance blockade throughout the year, at a time when most naval operations were suspended in winter. His victories at Porto Farina and Santa Cruz displayed excellent planning and assessment of risk, combined with a growing maturity in command. Although Blake's intolerant and autocratic nature gave him problems in his relationships with colleagues and subordinates throughout his career, by its closing stages he was demonstrating a confidence and sureness of touch which made these failings less important.

Campaign in Flanders
The victory at Santa Cruz gave Cromwell momentary cause for optimism regarding a conflict which otherwise was not going as he had hoped. By the summer of 1657, indeed, it was clear that the Lord Protector's overall strategy had failed. Spanish privateers based in Flanders, and especially at Dunkirk, were doing serious damage to English trade. During the course of the war between 1,500–2,000 English merchant ships were taken by the Spaniards, and mostly sold to the Dutch to replace the 1,200–700 ships they had lost to English privateers in the earlier war. The bulk of Spanish maritime trade was now carried by Dutch ships, which Cromwell dared not attack without provoking a new war with the Netherlands.

It was the lack of success in his maritime war with Spain which in March 1657 led Cromwell to conclude a full alliance with France, which in turn involved him in a major land campaign in Flanders. The alliance provided for a joint attack on Gravelines, Mardyke and Dunkirk, with the latter two places to be awarded to England.

Mountagu, on his return from Cadiz, was given command of the home fleet, whose main task was now to support the Army's operations in Flanders. A detachment under Vice-Admiral Goodwin attempted to blockade Dunkirk and Ostend. Mountagu's principal task was to supply the 6,000 English troops operating with the French, a mixture of veteran regulars and volunteers under Sir John Reynolds and Major-General Thomas Morgan, to assist them in reducing the Spanish coastal garrison of Mardyke. The French, however, were more interested in capturing Spain's inland fortresses, and left the English to struggle on with inadequate resources before Mardyke.

Within less than three months, disease and desertion had reduced English strength by a third, and many others were sick and unfit for duty, quartered as they were in damp and unhealthy conditions. The Navy could do little to assist, but fortunately General

Lockhart, the English Ambassador in Paris, managed to persuade Turenne, the leading French commander, to provide some assistance at Mardyke. Turenne appeared before Mardyke on 4 September, and the garrison fell four days later, its reduction assisted by a bombardment by the English fleet.

However, this success was not in itself decisive; Mardyke was merely the outpost of the much stronger fortress of Dunkirk, three miles away, which now became the main objective of the campaign. The English commanders wished to launch an immediate assault on Dunkirk; the more cautious Turenne wished to safeguard his rear by first capturing lightly-held Gravelines. By the end of the year relations were strained, with Turenne blaming the difficulties encountered by the English on their own laziness and incompetence. But the Spaniards thwarted both schemes by opening the dykes to flood the low-lying countryside, making an attack so late in the campaigning season impossible. The English were left in precarious possession of Mardyke, which was too small to contain a sufficiently strong garrison to protect it against attack from Dunkirk.

The open sandy terrain of the locality made it difficult to erect either stronger defences or housing for the troops, and there was a steady stream of desertions as morale slumped. Even the English commander, General Reynolds, was under suspicion of disloyalty following a clandestine meeting with the Duke of York. Called home to account for his actions, Reynolds was drowned en route.

Sir William Lockhart, his successor, was both more capable and on better terms with the French. The lingering threat of a Spanish-assisted invasion of England by Charles II's Royalist army in exile was removed in February when Vice-Admiral John Lawson with twelve frigates appeared before Dunkirk and destroyed two and captured three others of a flotilla of Dutch transports hired by the Spaniards to transport the Royalist troops. With his army brought up to strength on 4 June Lockhart was present with Turenne at the crushing Spanish defeat at the Battle of the Dunes, which at last forced the surrender of Dunkirk.

But the victory brought little respite for English merchant shipping, as the privateers transferred their operations to Ostend. Cromwell died on 3 September 1658. Even Clarendon admitted that 'his greatness at home was but a shadow of the glory he had abroad. It was hard to discover which feared him more, France, Spain, or the Low Countries, where his friendship was current at the value he put upon it.'[25] But with Cromwell's death, the English Republic was facing an increasingly uncertain future.

Chapter 8
Restoration

'. . . the King enjoys his own again . . .'
(Royalist song)

It is sometimes assumed that following the death of Oliver Cromwell the restoration of the monarchy in England was an inevitable, if prolonged, outcome. In fact for some eighteen months it was far from certain, and the feverish political debates and manoeuvrings which filled this time led to several changes of regime, and could have ended in rule by the Army, by some form of Parliamentary system, or by a hereditary Protectorate.[1]

The Navy would play an important role in deciding the outcome of these events. Its own attitude was uncertain, not least because its two most influential figures, Edward Mountagu and John Lawson, had sharply differing views on the future of the English Republic. Although he remained enigmatic until almost the end, for Mountagu the Restoration of Charles II was always the preferred outcome following the death of Oliver Cromwell. For Lawson, however, it would represent the defeat of the political ideals which he had held dear, but was ultimately a lesser evil than the alternative of naked military rule.

Following the accession of Cromwell's son, Richard, as Protector, Mountagu became one of the leading figures in his regime. His rise during the 1650s had been rapid; as well as being a General at Sea, Mountagu was also a member of the 'Other House' which had replaced the House of Lords in Parliament, and had been promised by Oliver the colonelcy of a regiment of horse.

He became a close confidante of Richard Cromwell, whose moderate views Mountagu found attractive. However, the majority of senior army officers, headed by Lambert, opposed Richard, and as a result Mountagu found himself increasingly isolated.

The tense political atmosphere in the months following Oliver's death, during which his son's Protectorate tottered towards its fall, meant that personal and ideological clashes were inevitable, with mutual accusations of disloyalty hurled between Mountagu and the largely republican military leadership, who were eager to challenge Richard Cromwell's nominal control of the armed forces.

The Royalists, eyeing the political ferment from exile, believed the time ripe to sound out senior naval commanders with a view to gaining their support, but were firmly rebuffed. However, in April 1659 Richard Cromwell's rule foundered amid a continuing struggle between Parliament and Army, and with the remnants of the old Rump Parliament recalled to office, by the end of the summer Richard had retired into private life.

The Navy had remained aloof from the political infighting, but the Rump, aware of the hostility of large sections of the Army, attempted to woo the Navy by offering to pay off the seamen's long-standing pay arrears, although it in fact proved unable to do so.

Some of the more radical naval officers had been glad to see the Protectorate overthrown; to Commissioner Nehemiah Bourne Richard Cromwell's removal was 'the clearest hand of God that ever was seen.'[2] However, only the naval squadron in the Downs commanded by his brother, Vice-Admiral Robert Bourne, seems to have actively come out in support of the change. Mountagu was with a squadron despatched to the Baltic to observe the ongoing struggle between Denmark and Sweden when news of Richard's fall reached him. A council of war with his captains proved that most of them were unenthusiastic both with the new order or in making any direct challenge to it. Though Mountagu agreed to receive civilian commissioners despatched to the fleet by the Rump (largely to keep an eye on his activities), he also insisted that his fleet should remain at sea, in order, so its commander claimed, to guard against any hostile action by the Dutch.

At the end of August Mountagu commented to the Speaker of

the newly returned House of Commons that Richard's removal filled him with 'fears and sorrow',[3] but he continued to keep a low profile, while emphasising that his loyalty was primarily to the English nation rather than to Parliament. The Rump was naturally deeply distrustful of Mountagu, but could not risk a direct confrontation with him at this stage. Instead attempts were made to appoint trusted officers to key commands, and John Lawson, a known opponent of the Protectorate who remained highly popular with the ordinary seamen, was by the end of July put in command of a squadron of sixteen ships with orders to cruise off the coast of Flanders, nominally to guard against activity by the Republic's increasingly hostile European neighbours, but also to counter any unfriendly action against the regime by Mountagu.

The Rump found itself in a situation frighteningly reminiscent of that which had faced its infant predecessor in 1649. But unlike the bellicose reaction of a decade ago, the Rump was unwilling to become involved in any new hostilities. The nominally continuing war with Spain was quietly allowed to die down, while efforts were made to conciliate the Dutch.

In fact the potential enemy most feared by the Rump was Edward Mountagu. His relations with the Commissioners despatched to join him in the Baltic were strained from the beginning, the latter suspecting Mountagu of secret contacts with the Royalists. Mountagu was indeed approached by Thomas Whetstone, a former naval officer now acting as an emissary from Charles II. But Mountagu rightly suspected that his enemies were looking for an excuse to remove him from command, and refused to be drawn by Royalist blandishments, going no further than to send a personal message of goodwill to Charles.

Mountagu was aware that there were no immediate prospects of winning over the great majority of his officers and men to the idea of supporting a restoration of the monarchy, and he knew that for the present the Army would block any such attempt. Further evidence of this came during August 1659, when a series of pro-Royalist uprisings were put down with relative ease by the military. Mountagu's own attitude to these events was extremely ambivalent. No naval units joined in the rebellion, but Mountagu and his squadron suddenly left the Danish Sound on 24 August and returned home. Mountagu gave as his reason shortage of supplies, and no clear evidence of his deeper intentions survives. He certainly knew of the planned uprisings, and probably intended his fleet to be on hand to support the risings if they succeeded in overthrowing the Rump.

Mountagu's action convinced the Rump that his loyalty was doubtful at best, and three commissioners were despatched to the fleet's anchorage in Southwold Bay to question its commander. But hard evidence of Mountagu's intent remained elusive, and he was eventually allowed to quit his command and retire to his country estates.

Although it had succeeded in removing one of its most serious potential opponents from active command, the Rump's deeper problems remained. It was still unable to settle the pay arrears of its soldiers and seamen, and both sailors and dockyard workers were becoming increasingly discontented. The fleet required one and a quarter million pounds to maintain it until the end of the year, but less than half this amount was actually available, while lack of naval stores meant that the whole of the fleet was threatened with gradual disintegration.

It was in this state of increasing governmental breakdown that in October the Rump was overthrown by a hardline republican military regime, which set up a Committee of Safety to run the country. This proved from the beginning to be deeply unpopular and divisive, and met with widespread opposition, both from within the Army and from the majority of the civilian population, but especially from the Navy, where that long-standing supporter of parliamentary rule, John Lawson, and, as yet more circumspectly and ambivalently, former General at Sea George Monck, still commanding military forces in Scotland, were serious potential opponents.

From the beginning the bulk of the Navy remained aloof from the new regime, which had no obvious supporter within the fleet able to rally resistance to Lawson. However, with many ships absent on convoy duty, Lawson was for the moment equally unready to take action, and remained quietly at his anchorage in the Downs, nursing his own and his seamen's resentments, and biding his time while the crisis between Monck and the Committee of Safety deepened.

While a few individual naval officers appeared willing to give grudging support to the military regime rather than face the prospect of renewed civil war, they were very much in the minority, and as winter approached opposition to the military was growing rapidly, coming to a head when the dockyard at Plymouth, and the ships in it, declared for a restored Rump. The naval threat presented by this in fact dwindled rapidly, as most of the crews quit their ships in order to march to London to demand their arrears of pay, which rendered their ships for the moment useless to Rump supporters.

However, the unrest served to trigger action by Lawson. On 9 December he told an emissary from General John Fleetwood that only a restoration of parliamentary rule would defuse the crisis, and four days later, having received a number of messages of support from the Speaker of the Rump Parliament, Lawson made a public declaration in its support, joined with demands for sweeping social and political reforms. These, however, met with little support from the civic leaders in London to whom they were addressed, and on 14 December Lawson upped the stake by leading his fleet into the Thames in a clear challenge to the authorities in the capital and to the regime itself.

The Committee of Safety knew that Lawson could blockade London, with massive economic and political effect, and on 17 December sent envoys, headed by the veteran Admiralty Commissioner Sir Henry Vane, to hold talks with Lawson. The latter remained obdurate in his demands, and with the failure of talks the nerve of the majority of the Army rulers collapsed. With both troops and civilians across the country demanding a return of Parliament, and Lawson openly blockading the Thames in their support, on 26 December the members of the Rump Parliament resumed their seats at Westminster.

For several weeks, however, they remained reliant on Lawson to secure their position. On 2 January 1660 both Lawson and Monck, respectively the naval and military pillars of an uncertain regime, were elected to the new ruling Council of State and voted lands worth £500 a year, as well as joint command of the fleet. By now it was widely expected that the political uncertainty would eventually be resolved by a restoration of the monarchy, and the Royalists continued to put out feelers to leading naval and military figures. Lawson, however, as a Republican of long conviction, remained seemingly obdurate, and it was clear that nothing would be resolved until Monck eventually showed his hand.

Lawson was not the only leading figure to have been convinced by Monck's professed devotion to the Rump, perhaps not surprisingly, as many of Monck's own political thought processes remain unclear,[4] and it certainly came as a shock to the admiral when the long-excluded moderate MPs were recalled. Lawson hesitated, but in the end made no attempt to oppose these developments. He probably hoped that the outcome might still be either a republic or at worst a constitutional monarchy, and also realised that in practice there was very little that he could do to oppose moves which had such widespread popular support.

Lawson can have gained little comfort when on 2 March Monck and Edward Mountagu were named joint Generals at Sea by Parliament, with Lawson himself demoted once more to Vice-Admiral. Lawson quietly submitted to the inevitable. By now, indeed, feelings of self-preservation may have been at the forefront of his thoughts. By April he had resigned himself to the return of the monarchy.

Mountagu, on his reappointment as General at Sea, was unclear how far his authority would be recognised, and in this Lawson's support proved decisive. With his assistance Mountagu was able to remodel the officer corps intended for the Summer Guard that year to ensure that his supporters occupied key posts. He had found that there were still a significant number of prospective malcontents in place, but he was now able to remove the majority of them. Of the twenty-one captains under Lawson, all but seven had been removed by the time Mountagu took the fleet over to Holland to collect the king in May.

After the relatively moderate Declaration of Breda issued by the king on 1 May 1660, the Convention government in England declared Charles II restored. None of the officers under Mountagu's command actively opposed the Restoration, though Pepys, who accompanied the fleet over to Holland, noted that 'not one man seemed to say no to it, though I am confident many in their hearts were against it.'[5] The ordinary seamen, however, proved to be strongly pro-monarchist in the coming days.

The ships selected to meet the king and the rest of the royal family and bring them over to England were prepared with care. Some accounts suggest that the figurehead of Oliver Cromwell was temporarily removed from the bows of the fleet flagship, *Naseby*, although Pepys recorded its removal in 1663 when he noted: 'God knows it is even the throwing away of £10,000 of the King's purse.'[6]

On 8 May Charles II was officially declared king. Undoubtedly its parlous financial condition had a significant role in the Navy's decision to support the Restoration. The ordinary seamen were desperate for some assurance of stability, while the officers on the whole were too demoralised and disillusioned to mount any opposition. A minority, however, remained defiant for as long as possible. Captain William Barker of the *Lichfield* captured a privateer belonging to James, Duke of York, in mid-May. Mountagu also had well-founded doubts of the loyalty of some junior officers, and there were fears of an assassination attempt on the royal family during their voyage back to England. However, if only because Charles had joined the long list of those in authority who had promised them their arrears of pay, the ordinary seamen were relatively enthusiastic about his return.

Mountagu and his squadron set sail on 12 May, and arrived at the Dutch port of Scheveningen two days later. On 23 May Charles and other members of the royal family embarked, the State's Navy ensign was replaced with the royal banner, and, in a sign of things to come, a number of politically contentiously named ships were rechristened. *Naseby* became *Royal Charles*, while *Marston Moor* and *Dunbar* were renamed *James* and *Henry* after the king's brothers.

On 25 May the royal party landed safely at Dover. Mountagu reaped the first rewards for his support when he was made Earl of Sandwich and awarded the Order of the Garter, as well as numerous public offices. Within a few months Pepys was describing the new Earl of Sandwich as 'the perfect courtier'.

Charles now faced the task of turning the Commonwealth State's Navy into the Royal Navy, a task made potentially more difficult as its officer corps still retained many former Army personnel among whom republican and radical sentiments had always been strong. In July a Navy Board, presided over by the Duke of York, was set up to replace the Admiralty and Navy Commissioners. Among its members were William Penn and the old

Parliamentarian turned Royalist, Sir William Batten. Most of the Navy's permanent officials proved ready enough to continue working under the new regime. There was some weeding out of known Radicals and Anabaptists among dockyard workers, but many were kept on, including the famous shipbuilding Pett dynasty, who had always proved suitably adaptable in their loyalties.

Officers were expected to swear oaths of supremacy and allegiance, which served to remove or silence some of the more radical elements, with less than one percent actually refusing to take the oath.

These initial checks were followed by a much more intensive investigation, which led to the dismissal of such recalcitrants as captains King, said to be 'ashamed of his own name,'and Coppin, 'an old king hater'. Warrant officers and chaplains were also investigated, many of the latter, as might be expected, proving unsatisfactory.

The other most urgent task for the new Government was to arrange for the paying off of many of the armed forces, which were much too large for the needs of the new regime, and whose continued existence was a potential threat. So far as the Army, the most urgent possible danger, was concerned, the task had almost been completed by the end of 1660. It took longer for the Navy. There were about 109 ships in commission in May 1660, of which only eight had been paid off by the end of the year. Over £3,400 would be needed to clear all of the arrears of pay owed to the seamen, and as it became apparent that their expectations would not be speedily met, there were frequent outbreaks of disorder among the crews. But once the immediate needs of the Army had been dealt with, the task proceeded at a faster rate, and by the end of July 1661 Cromwell's Navy was effectively no more.

However, an effective officer corps was needed for the new Royal Navy. The most immediate problem was that most of the experienced and suitable men had served under the Commonwealth, although there were also a large number of former Royalist privateer commanders demanding employment as recompense for the sacrifices which their loyalty had cost them. Both categories had to be employed, and the task of reconciling these formerly bitterly opposed factions in one unified command in a much smaller peacetime Navy might potentially have been much more difficult than actually proved to be the case.

Over the next few years steady progress was made. Not re-employed were thirty-six Commonwealth captains and lieutenants commissioned in the spring of 1660, and many of the ninety-one newcomers commissioned in 1661–3 were former Royalists. Mountagu, probably to his surprise, found difficulty in maintaining his former pre-eminence. The plain-speaking James, Duke of York, favoured unpolished experienced seadogs to courtier commanders, and, perhaps to his own amazement, the blunt, vastly experienced John Lawson rose steadily in James's estimation, a classic example of poacher turned gamekeeper.

Much less fortunate was one of the principal architects of Cromwell's Navy, Sir Henry Vane. Exempted from pardon, he was convicted of treason and excuted on 14 June 1662. Charles II paid reluctant tribute to Vane's ability when he commented before his trial that he was 'too dangerous a man to live if he could be put honestly out of the way.'

Of the many ex-Commonwealth officers who found themselves unable or unwilling to serve in the new Royal Navy, some entered or re-entered the merchant service while others sought fresh beginnings in the colonies of the New World. Some, stumbling along the fringes of legality, became privateers. Others accepted the inevitable and stayed on in the Navy, albeit at a lower rank. In many cases the officers of Cromwell's Navy met with considerable hostility from some of their new Cavalier colleagues. Particularly noted for his animosity was Sir John Mennes, now Comptroller of the Navy, who had commanded the fleet of King Charles I in the days before the Civil War, and who particularly disliked Mountagu. However, the Duke of York appreciated the value of the vast store of experience represented by Cromwell's veterans, despite fears that radicals among them might attempt to suborn the fleet.

Indeed, a few ex-naval personnel were involved in the various republican-motivated plots which marked the early years of the Restoration, and there remained some underlying discontent in the fleet, which came to the surface in drunken brawls when tongues ran loose.

The approach of renewed conflict with the Dutch in 1664

necessitated a massive re-expansion of the fleet, and led to concerns regarding the loyalties of some of those who had to be re-employed. Command was shared by the old Generals at Sea, Mountagu (now Earl of Sandwich) and Monck (now Duke of Albemarle) serving alongside their former most inveterate foe, Prince Rupert. Eleven out of seventeen flag officers during the war were ex-Parliamentarians, and some ninety of their captains had served under the Commonwealth. Perhaps in part because of command friction, the success of the Second Dutch War did not match that of the earlier conflict. An initial victory gained off Lowestoft in 1665 was not followed up, and the Four Days Battle of June 1666 ended in bloody defeat. In the late spring of 1667 English humiliation reached new depths when the Dutch raided the Medway, burning the dockyards and some ships in them.

The old veterans had a mixed record in this new conflict, and none of the senior commanders proved particularly effective. Indeed at times it seemed that more energy was being expended on seeking scapegoats than in fighting the enemy. Though disputes and ill-feeling crossed party boundaries, it was clear that old Civil War enmities played a part. Religious non-conformists were seen as seeking an English defeat, while a handful of renegades actually served with the Dutch. As on earlier occasions, there were numerous allegations of backwardness and unwillingness to engage in battle, and there were one or two cases of defection to the enemy.

However, the vast majority of the veterans of Cromwell's Navy served the new king loyally. Some sixteen of them, including John Lawson, died in action, and many others won promotion as a result of their actions.

The Third Dutch War of 1672–4 saw some of the old Commonwealth men in action again. But their numbers were dwindling with the passing years. Sir George Ayscue, veteran of the First Dutch War, died before he could take up a new command, and Mountagu was killed in action at the Battle of Sole Bay. However, the old enmities were at an end, and this more successful conflict saw none of the accusations of treachery which had marked former years.

The 'Glorious Revolution' of 1688, bringing about the overthrow of James I, might have been seen as sweet revenge for the men of Cromwell's Navy. But few of them were still in active service, and none of them were involved in the events which brought William and Mary to the throne of England. At least one of Cromwell's seadogs, Richard Haddock, lived to see the establishment of the Hanoverian dynasty in 1714.

The legacy of Cromwell's Navy was deep and permanent. For the first critical decade following the Restoration, the Commonwealth veterans provided vital experience and discipline in a fleet which might otherwise have been dominated by the less savoury outlook of Rupert and his privateers. As well as practical examples, the old Cromwellians brought with them a tradition of an always victorious Commonwealth Navy, and, more tangibly, a reputation for decency and honesty which would establish an enduring tradition for those who succeeded them.

During the critical birth pangs of the English Republic, the State's Navy had played the leading role in establishing the reputation of the vulnerable new nation as a power to be reckoned with by its European peers. Its own steady growth in self-confidence after early victories against the admittedly inferior naval forces of the Royalists had boosted the resolve of the men of the State's Navy, which enabled them to meet the sterner challenges presented by the Dutch and Spanish, and for years played a major role in shaping the foreign policy of the English Republic.

Cromwell, as Lord Protector, although he never fully grasped the potential or limitations of seventeenth-century sea power, used the burgeoning reputation of his navy to press his demands on European nations, and was the first regular English practitioner of what would in a later age be known as 'gunboat diplomacy'. Indeed, Cromwell's period of rule saw a significant early example of what would later be common English colonial-based strategy with the ill-fated Western Design and its almost accidental sequel, the conquest of Jamaica.

At home, the successes of the Navy overrode political divisions, and seemed to promise a return to the retrospectively rosy days of Good Queen Bess. More realistically, the potential of England's maritime destiny became increasingly obvious. For the only time in its history, the Navy was a strong radical instrument with many of its officers and men fired and inspired by their political and religious beliefs. Or at least this was the overriding case in peacetime; in times of war more immediate national interests generally took priority, while in 1660 realism came to the fore as the vast majority of the Navy's personnel bowed to the inevitable Restoration.

The Commonwealth era, while patronage still had an important role to play in naval appointments, saw much greater opportunities for the 'tarpaulin' officer than for many years to come. There was, of course, a good deal of the corruption and embezzlement inevitably associated with naval administration, though probably less of both than at other periods. This manifested itself to some extent in a more lenient approach to disciplinary matters than was to be the case for most of the next two centuries. Officers tended to appeal rather to the sense of community among their men than to threaten draconian punishments. One result was that a captain had to rely heavily on his personal powers of leadership when dealing with seamen readily prepared to voice their grievances against superiors.

Overall, Cromwell's Navy had a unity and cohesion which would not be matched for at least the remainder of the seventeenth century. It was the real beginning of the professional Navy, which over the following centuries would play such a vital role in the history of Britain.

Notes

Chapter 1

1. See Austin Woolrych, *Britain in Revolution*, Oxford, 2002, chapters 15 and 16
2. Ibid, pp437–8
3. Jane Ohlmeyer, 'The Civil wars in Ireland', in *The Civil War* ed. John Kenyon and Jane Ohlmeyer, Oxford, 1998
4. Woolrych, pp508–9
5. J.R. Hill (ed), *Oxford History of the Royal Navy*, Oxford, 1996, pp53–5
6. J.R. Powell, *The Navy in the English Civil War*, London, 1962
7. Bernard Capp, *Cromwell's Navy*, Oxford, 1989, Chapter 1
8. Ibid.
9. Ibid, pp16–21
10. Ibid, Chapter 3
11. *DNB*
12. Ibid.
13. See Michael Baumber, *General-at-Sea Robert Blake*, London, 1989, pp3–53
14. N.A.M. Rodger, *The Command of the Sea*, London, 2004, pp2–3, gives an excellent précis of this ambiguous title.
15. Capp, pp58–62
16. Capp, p22

Chapter 2

1. Rodger, *op cit*, p35
2. Capp, *op cit*, p4
3. Ibid, pp9–10, 341–2
4. A.W. Johns, *The Constant Warwick*, in Mariner's Mirror, vol. 18, 1952, pp254–66
5. See p??
6. Capp, p121
7. CSPD, 1652–3, p565
8. Woolrych, *op cit*, pp523–36
9. Declaration of the Generals-at-Sea, 1652

10. Oldmixon, *History and Life of Robert Blake Esq*, 1740, p72
11. *Moderate Publisher*, 3–10 June 1653
12. Capp, p131
13. Capp, pp52–3, 134.
14. Significantly, following the Restoration, it would not be until the 20th century that another *Newbury* and *Dunbar* would be added to the Royal Navy, while King George V reportedly angrily rejected the suggestion that a dreadnaught should be named *Oliver Cromwell*.
15. Capp, p139
16. See Chapter
17. Ibid, p158
18. Ibid, p167
19. Ibid, p166
20. Ibid, pp172–3
21. Ibid, p178
22. Ibid, pp183–5
23. Ibid, p195
24. Ibid, p196
25. Ibid, p199
26. Ibid, p204
27. Ibid, p215
28. Ibid, p217
29. Ibid, p219
30. Ibid, p223
31. Ibid, p245
32. Ibid, p246
33. Ibid, pp253–4
34. Ibid, p272–4
35. Ibid, p273
36. Ibid, p299
37. Ibid, p323
38. Ibid, pp326–8

Chapter 3

1. See John Barratt, *Cavalier Generals*, 2004, Chapter 3
2. Ibid, p326
3. Clarendon State Papers II, p415
4. Eliot Warburton, *Memoirs of Prince Rupert and the Cavaliers*, III, p266
5. See R.C. Anderson, The Royalists at Sea 1649, in *Mariners Mirror*
6. Warburton, *op cit*, pp263–4

7. In a daring raid, the Antelope would later be burnt by a Commonwealth boarding party.
8. Quoted Anderson, *op. cit*, p324
9. Declaration of His Highness Prince Rupert, p2
10. Anderson, *op cit*, pp326–7
11. CSPD 1649-50, pp98, 102, 110
12. Anderson, p329
13. Letters, p56
14. Warburton, *op cit*, III, p293
15. Letters, p57
16. TTE 533.4
17. Warburton, III, 311
18. BL Add. MS 18983, f
19. S.R. Gardiner, Prince Rupert at Lisbon, *Camden Miscellany*, X, p1.
20. Letters, p53
21. Thurloe, I, p34
22. Gardiner, *op cit*, p10
23 Ibid, p15
24 Warburton, III, p303.
25 Ibid, p313
26 Letters, p57
27 Ibi
28 Ibid, p58
29 Ibid, p305
30 Prince Rupert's Declaration, p4
31 Gardiner, *op cit*, p18
32 Letters, p61
33 Anderson, p140
34 Dutch Wars
35 Warburton, III, p313
36 Anderson, *op cit*, pp166–7
37 William Penn, Memorials I, 380–1.

Chapter 4
1. Letters, *op cit*, p91
2. Peter Newman, *Biographical Dictionary of Royalist Officers*, New York, 1981, item 381. J. Putley, *Scilly Isles in the English Civil War*, nd. pp1–2
3. Ibid.
4. J.R. Powell, 'Blake's Reduction of the Scilly Isles', in *Mariner's Mirror*, vol. xvii, 1931, pp205–220
5. Ibid.

6. Ibid.
7. TTE 875, No.24
8. Powell, *op cit*
9. Letters, p113
10. Lereck's *Account*, quoted Powell, p212
11. *Special Hands*, quoted Powell, p213
12. Ibid.
13. Lereck, ibid, p214
14. Bishop Leslie's Account, ibid, p214
15. TTE 292, 25
16. Several Proceedings, p85
17. Ibid.
18. CSPD 1651, p451
19. Letters, p136
20. Ibid.
21. Ibid.
22. Ibid, p141
23. Ibid.
24. Clarendon State Papers, I
25. Ibid.
26. Ibid.
27. Ibid.
28. Letters, p111
29. Ibid, p140
30. Edward Chevalier, *History of the Channel Islands*, 1899, 2, 963
31. Letters, p139
32. Clarendon State Papers, 4
33 TTE 651, 9
34. Clarendon State Papers, 4.
35. Ibid.
36. J.R. Powell, 'Sir George Ayscue's Capture of Barbados', in *Mariner's Mirror*, xxv, 1935, pp206–31
37. Ibid.

Chapter 5

1. See John D. Grainger, *Cromwell Against the Scots*, East Lothian, 1997
2. Rodger, *op cit*, pp9–10.
3. Ibid, p11
4. C.R. Boxer, 'Van Tromp', in *History Today*, vol. VII, pp211–15
5. C.R. Boxer, 'M.A de Ruyter', in *Mariner's Mirror*, vol. XLIV, 1958,

pp3–17. The 'de' was added to his name by contemporaries, but was not apparently used by Ruyter himself.

6. Baumber, *op cit*, p114
7. Rodger, p12
8. Blake, Letters, 16
9. The latter were small vessels, filled with combustible materials, and intended to be run among enemy ships in order to set them ablaze.
10. Baumber, p132
11. DW, I, 403
12. Mercurius Politicus
13. Baumber, p135
14. C. Ronciere, *Histoire de la Marine Francaise*, vol. V, pp190–5
15. G. Penn, *Memorials of Sir William Penn*, vol. 1, p440.
16. DW, 2, 357.
17. Ibid, 2, 235–6
18. Ibid, 2, 360
19. Ibid.
20. DW, 2, 268–72
21. Rodger, p14
22. Penn, *op cit*
23. q. Rodger, p14
24. Penn, p446
25. DW, 2, 271.
26. Ibid
27. Ibid.
28. Rodgers, p14
29. See R.C. Anderson, First Dutch War in the Mediterranean, in *Mariner's Mirror*, XLIX, 1963, pp241–65
30. Rodgers, p14
31. Ibid.
32. Letters, 184
33. Mercurius Politicus: Letter from the Fleet.

Chapter 6
1. Letters, 184
2. Ibid.
3. DW, 3, 293–301
4. see p24
5. Rodger, p54
6. Dr Eric Gruber Von Arni, 'Soldiers at Sea and Inter-Service Relations During the 1st Dutch War', in *Mariner's Mirror*, LII, 2001, 126–32
7. Dutch Wars, 3, 393

8. Edgar K. Thompson, 'Lashing a Broom to the Foretopmast', in *Mariner's Mirror*, LIX, 1973, pp441–2
9. R.C. Anderson, 'The English Fleet at the Battle of Portland', in *Mariner's Mirror*, XXXIX, 1953, pp171–77
10. Letters, p206
11. DW, 4, 180–81
12. Ibid, 121
13. Ibid.
14. Relation of the Late Engagement, p80
15. DW, 4, pp180–1
16. Ibid.
17. Rodgers, pp16–17
18. DW, 4, p69–70
19. Letters, 200–204.
20. DW, 4, 262–72
21. quoted Rodger, p17
22. DW, 5, 367
23. Ibid.
24. Quoted J.R. Powell, Robert Blake, London, 1959, p245.

Chapter 7
1. C.S.P. Venetian 1655–6, p10
2. Ibid, p19
3. Letters, pp294–6
4. Baumber, p205
5. Letters, pp296–8
6. Thurloe, Papers, iii, p547
7. Woolrych, p506
8. Rodgers, p27
9. Letters, p298
10. Ibid, p311.
11. See Richard Ollard, *Cromwell's Earl*, London, 1969
12. Thurloe, V, 216
13. CSPD, 1656–7, p126
14. Thurloe, V, 213–4
15. Ibid, V, 363–4
16. Rodgers, p26
17. C.H. Firth, 'Blake and the Battle of Santa Cruz', in *English Historical Review*, XX, 1905, pp228–50
18. Richard Stayner, Account in Navy Record Society, vol xi, 1910, p134
19. *The Fighting Sailor*, pp8–9
20. Ibid, pp38–9

21. Stayner, *op cit*
22. Ibid.
23. Clarendon, *History of the great Rebellion*, VI, 36
24. CSPD, 1657, pp58–9
25. Clarendon, *op cit* VI, 94

Chapter 8

1. Woolrych, *op cit*, Chapter 19
2. Clarke Papers, iii, 209
3. Ibid, iv, 279–80
4. Diary, I, 123–4
5. Ibid, II, 164

Bibliography

Anderson, R.C., 'Blake's Capture of the French Fleet Before Calais', in *Mariner's Mirror*, xlviii, 1962, pp192–207.

—— 'English Fleet at the Battle of Portland', in *Mariner's Mirror*, xxxix, 1953, pp17–77.

—— 'First Dutch War in the Mediterranean', in *Mariner's Mirror*, xlix, 1963, pp241–65.

—— 'Royalists at Sea, 1649', in *Mariner's Mirror*, xiv, 1928, pp320–8.

—— 'Royalists at Sea, 1650', in *Mariner's Mirror*, xvi, 1931, pp135–68.

Arni, Dr Eric Gruber von, 'Soldiers at Sea and Inter-service Relations during the First Dutch War', in *Mariner's Mirror*, xliii, 2003, pp32–61.

Ashley, Maurice, *General Monck*, London, 1977.

Baumber, Michael, *General-at-Sea, Robert Blake*, London, 1989.

Birch, T., *Letters and Papers of John Thurloe*, 7 vols, London, 1742.

Boxer, C.R., 'M.A. de Ruyter, 1607–76, in *Mariner's Mirror*, xliv, 1958, pp3–17.

—— 'Martin van Tromp', in *History Today*, vii, 1959, pp23–7.

Capp, Bernard, *Cromwell's Navy*, Oxford, 1988.

Chevalier, Edward, *History of the Channel Islands*, London, 1893.

Corbett, Sir Julian, *England in the Mediterranean*, 2 vols, London, 1904.

Firth, Sir C.H., 'Blake and the Battle of Santa Cruz', in *English Historical Review*, xx, 1905, pp228–50.

—— (ed.) *Clarke Papers*, Camden Society, N.S. vols 49 and 54, 1891–1901.

—— *Last Years of the Protectorate*, London, 1909.

—— (ed.), 'Richard Stayner's Account of the Battle of Teneriffe', in *Naval Miscellany*, vol. ii, Navy Records Society, vol. 40, 1910.

Gardiner, S.R., *History of the Commonwealth and Protectorate*, 3 vols, London, 1894–1903.

—— 'Prince Rupert at Lisbon', in *Camden Miscellany*, Camden Society, 3rd Series, vol. x, 1902.

—— and Atkinson, C.T., (eds), *Letters and Papers relating to the First Dutch War*, 6 vols, Navy Records Society, vols 13, 17, 30, 37, 41 and 66, London, 1899–1930.

Green, M.A.E., (ed.) *Calendar of State Papers, Domestic, Commonwealth Series*, 13 vols, London, 1867–86.

Hinds, Allen B., (ed.), *Calendar of State Papers, Venetian*, London, 1896.

Johns, A.W., 'The Constant Warwick', in *Mariner's Mirror*, xxvii, 1952, pp254–66.

Macray, W.D., (ed.), *Calendar of Clarendon State Papers*, vols i and ii, Oxford, 1872.

Morrah, Patrick, *Prince Rupert of the Rhine*, London, 1971.

Newman, Peter, *Biographical Dictionary of Royalist Officers*, New York, 1981.

Oldmixon, John, *History and Life of Robert Blake, Esq*, London, 1740.

Ollard, Richard, *Cromwell's Earl*, London, 1971.

Penn, Granville, *Memorial of the Professional Life and Times of Sir William Penn*, 2 vols, London, 1830.

Powell, J.R. 'Blake's Reduction of the Scilly Islands', in *Mariner's Mirror*, vol. xvii, 1931, pp205–20.

—— 'Blake's Reduction of the Channel Islands', in *Mariner's Mirror*, vol. xvii, 1932, pp121–36.

—— (ed.) *Letters of Robert Blake*, Navy Records Society, vol. 76, 1937.

—— *Robert Blake, General-at-Sea*, London, 1972.

Rodger, N.A.M., *The Command of the Ocean*, Oxford, 2004.

Thompson, Edgar K. 'Lashing the Broom to the Fore Topmast', in *Mariner's Mirror*, mmlix, 1973, pp441–2.

Warburton, Eliot, *Memoirs of Prince Rupert and the Cavaliers*, London, 1849.

Warner, Sir George F. (ed.), *The Nicholas Papers*, 4 vols, Camden Society, New Series, 40, 50, 57 and third series, 31.

Woolrych, Austin, *Britain in Revolution*, Oxford, 2002.

Index